HERBERT SPENCER:

Structure, Function and Evolution

HERBERT SPENCER:
STRUCTURE, FUNCTION AND EVOLUTION

Edited and with an introductory essay by
STANISLAV ANDRESKI

Charles Scribner's Sons · New York

CONTENTS

v

Introduction by Ronald Fletcher

After Comte, Herbert Spencer was undoubtedly the scholar chiefly responsible for the foundation of sociology during the nineteenth century. It was the work of these two men—not always in agreement—which most stimulated the growth of the subject throughout Europe, Britain, and America. The range of Spencer's influence was enormous, and is difficult now to imagine. He was the dominating figure in England, and it was on his death— as though at the end of an epoch—that the British Sociological Society was founded at the London School of Economics to which continental scholars—such as Durkheim and Tönnies, as well as the first English professors of the subject—Westermarck and Hobhouse, and a wide range of scholars in all fields (Maudsley, McDougall, Marett, Graham Wallas, Beatrice Webb, William Beveridge, Branford, Geddes, Booth, Rowntree—to mention but a few) contributed. Durkheim was greatly influenced by his detailed observations on the division of labour in society, as well as by his 'structural-functional analysis' and, quite fundamentally, by his evolutionary theory. Pareto also owed much to him. In America, the earlier sociologists like Ward and Giddings, and also those who developed the subject early in the present century, like Cooley, though far from being uncritical, acknowledged their great indebtedness to him. In 1952, no less a scholar than Radcliffe-Brown acknowledged his rootedness in Spencer (as well as in Comte), and accepted and adopted his structural-functional analysis and his conception of social evolution.

When Talcott Parsons wrote in 1937—'Who now reads Spencer?'—his question could have been given a fuller answer than he thought. Spencer's ideas have never been dead in the making of sociology, and it is particularly salutary and instructive to reconsider his ideas now: at this juncture in the critical re-assessment of the subject.

I

A fallacy is deeply entrenched in the minds of many that 'structural-functional analysis' is a *static* analysis of society, or considers society in a *static* condition, and is inapplicable to studies of social change. Ward long ago dismissed this, and attacked it, as 'The Fallacy of the Stationary'. And we find, in fact, that Spencer offered as clear as possible a statement of structural-functional analysis, including a significant grouping of institutions for the purpose of constructing 'types' of society for classification and comparative study, whilst at the same time considering societies as being *essentially* processes of change; *essentially* involved in the complex sequences of order and change in evolution. A similar fallacy is abroad that Spencer borrowed the biological theory of evolution and applied it falsely to the study of societies; misconceiving societies as biological organisms, and the like. But Spencer's conception of 'evolution' was much more profound than that, and is more akin to the conception underlying Whitehead's 'Process and Reality', for example, than to any simple-minded misuse of biology. Spencer is sometimes thought, too, to belong to what one might call the *historicist* club: believing in the *inevitability* of a *single line* of social evolution, and claiming, on the basis of this, to predict the future course of history as a matter of *necessity*. But this is a nonsensical criticism, and no one who knew his work could make it. Spencer is not something to be pulled from under the dust-sheets in a Victorian lumber-room. He is a living thinker, who established ideas of perennial worth to the subject.

Professor Andreski knows Spencer's work well, and has always, himself, been committed to the same comparative and historical sociology. His own first book—*Military Organisation in Society* took its starting point from Spencer's ideas, and he has also recently produced an abridgement of *The Principles of Sociology*. This new selection and introduction provides a clear picture of Spencer's basic conceptions, and also conveys the quality of Spencer as a person always sensitive and alert to the social and political issues of his time, and always lively and acute as a critic and commentator. The basic conception of evolution was outlined in *First Principles*, and is here. The analysis of society in terms of structure and function, the methods of classifying societies for comparative study and the analysis of the processes of order and change, were chiefly outlined in the section on 'The Inductions of Sociology' (in *The Principles*) and are substantially here. But Spencer was far from being the dried-up stick of an abstract theorist and agnostic that many think him. He was a well-liked and good-humoured figure in country-house parties, and his sociological thinking had biting teeth for his critical attack on political policies and practices in his time. It is fitting, therefore, that the last section of essays should dwell especially on his concern for the problems of power in society. For Spencer feared above all the threatened dominion over the individual in the growing processes of 'collectivization' and 'militancy' in modern society, and his comments on 're-barbarization'—as evidenced in the dwelling on violence in press and novels, and even in football, as well as in imperialism and slavery (as applicable *now* in Czechoslovakia as it was *then* in South Africa)—will be seen to have a striking relevance to the problems of our own time.

Spencer was ambiguous in many ways, ethically unseeing in certain directions, and his extreme 'liberalism' could not now be upheld. But—for better, for worse—he *was* a liberal to the *core*, and his clear views, his telling criticisms, the compelling concern for truth and reason in his voice, quickly persuade the reader that his is a position worth listening to. There is another fallacy abroad: that only left-wing movements on behalf of the masses possess realism and humanity. But it was not Marx only who desired a humane society, and there are differing approaches to its achievement. Spencer's 'liberalism' is decidedly not in the fashion, but perhaps it ought to be more so.

What is certain is that here is a contribution to the making of sociology, and to the clear statement of a particular political position which is of great and permanent worth. If we forget the first, our conception of sociology will be impoverished. If we ignore the second, we do so at our peril—which is, of course, far from saying that we should accept it in its totality.

Here, at any rate, is a book which gives the reader a basic and reliable grasp of Spencer's work.

Introductory Essay:

Sociology, Biology and Philosophy in Herbert Spencer

THE UNITY OF SCIENCE AND THE KEY
CONCEPT OF EVOLUTION

Herbert Spencer firmly believed in the unity of all science: not only in the sense that the basic logical methods are the same in all fields of scientific inquiry, which was the chief message of his somewhat resented illustrious forerunner Auguste Comte, but also in the sense that the basic processes in all the realms of being are essentially identical, which he proceeded to prove in the successive parts of his *System of Synthetic Philosophy*. With the aid of numerous examples from all branches of knowledge—ranging from astronomy, physics and chemistry to linguistics, technology and the history of art—he shows the ubiquity of the fundamental processes of integration, dissolution, equilibration, segregation and differentiation.

Whether these are emanations of our own minds—as time and space are according to Kant—or immanent attributes of reality (whatever that means), the truth remains that they are universal components of our picture of the world. However, whether we can get very far by contemplating them is a difficult question which leads straight into the fundamental problems of the nature of reality, a discussion of which would call for a lengthy philosophical treatise. Consequently, despite my feeling that Spencer's *First Principles* have been unjustly neglected by the philosophers, I shall leave aside his most general ontological ideas and concentrate on the relationship in his thought between biology and sociology; on which topic his views can be examined in the light of empirical evidence, notwithstanding their extraordinarily far-reaching scope. Moreover, not being qualified to judge the details of his contributions to biology (for the assessment of which I can refer the reader to P. Medawar's recent book of essays *The Art of the Soluble*) I shall deal only with their applications to sociology.

This selection has been inspired by the desire to show that sociological knowledge has not become cumulative only in this generation but has always been so; and that if we cut out from works of old masters what has become untenable in the light of later studies their contributions dovetail like parts of a jig-saw puzzle. What is required for such a synthesis is a correct mixture of admiration for the great pioneers and criticism. In this way we

7

can learn from Aristotle as well as from Marx, from Saint Simon as well as Pareto and Weber. Every kind of ancestor worship—in fact anything ending in 'ism'—inevitably produces a stagnant orthodoxy: but generalized patricide also precludes progress by giving rise to an endless re-discovering of America. In passing a judgment on a thinker we must bear in mind that a single contribution of lasting value outweighs in the long run a hundred gross errors because many more people can spot mistakes than produce an original idea.

Spencer's key concept was 'evolution', by which he meant the process of increasing differentiation (that is to say specialization of functions) and integration (by which he meant mutual interdependence of the structurally differentiated parts and coordination of their functions.) He believed that evolution as thus conceived could be discerned in all the realms of the universe, including inanimate nature, but we need not dwell upon the questions of cosmology because the relevance or irrelevance of this concept to physics or astronomy in no way prejudges its applicability to the history of human society. As far as biology is concerned, no one nowadays contests the view that the more highly differentiated and integrated organisms have come into existence by originating from the simpler through a process of growth in complexity extending over countless generations.[1]

In the study of society the word 'evolution' fell out of fashion although every complex society or even institution can be shown to have originated from something simpler. Actually, the process of evolution in Spencer's sense is much more visible in human social aggregates than in the realm of organic nature. The bio-

---

[1] Another example of fertilization across the boundary between fields of learning deserves mention. Spencer arrived at his concept of evolution—as the trend towards increasing differentiation coupled with integration—by giving greater generality to the idea of progress as the product of advancing division of labour, which Adam Smith has made into a commonplace among the economists. Now, one of the more curious ramifications of Spencer's theory of evolution was his notion that heterogeneity is more stable than homogeneity, which would explain the trend from the latter to the former condition, which according to him was manifesting itself throughout the universe, and accounted among other things for the differentiation of the animal species. At the time of publication of his *Principles of Biology*, this view had no empirical foundation but, curiously, it fits exactly with what the ecologists have recently found: namely that ecological communities containing a large number of interdependent species exhibit great stability, whereas those which comprise only a few species are subject to violent fluctuations, often ending with the extinction of populations.

logical theory of evolution has been accepted because it accounts for a myriad of facts registered by palaeontology, anatomy and comparative physiology, but none of the greater transitions which it presupposes has ever been directly observed: nobody has ever seen an emergence of a new genera or even of a new species of a multicellular organism. Only the ontogenetic process of differentiation and integration—that is to say, a transformation of the fertilized egg into an adult individual—can be seen, whereas (apart from small modifications) our knowledge of phylogenesis rests solely upon inference. In contrast, in the realm of human social aggregates we not only have historical records describing numerous cases of transition from the simple to the complex, but many people alive today have seen such changes with their own eyes.

The social analogy of ontogenesis (i.e. of individual reproduction and growth) is the process of replication of organizational units in accordance with a pre-existing pattern, such as takes place when a firm opens a new branch, or an army sets up a new regiment. It might be worth noticing that such occurrences exhibit a further analogy to organic ontogenesis in that here too an organizing nucleus comes into existence first, and then proceeds to arrange the accruing materials in accordance with a blueprint. Apart from this kind of replication however, we can see many examples of transformations from the simple to the complex which are analogous to phylogenesis when new types of social structure arise which are more complex (i.e. more highly differentiated and integrated) than those from which they have emerged. This can best be observed in the field of industrial or military organization.

The evolution of human social aggregates displays the trend from the simpler to the more complex more conspicuously than organic evolution does because although the more complex species have originated from the simpler, they have not displaced them, and there is no reason to believe that they will do so in the future. Thus through the process of involving a growth in complexity the vertebrates have gradually evolved from unicellular organisms, but the latter still exist. Assuming the truth of the biological theory of evolution, we can surmise that the lions came into existence later than the amoebas, but there is no evidence that, by multiplying, the lions have ever threatened the existence of the amoebas. In the realm of human social aggregates, on the other hand, the complex formations have not only come into existence later than, and have originated from, simpler structures, but they have been for millennia, and still are, displacing the latter by absorbing or exterminating them. States, for instance, have not only originated from tribes, but have also replaced them, so that there are no tribes as independent political entities left.

Beginning with the earliest traces of mankind, we can discern a general (though by no means constant) trend towards increasing size and complexity of human societies, whereby a larger and larger proportion of the globe is taken over by increasingly complex entities. Though occasionally interrupted—as when, for instance, the Roman Empire was replaced by the numerically smaller as well as organizationally simpler feudal principalities— the trend towards increasing size, differentiation and integration is unmistakable in the history of civilization, and attested beyond doubt by written records as well as the findings of archaeology.

It is strange that precisely at the time when the movement from the simple to the complex was gathering speed—when the remaining tribes as well as the much larger traditional kingdoms were being rapidly devoured by the industrial civilization—that 'evolutionism' has been consigned to the museum and labelled as an antiquated nineteenth-century pre-conception. As often happens, however, what really occurred was that the articulated concept was shelved and replaced by a set of cruder and tacit assumptions about the direction in which the world is moving, which roughly mean the same thing but without the benefit of explicit and clear formulation. Evolution and progress are out of fashion but development and growth are in. Why? The most common reason for purely verbal changes is that they enable people to delude both themselves and others that they are making discoveries when in reality they are merely echoing their ancestors, sometimes rather ineptly.

Rediscovering America is one of the most popular occupations among the practitioners of the social sciences and it requires that the original discoverer should be consigned to oblivion. (There is, incidentally, a curious parallel here with the naming of the new continent which was baptized not after its discoverer but after Amerigo Vespucci, who was much better than poor Columbus at putting himself in the limelight). So, Herbert Spencer has been recently kept in oblivion largely because he said more clearly, as well as somewhat earlier, what some of the influential theorists of today claim as their discoveries. For, as the reader will see from the text which follows, Spencer not only introduced the concepts of what is now called 'structural-functionalism', but also laid foundations for a cybernetic analysis of social phenomena; in addition to developing the ideas which in an inarticulate (and therefore bastardized) form underlie most of contemporary thinking about such matters as 'development' and 'resistance to change'.

EVOLUTION IN CULTURE AND SOCIETY .

On the assumption that what the biologists and palaeontologists tell us about the origin of human species is true, it is quite clear that all the items of culture that have ever been recorded must have evolved from simpler forms, that none of them has sprung into existence fully fledged like Pallas Athene from Zeus's forehead. As far as tools are concerned, we can see this by walking around a museum. The early stages in the development of languages, beliefs and customs have left no traces, and hence we have no means of finding out any details; but, though condemned to never knowing the exact routes, we can remain sure that a gradual evolution from simpler to more complex forms has taken place, because the only alternative would be a whole series of ready-made creations by a supernatural power. In other words, if we accept that human beings descend from cultureless ancestors, we cannot doubt the reality of the evolution of society and culture (including, of course, language) from the simple to the complex.

Though true of the entire socio-cultural realm, the principle of evolution sheds more light on those of its provinces where we are not confined to imagination and deduction, and can rely on fairly well authenticated and detailed data. Thus we can trace in detail the evolution of the art of writing, and explain the origins of various scripts, whereas the question of the origins of speech has been given up as insoluble because of the complete lack of evidence. Some developmental stages must have intervened between the limited repertoire of signs of our pre-human ancestors and the highly complex syntax and vocabulary exhibited by all the languages that have ever been recorded, but we are condemned to ignorance on this matter.

There are some aspects of social structure where, during the era encompassed by our historical records, the trend of change has been from the complex to the simple rather than the other way round as normally happens, the most notable example being the webs of kinship. All the tribes known to historiography and ethnography had complex networks of kinship, with an intricate distribution of rights and duties and an elaborate nomenclature, which lost many of their fuctions when centralized states came into existence, and which were finally destroyed by industrialism. The Occidental nuclear family is something extremely simple in comparison with the clans and phratries of old. Nevertheless, we must remember that the simplification of kinship has been connected with the growing complexity of other social networks, so that it has entailed no reduction in the complexity of the social structure as a whole. Moreover, the relatively complex webs of kinship found in the most primitive of known societies must have developed from simpler forms which bridged the gap towards the societies of our pre-human ancestors.

There are other aspects of culture, apart from webs of kinship, which exhibit no trend towards greater complexity as far as the extant records are concerned: in language the tendency towards grammatical simplification seems to have been more pronounced than its opposite, although vocabularies have no doubt grown with the advance of civilization. We must remember however that it is only collective vocabularies which have grown in quantity, not those of the individual; and there is no evidence that an average Londoner knows more words than a Somali shepherd . . . rather the contrary. If we take such aspects of culture as manners, poetry or amusements it is difficult to discern any historical trend from the simple to the complex. Even in music and painting the highest level of complexity seems to have been reached in the past centuries, even if we disregard the question of rhythm, the most complex form of which seems to be West African drumming.

The mistake of most of the nineteenth-century evolutionists consisted not in their use of the Spencerian concept but in focusing on those aspects of culture—such as morals, religion and family—to which it was least applicable. No matter how interesting, their speculations remained unverifiable, and therefore could scarcely provide a basis for further progress. The sterility of the evolutionary approach to the non-cumulative provinces of culture has brought the entire concept into disrepute despite its undeniable relevance to such spheres as the economy of the state, where the movement from the simple to the complex can be traced in detail in the full light of historical records. Unlike, for instance, Westermarck, Herbert Spencer did fortunately write a great deal about political and economic institutions, and social structure in general. What he has to say about the origins of religion is quite interesting and plausible but unprovable, and cannot therefore be regarded as a bequest of undoubted value. The fairly long discussion of the origins of the professions has better evidential foundations but is not particularly illuminating because his master key of differentiation and integration can be applied to the occupational structure as a whole but not to single jobs as such.

Spencer's treatment of the family shows him at his weakest; firstly because of the inapplicability of his master concept to this matter, and secondly because it was precisely in this field that the sentiments of a Victorian bachelor most strongly interfered with his judgment. He accepted as self-evident that a rather idealized family pattern of Victorian England was the resting point of human history, and arranged other forms of family in accordance with a preconceived sequence, assuming without any good argument that humanity followed the route from promiscuity to life-long monogamy passing through polygamy. Apart from in no way exemplifying growing complexity, this sequence is non-concatenated, as none of these forms of marriage requires an antecedent existence of any of the others, and all of them can be found at various levels of material culture.

Actually, as shown by Hobhouse, Ginsberg and Wheeler, in their *Material Culture and Social Institutions of Simple Peoples* (1915), monogamy and relative equality between the sexes prevail among the simplest peoples; whereas massive polygamy and extreme subjection of women go together with a more complex material culture and political structure. Furthermore, polyandry as a predominant pattern is so rare as far as our records go that there are no grounds whatsoever for assuming that there has been a period or a level of material or structural simplicity at which this was the most widespread form of marriage.

In contrast to family and kinship, the techniques of organization and administration exhibit an unmistakable evolutionary trend from the simpler towards the more complex forms with a determined concatenation of stages. If we study the history of business management we can see very clearly how the methods of supervision, accountancy forecasting, stock-control, communication and so on have developed through a necessary sequence of stages, and how each step entailed an increase in differentiation and integration of functions. The same is true of military organization which, incidentally, is the only kind of organization whose evolution has been systematically surveyed. We have historical treatises which describe how the Roman manipular 'ordre de bataille' developed from the Greek phalanx, and how many centuries later it was revived in a more elaborate form by the Spanish infantry; or how the organization and tactics of Swedish squadrons under Gustavus Adolphus had to precede those of Frederic II of Prussia's troops; which in turn provided a necessary foundation for Napoleon's innovations. There are, of course, many good works on the history of civil administration but they deal with individual historical cases, and I have seen none which treats that subject from an equally general developmental viewpoint.

The above-mentioned examples from military history show that, though necessarily concatenated, the successive evolutionary steps need not take place in the same society; and so we come to the question of the alleged assumption of 'unilinearity' for which the nineteenth-century evolutionists continue to be castigated in histories of sociology and anthropology. Though often repeated this accusation is unjust. Neither Spencer nor Tylor ever entertained the idea that all the peoples of the world (or polities, if 'people' seems too vague) must traverse exactly the same historical trajectory. Spencer's emphasis on the part played in social evolution by war—through which 'unfit' polities and institutions are eliminated, and smaller entities are welded into larger—rules out the possibility that he might have thought that all social units have to go through the same stages of development. He knew very well that the Anglo-Saxon tribes never reached the stage of elaborate division of labour because they were destroyed as social entities at a much lower evolutionary level. He knew equally well that the French nation never passed through a tribal stage because it did not exist when the territory which later became France was peopled by tribes.

What Spencer was trying to reconstruct was not a history of concrete social aggregates but a genealogy of types of social structure, although he never explicitly made this distinction. In contrast to Henry Summer Maine, who used Indian analogies to reconstruct the institutional history of the European peoples, Spencer resorted to the comparative method solely to classify the types of structure and to establish their sequences. True, generality is a matter of degree, and the gap between Maine's conjectural history of institutions and Spencer's evolutionary typology is by no means unbridgeable; nonetheless, the difference remains fundamental.

EMPIRICAL DATA AND COMPARATIVE METHOD

Auguste Comte and Herbert Spencer are the only two sociological writers who also occupy an important place in the history of philosophy and have constructed systems encompassing all the sciences. Marx, of course, is often treated as a great philosopher, but this is a simple 'halo effect' stemming from his eminence as a sociologist and above all from his status as a founder of a secular religion. In comparison with Comte's or Spencer's subtle argumentation, Marx's philosophical pronouncements appear inept and often meaningless, as in the case of the celebrated dictum that 'existence determines consciousness' . . . as if consciousness could be anything but a part of existence.

Having invented the word sociology, Comte is often treated as the founder of the study itself, although his contribution to empirical knowledge is meagre, and cannot be even remotely equated with that of Montesquieu or John Millar. His excellence lies in methodology in which field he laid the foundations for the systematic (or scientific, if you like) study of society. For example, his classification of the sciences—showing the coincidence of the degree of complexity of the subject matter with the chronological order of maturation—remains valid to this day and was a real stroke of genius. Spencer's system of synthetic philosophy was obviously an attempt to re-write *Le Cours de la Philosophie Positive*, but, as far as the philosophical and methodological foundations of sociology are concerned, Spencer did not succeed in improving upon Comte. Actually, reading Spencer's essay 'On the Reasons for Disagreeing with M. Comte', one is struck by the latter's superiority as a philosopher of science. In empirical sociology, on the other hand, it was the other way round: and here Spencer's theorizing was much more scientific even when it was mistaken; because he made a serious attempt to base his theories on factual information, which is scanty in Comte.

With their mass of details about the customs and institutions of all kinds of peoples, Spencer's *Principles* seem to descend from Montesquieu's *De l'Esprit des Lois* or Adam Smith's *Wealth of Nations* rather than from Comte's utopia. The importance which Spencer attached to empirical material is demonstrated by his founding of the series on *Descriptive Sociology*, the later volumes of which were financed out of his bequest. True, he was undeniably narrow-minded about how the collecting and collating of data ought to be done, but it was a remarkable enterprise in its day.

The notion of the mutual dependence of the parts of the social system had already been formulated by Comte; and Spencer's improvement upon his predecessor consisted, firstly, of putting empirical flesh into this notion, secondly, of working out more specific theorems on this basis, and thirdly, of shifting the emphasis from purely intellectual factors to social structure.

In *The Principles of Sociology*, then, Spencer tries to demonstrate three main points: firstly, that societies can be classified in terms of increasing differentiation and integration, secondly, that there is a necessary filiation of the types of total social structure as well as of the types of partial structures such as industrial, political or ecclesiastic, and thirdly, that a general trend towards growing complexity can be discerned in the long run.

The idea of stages of civilization was by no means new when Spencer was writing; and much earlier writers like Adam Ferguson and Condorcet have propounded very reasonable classifications of them. Spencer's contribution to social morphology was to introduce structural complexity as the unitary semi-quantitative bases of classification, whereas other writers' schemes exhibited no such underlying unity.

The stress on structure—which makes Spencer the founder of contemporary sociological analysis—has led him to gloss over the factor which many earlier as well as later thinkers have regarded as the mainspring of progress—namely, the development of productive forces. Not that Spencer denied or ignored the importance of technical progress and the growth of wealth, but he simply does not say much about the impact of technology upon society—which seems very strange on the part of an assiduous student of the natural sciences and an inventor of mechanical gadgets; particularly as it stands in such contrast to the viewpoint of Marx who had no direct acquaintance with science and technology. The explanation seems to be that Spencer was interested in social evolution as an exemplification of an omnipresent cosmic process rather than for its own sake. We must remember that Spencer regarded himself as an all-embracing philosopher rather than a mere sociologist, and that *The Principles of Sociology* came at the end of his series on Synthetic Philosophy, preceded by *Principles of Biology*, *Principles of Psychology* and the *First Principles*, and followed by *Ethics*. Technical progress fitted the scheme of cosmic evolution expounded in the *First Principles* only in so far as it translated itself into increasing division of labour and economic interdependence. This *a priori* approach to social evolution was also the reason why Spencer did little to analyse the social mechanisms which produce it, with the exception of the factor of war and conquest through which a selection of the fittest polities and institutions takes place; for if social changes simply follow the lines of an omnipresent cosmic trend, then a fundamental explanation must be cosmological rather than merely sociological.

Apart from the logical reasons, the intellectual climate did not favour an inquiry into social conditions of technical progress. To the thinkers of the eighteenth and the early nineteenth centuries— Hume, Turgot, Adam Smith, Charles Comte, Volney—technical progress and the growth of wealth were sufficiently new to elicit a questioning as to why they were occurring, whereas their successors of the middle of the nineteenth century (with the exception of Thomas Henry Buckle) began to take this onward march for granted. In Marx's system the development of the forces of production plays the role of an irresistible prime mover which breaks the social forms which hinder its forward march— which was (and remains) a valid vision of social mechanics within the institutional setting of contemporary industrial civilization. The question of why (not merely how) this setting has come into existence, and whether it was not in some sense accidental, attracted neither Marx's nor Spencer's attention.[1] Nonetheless, their respective emphases—on the development of productive forces and on the increasing structural differentiation and integration—not only retain their validity but complement each other, pointing out correlated facets of social reality.

Marx's and Spencer's visions complemented each other in another way too. Marx, as everybody knows, declared that 'all history is the history of class struggles'—which can be taken as a rhetorically exaggerated statement of the undeniable truth that in all states recorded in history some form of struggle between classes has been going on. Spencer on the other hand (though by no means oblivious of the phenomena of exploitation, oppression and rebellion) did not pay much attention to them, and focused on the ubiquity of war and its role in furthering progress towards greater differentiation and integration by eliminating weaker polities and institutions. However, it is neither necessary nor even possible to decide which contention is more valid because neither the present state of mankind nor its past condition can be understood without taking *both* factors into account.

There is a further parallel between Marx and Spencer in that both expected their chief driving forces to come to rest before very long. Spencer confidently hoped that industrial societies would give up wars, while Marx believed that an abolition of private ownership of the means of production would put an end not only to class conflict but to social inequality itself. Both, of course, have proved to be wrong, and we can see that neither has industrialism put an end to wars nor has socialism eliminated exploitation and conflict between the privileged and the burdened. As makers of blueprints for a future society neither Marx nor

---

[1] True, in the so-called theory of primitive accumulation Marx tried to answer the question of how the initial accumulation of capital came about by surveying the pre-capitalist forms of exploitation of labour. Nonetheless, though broadly true, the assertion that the pre-capitalist forms of exploitation constituted a necessary prelude to the rise of capitalism does not provide an explanation of why the capitalist system should have arisen where and when it did, because Marx made no effort to show that pre-capitalist exploitation was greater in the countries where capitalism arose than where it did not. Moreover, by not considering the possibility that capitalism might not have arisen at all, had some fortuitous confluence of circumstance not have occurred, Marx makes the implicit assumption that the general march of civilization is predetermined rather than in some sense accidental.

Spencer has been much good, in contrast to Auguste Comte whose utopia of a society-worshipping, thought-controlling, ruling, lay priesthood, armed with a sociological doctrine in lieu of the Bible, bears some resemblance not only to the Soviet reality but also to the condition towards which the capitalist societies seem to be evolving.[1]

The idea that a society oriented towards industrial production must differ from the traditional warlike type stems from Saint-Simon, and remains fruitful if we treat this dichotomy (in accordance with Otto Hintze's sixty-year-old suggestion) as specifying polar types between which the historical reality has oscillated, rather than a chronological sequence.[2] True, unaggressive states have come into existence only after industrialism, but the extreme warlikeness of so many industrial nations rules out the possibility that industrialism may be a sufficient (rather than merely a necessary) condition of peacefulness. However, Spencer was on the whole right about structural correlates of militancy such as centralization of authority, extension of governmental regulation of social life; and not altogether wrong about its connections with forms of inequality. To fit the empirical evidence available now, Spencer's theories have to be qualified and inserted into a wider framework comprising other factors, which I have tried to do in my *Military Organisation and Society*.[3] Unfortunately, a summary of the arguments presented there would take up more space than can be spared here.

FUNCTIONALISM

In addition to making evolutionism into the dominant approach to the study of society during his lifetime, Herbert Spencer begat a more remote offspring: namely, functionalism. Not that he invented either the term or the concept of function or social structure any more than Marx the idea of class struggle or of the

See on this point my *Elements of Comparative Sociology*, Ch. 24—'Communism and Capitalism Are they Converging?' Weidenfeld & Nicolson, London, 1964. Published by California University Press under the title of *The Uses of Comparative Sociology*.
[2] See *Staat und Verfassung*, Göttingen, 1966.
[3] Routledge & Kegan Paul, London, and University of California Press, 2nd augmented edition, 1968.

economic determination of politics. What both of them did was to take ideas casually adumbrated by their forerunners and to erect them into cornerstones of a specific vision of social mechanics, and to interpret vast cultural processes from this viewpoint. This does not detract from their greatness, for no thinker, no matter how gifted, can build out of nothing or outclass completely all the other great minds which humanity has produced. Moreover, apart from his dependence on the bequest of his forerunners, every outstanding writer has derived assistance from a large number of more modest contributors—some very modest indeed, others not far removed from his excellence. The accumulation of knowledge is a collective enterprise, and the great figures resemble the peaks of the mountains rather than their entire mass. However, there is no need to labour this point in connection with Spencer because he is nowadays in no imminent danger of becoming the focus of a cult of personality like the one practised by the crowd still suffering from an infantile fixation on grandpa Karl.

The migrations of the word 'function' show how intimate has been the cross-fertilization of sociological and biological thought. The recourse to organic analogies for grasping the nature of society goes back (as Spencer himself has pointed out) at least to Hobbes and Francis Bacon as far as explicit analogies are concerned, while casual similes can be found in the Bible. But until the organic analogy was brought by Spencer to bear with full force upon the study of society, the current of stimulation ran mainly in the opposite direction, and the inter-dependence of bodily organs was described by metaphors drawn from the realm of collective action. Thus in old books on physiology one can find the very anthropomorphic word 'office' employed in such sentences as 'the office of the liver is . . .'. Furthermore, not only Malthus (whose law of population suggested to Darwin the idea of natural selection) but also Adam Smith, exerted influence on the study of living things, revealed by the expression 'physiological division of labour' in common usage among biologists of the early nineteenth century.[1]

Owing to its incorporation into the biological vocabulary, 'function' ceased to be confined to designating a consciously assigned and assumed task, and began to mean any process which

[1] See on this point J. B. Burrows, *Evolution and Society*, Cambridge University Press, 1966.

is essential to the maintenance of a living system. And it was in this wider and more abstract sense that it was brought back into discussion of human affairs by Spencer. Whereas Adam Smith thinks only in terms of a division of labour between individuals and groups, Spencer adumbrates a much more abstract co-ordination of processes when he speaks of the functions of religion or music. True, like the sociological writers of today, he does not entirely forgo the older meaning and does not explicitly distinguish between the abstract and the concrete sense. Nevertheless, all the shades of meaning given to this word by the contemporary functionalist anthropologists are already there; and as far as the concept itself is concerned (though not its applications) the only subsequent addition was Radcliffe-Brown's definition which clarified the terminology. However, in contrast to some more recent self-proclaimed founders of structuralism-functionalism, Radcliffe-Brown did not conceal his debt to Spencer, although he was more directly influenced by Emile Durkheim who (among other things) acted as an intermediary between Spencer and the functionalist school of social anthropology founded by Malinowski and Radcliffe-Brown.

In relation to Spencer's *Principles*, Durkheim's *Division of Labour* represented a step forward in some respects and backwards in others—forward because Spencer was primarily a synthetic philosopher interested in the social manifestations of a cosmic principle, whereas Durkheim was a full-time student of society able to marshal empirical evidence for his theories with more skill and reliability. Despite the profusion of factual material in the *Principles*, Spencer baldly 'lays down the law' whereas Durkheim presents subtle inductive arguments. Durkheim's superlative quality as an inductive reasoner reveals itself particularly in *Le Suicide*, which goes far beyond the sphere of Spencer's pre-occupations but it is fully visible in *Division of Labour*, which takes Spencer as the starting point and relates the progress of social differentiation to a number of social phenomena which he did not touch, such as penal and civil law. We must not forget, however, that taking some questions further constitutes no proof of greater merit when the next step is no longer, and the continuity is not only clear but also quite conscious as can be seen in this case from frequent references.

Recoiling from the overemphasis on biological analogies to

social phenomena, Durkheim has re-directed sociological work towards studies in depth and induction as opposed to mere factual illustration. The so-called 'organicism', which was highly fruitful at an earlier stage of development of sociological thought (and which as we shall see later, continues to hold certain possibilities) had by then become a stultifying blind alley barring immersion in empirical data.

In contrast to these strong points, Durkheim's dichotomy of organic versus mechanic solidarity appears jejeune in comparison with Spencer's conceptual framework. Firstly, because the term 'solidarity' confuses the fact of interdependency with sentiments which may or may not accompany it. To impute organic solidarity to a slave plantation or a forced-labour camp simply because it has a relatively advanced division of labour (as we must if we follow Durkheim's terminology) amounts to an unconscious smuggling of the entirely unproven value assumption that 'all is for the best in the best of possible worlds', apart from doing violence to etymology. Equally gratuitous are the semantic insinuations implicit in affixing the label 'mechanic' to the social bonds holding together a tribe or a peasant village as opposed to an industrial city. In any case there is nothing original in this dichotomy which merely replicates Tönnies' scheme of *Gemeinschaft* versus *Gesellschaft* (published a few years earlier) with the meaning of 'organic' simply transposed: Tönnies describes the bonds within a *Gemeinschaft* as organic whereas Durkheim calls them 'mechanic solidarity', while 'organic solidarity' corresponds to *Gesellschaft* characterized by the artificiality (in other words mechanicality) of the social bonds. Tönnies' usage undoubtedly harmonizes better with the semantic nuances inhering in the words in question, but anyway Spencer's classification in terms of one continuous variable of differentiation combined with integration through interdependence surpasses in sophistication as well as heuristic usefulness this rather crude dichotomy. Even Durkheim's own disciples, especially Celestin Bouglé, employed Spencer's variable more often than their master's scheme; and it is arguable that the same is true about Durkheim himself.

Although Spencer's conception of structure, function, system and self-regulation created the framework of modern sociological analysis, he never produced an analytical description of a society or even of an aspect of a society. Curiously it was his somewhat earlier and entirely unphilosophical contemporary Alexis de Tocqueville who first practised functionalism *avant la lettre* without bothering about a conceptual framework. *Democracy in America* resembles Max Weber's volumes on China or India in being a piece of 'comparative functionalism': that is to say, a work which attempts to disentangle the relationships of interdependence between various aspects of a social order by comparing the situation in focus with other configurations of circumstances: with the old Europe in the case of Tocqueville and with whatever he saw fit in universal history in the case of Weber. As Raymond Aron has shown in his lectures (now published as *Les Grands Étapes de la Pensée Sociologique*), Tocqueville was one of the greatest theoreticians despite his unconcern for formalization and methodology.

Durkheim's importance in the history of sociology derives from the fusion of Tocqueville's unconscious empirical functionalism with Spencer's conceptual framework, in addition to the substantially enhanced sophistication of inductive reasoning as evidenced especially by *Le Suicide*. His *Les Formes Elémentaires de la Vie Réligieuse* constituted the first explicit attempt to interpret a social reality in terms of structure, function and system, showing in this case how a set of beliefs was essential for perpetuation of a specific structure, and therefore somehow determined by it. In contrast to Tocqueville who relied to a considerable extent on personal observation, this was done from a distance and based solely on the existing printed information. The next step in fusing Spencer's heritage with that of Tocqueville (as transmitted through Durkheim) was taken by Malinowski and Radcliffe-Brown who were the first to gather and order ethnographic data with an explicit purpose of disentangling the relationships of mutual dependence between various customs and beliefs. This sounds simple enough but it was neither an easy nor an unimportant step as can be seen by confronting their works with older ethnography (or later but unaffected by their influence) where one finds each institution or custom described in isolation without any attempt to view society as a system. Living among the Trobrianders for four years and learning their language, Malinowski also set a new standard for data-collecting, but Radcliffe-Brown was less outstanding as an observer, and the importance of his contribution resided in introducing sociological theory into ethnographic fieldwork. He, as well as Malinowski (whose mind was less precise and more prone to errors but more fertile in ideas) put forth a number of theories about the functioning of specific customs and institutions, but their most general concepts were those to which Herbert Spencer had given currency before they were born.

A number of critics have voiced objections to the functionalist doctrine, but the issue cannot be examined here, and as far as my own views on this matter are concerned I must refer the reader to chapter IV of my *Uses* (*Elements*) *of Comparative Sociology*. I must say, however, that in contrast to modern functionalists—and I mean the respectable representatives of this school rather than the ponderous jargon-mongerers who reiterate the words 'structure' and 'function' (often illogically hyphenated) to adorn their ponderous platitudes—Spencer cannot be accused of propounding a theoretical framework which excludes change. On the contrary: his transformist orientation (derived from Lamarck and re-inforced by Darwin) explains social change very well: societies and institutions are struggling for living space, and only those survive which are able to adapt themselves to the changing environment. The extension of the notion of natural selection to the competition between polities and institutions positively entails change rather than merely allowing for it. What is equally important, the selectionist viewpoint provides a justification for the otherwise gratuitous functionalist assumption that every enduring institution must have a function—in the sense of Radcliffe-Brown's definition of 'making a contribution to the continued existence of the whole'. We must reject the view of the so-called diffusionists that a culture is an accidental assemblage of customs and beliefs, if we accept Spencer's theory of the survival of the fittest, according to which a system consisting of structural parts whose functions are not adjusted to each other or to the demands of the environment will be destroyed by its competitors.

In addition to providing a justification for the fundamental assumption of functionalism, the notion of natural selection of social systems and institutions constitutes the cornerstone of evolutionism because it accounts for the secular evolution of social systems towards greater complexity, provided we accept the additional assumption (more than plausible in sociology though debatable in biology) that an increase in differentiation and integration—or to use Spencer's favourite expression 'an advance in organization'—more often than not bestows a superiority of power in the struggle for survival.

Montesquieu's monumental contribution towards laying the foundations for sociology consisted of demonstrating (though not analysing) the idea that different institutions depend on one another. For our taste his treatment is too legalistic—too much in terms of laws, and not enough in terms of less obvious characteristics of society—and too static. He was the last of the great social philosophers to view humanity statically; for all the subsequent proto-sociological thinkers of note (beginning with Adam Ferguson, Hume and Turgot) were very much concerned with the onward march of mankind. Condorcet, Auguste Comte and Buckle were thinking primarily about the progress of knowledge, although Comte did discuss the problem of coherence of social institutions. John Millar, Adam Smith and later Marx and Engels focused on the improvements in the production of wealth. Spencer's concept of evolution combined Montesquieu's idea of a closely knit interdependence of institutions with Condorcet's and Comte's version of progress, by postulating a global and permanent trend towards increasing inter-dependence—or, to use his term, integration.

If we take the three great near-contemporaries—Comte, Marx and Spencer—we can see that each focused on an aspect of the global trend which in fact entails the other two: Comte on the progress of knowledge, Marx on the development of productive forces, and Spencer on the increase of structural integration. With his insufficiently analysed and ill-defined concept of 'rationalization' Max Weber seems to have been grouping for an idea encompassing all three master keys of his great predecessors.

Whereas Comte drew a plan for a social system conducive to moral improvement, and Marx attacked the very idea of universal moral standards, Spencer attempted to deduce ethical norms from the principle of evolution. He did not succeed in overcoming Hume's argument about the impossibility of deducing what ought to be from statements about what is, or was, or will be happening, without postulating an *a priori* standard of value. Nonetheless, even apart from various more specific valuable insights into ethical problems, Spencer's general assumption is by no means absurd; for if we want a non-fideistic and non *a priori* foundation

B

for ethics, then ascertaining the general direction of evolution of mankind (as well as of nature) is as good a method of finding it as any.

SOCIAL DARWINISM AND PROBLEMS OF ETHICS

Darwin's theory of natural selection supplied the conceptual ammunition for an ideology (later labelled as social Darwinism) which allayed the qualms of the rich about not helping the poor by telling them that the latter's sufferings were an inevitable price of progress which could occur only through the struggle for existence ending in the survival of the fittest and the elimination of the unfit. The fallacies underlying this ideology were exposed by its critics as soon as it was formulated. The Russian anarchist Prince Kropotkin has shown in his famous book on *Mutual Aid* that even among the sociable animals individual survival depends on solidarity within the group, while other writers have pointed out that victory in the race for wealth cannot be equated with natural selection because the poor procreate faster than the rich. Other critics have reminded the social Darwinists of the teachings of Condorcet and other writers of the Enlightenment that the progress of civilization depends on the accumulation of knowledge, and that the biological changes could not have been fast enough to account for the rise and fall of civilizations. Nonetheless, social Darwinism remained popular so long as the class of competitive free enterprise retained its ascendancy. Its enduring contribution to human knowledge was to raise the question of how social institutions affect the genetic composition of populations, which remain of great practical as well as theoretical importance.

Spencer did not escape the pitfalls of social Darwinism which mar parts of his later publications, including *The Study of Sociology*. These foibles, however, do not undermine the value of his true innovation which was to apply the concept of natural selection to the problem of survival of groups and, above all, of institutional arrangements. Looking at structural patterns in this way amounted to moving to a higher level of abstraction. To explain the prevalence of polygamy, for instance, Spencer does not rely on suppositions about the nature of males and females but points out that under conditions of constant warfare a tribe which practices polygamy can replenish its ranks much faster than one which does not, and therefore has a much greater chance of surviving. From this viewpoint the diffusion and permanence of a custom depends on its ability to enhance the power of survival of the group where it is established. The full implications of this valuable insight have not yet been worked out; and its neglect accounts to a large extent for the sterility of much recent theorising inspired by Spencer's notion of function.

Despite its usefulness in making people realize that society is a system where subtle processes of adaptation and equilibration take place which cannot be explained in terms of individual consciousness and purpose, the stress on organic equivalents of social structures and processes—labelled organicism by its critics —was leading sociology into a blind alley, because it was diverting attention from the need to analyse empirical material. The critics were right to insist that drawing analogies between society and organism proves nothing about either but they were wrong not to see that, even apart from its value as a source of suggestions for understanding each domain, this approach has a value of its own; for surely it is worthwhile to know that analogous processes (or mechanisms) operate in different realms of existence. Actually, cybernetics, or its most general form known as general systems theory, studies precisely that; and therefore Spencer can be regarded as its forerunner, if not the true founder. True, general cybernetics is both more exact (as it consists largely of mathematical formulae) and more restricted, as it only studies precisely defined self-regulating systems, whereas Spencer's *First Principles* attempted to encompass even such processes as the origin of the universe and the evolution of the galaxies. Nonetheless, the affinity is clear.

The founder of modern cybernetics, Norbert Weiner, did not give much thought to sociology despite having written a book called *Human Use of Human Beings*; and was interested, as the subtitle of his *Cybernetics* indicates, in 'control and communication in the animal and the machine'. Recently, however, the application of cybernetic concepts (or rather terminology) has become a fashion if not a craze. This is not the place to discuss the uses and abuses of cybernetics in sociology; and I must refer the reader on this point to Chapter I of *Uses (Elements) of Comparative Sociology* where I have tried to show that, despite its undeniable potentialities, up till now the chief use of cybernetic terms in the study of politics and society has been to blind the reader with pseudo-science and to give spurious weight to ponderous platitudes. Let us, however, leave these questions aside. What matters as far as Spencer is concerned is that the recent cybernetic interpretations of society are a continuation of his organicism; and that all the criticisms which have been levelled at the latter apply to the former too. In fact even more so because the analogies between society and machines are a great deal more tenuous than those between society and organism.

The advantages of organicism as well as of the cybernetic viewpoint in sociology are the same: namely that by contemplating analogies with phenomena which are (or seem to be) better understood we might discover relations between social phenomena, or ways of analysing them, which would not occur to us otherwise. The concept of feedback, however, adds nothing to what we can find in Spencer whose organicism takes fully into account the process of self-regulation through social homologues of afferent and efferent nerves. The recent writers who talk about the nerves of government are simply repeating Spencer.

As his contemporaneous admirers T. H. Huxley and Lester Ward have already noted, Spencer's organismic view of society stood in disharmony with his ideology of most extreme *laissez faire* in all respects (be it economics or educational policy or public health) because the organic analogy suggests the inevitability (if not desirability) of centralization of control, and of the subjugation of the parts (that is to say, individuals) to the interests of the whole as perceived by the central organ. Rather than to fundamentalist liberalism, Spencer's theory of society should have led him to espouse some form of authoritarian collectivism because the organisms regarded as higher display a greater centralization of the nervous system, and a greater subordination of the parts to the whole. Indeed, his system provides a much more logical justification for socialism (as it is practised rather than preached) than Marx's theory of class struggles; from which one could infer the paramount need to prevent an excessive accumulation of power in the hands of the rulers, and therefore to bolster up small private property as the bulwark against overweening bureaucracy.

When Spencer was widely regarded as the foremost philosopher of his time, and was setting the tone of progressive thinking, Karl Marx was living penuriously on charity, read only by a small band of alienated intellectuals. Now Marx has replaced Jesus or Confucius over a large part of the globe, while an influential contemporary American writer on the history of sociology asks rhetorically: 'Who now reads Spencer?' This reversal of fortunes certainly does not reflect the relative weight of their contributions to knowledge, but can be explained in terms of sociology of beliefs.

It stands to reason that a writer who rides on the crest of a wave and provides intellectual ammunition for the defence of the status quo has much more chance of acquiring fame during his lifetime than a prophet of revolution. But by the time the old bastions have fallen their extollers' fame will have lost its basis, whereas the standing of their one-time critics may rise because what they had been attacking can no longer hit back . . . although whether in fact it will rise, depends on the usefulness of the old critiques to the new establishments.

As suggested earlier, from a logical point of view, Spencer's organicism should be welcomed by the rulers of authoritarian collectivist states, but ideological affinities derive not from logic but from expressions of sentiments; and here the determining fact is that Spencer's explicit pronouncements favoured the ideals and interests of the free-enterprise, anti-statist, bourgeoisie (that is to say, independent, small and middling businessmen, farmers and artisans) who have since been thoroughly demoted. Whereas Marx thundered against this now defeated class, Spencer fulminated against bureaucracy which has turned out to be the winner. As the Polish anarchist Waclaw Machajski diagnosed towards the end of the last century, Marxism is an ideology of the bureaucratic intelligentsia which enables them to enlist the support of the workers for overthrowing landlords and capitalists, and usurping their place. By refraining from working out any plans for a future society, Marx has greatly facilitated the rise of his cult, because a vague blessing in the absence of a concrete blueprint amounted to drawing a blank cheque for anyone who wished to invoke his name. Furthermore, cults thrive on obscurity and ambiguity permitting all kinds of convenient interpretations . . . and these abound in Marx, whereas Spencer is much too clear, as well as too emotionally committeed to Victorian England to be a modern totem. Spencer's forthright opinions on the public affairs of his day show that thinking in terms of function, structure and system need not lead to a timorous fence-sitting, as one might suspect from the pronouncements of today's addicts to these words.

There was little that was startlingly original in Spencer's political opinions (despite the forceful ingenuity with which they are often argued) and the enduring heritage of liberalism has been more judiciously stated by John Stuart Mill. Nonetheless, his diatribes against the short-sightedness, inertia, pettiness and selfishness of politicians and bureaucrats retain their perennial topicality and (especially in socialist lands) make much more realistic and profitable reading than Marx's visions of the withering away of the state.

The merit of a pronouncement on current issues often stands in an inverse relation to the acclaim it elicits because what people need most to be told is what contradicts the prevalent prejudices rather than what confirms them, and originality usually puts a thinker at odds with the dominant opinion. So at the time they were written Marx's vituperations and exposures of the evils of capitalist exploitation were more meritorious than Spencer's eulogies of *laissez-faire* (then at its zenith) and his condemnations of bureaucracy (then at its nadir). Capitalist ownership was indeed the chief form of exploitation in the most advanced countries at the time, and Spencer's silence on this subject no doubt made it easier for him to win fame in his life time but also helped to discredit him in the eyes of social reformers. By now, however, the situation has been reversed in the highly industrialized countries where it is difficult to find tyrannical factory masters able to squeeze the last ounce of sweat out of their workers in exchange for a starvation wage. Furthermore, with capitalism becoming increasingly bureaucratized or replaced by various brands of state-controlled economy, bureaucracy is becoming the chief agent of oppression and exploitation, which makes Marx more and more out of date, while endowing Spencer's impassioned pleas for liberty, and his tirades against the bureaucratic octopus, with merit which they did not have when they were written.

Spencer's account of the evolution of social institutions had to be based on the historiography and ethnography existing at the time, the latter consisting mainly of reports from travellers and missionaries. But this adds to, rather than detracts from, the value of the book for the reader of today who can obtain from it a picture of what the primitive world looked like to the European of a hundred years ago. It must be remembered moreover that modern anthropology has not entirely superseded the old travellers' tales because the social reality has changed in the meantime. However, the main reason why the empirical parts of his *Principles of Sociology* retain their value is that to this day they remain the only account of the genesis of institutions such as representative assemblies, political headship, administrative machinery and ecclesiastic organization, which integrates historiographic and ethnographic materials from a world-wide perspective. And it must be added that whereas a number of sociological theorists, such as Max Weber, Otto Hintze or the forgotten genius John Mackinnon Robertson, had a wider knowledge of history, none of them equalled his acquaintance with the ethnographic data, in which respect he was surpassed only by more narrowly specialized students of primitive culture like Lewis Henry Morgan or Friedrich Ratzel.

The solidity of Spencer's treatment of social structures varied according to the evolutionary stage. He had relatively little to say that was new about the social circumstances of his days, and his accounts of the evolution of institutions peter out when he approaches the industrial civilization. As an observer and interpreter of current trends he does not attain the originality of Tocqueville or the Marx-Engels couple . . . except on two very important points, namely the dangers of bureaucracy and of a revival of absolutism brought about by a resurgence of warfare. Even on commercial pre-industrial Europe, he was not as well informed as Thomas Henry Buckle, while the much earlier writers, Charles Comte and Volney had a much deeper knowledge of the great civilizations of the East. His chief strength lay in the study of transitions from tribal to supra-tribal political, economic and ecclesiastic institutions, where he could integrate historiographic with ethnographic data, and illuminate them from the perspective of his theory. His account of the emergence of the administrative bodies, for instance, makes a very instructive companion to Weber's treatment of bureaucracy, of which it constitutes in a way an extension backwards: not chronologically but into a lower evolutionary stage.

As a global view of the genesis of the complex political, economic and ecclesiastic structures, Spencer's works have not yet been superseded, and remain an essential reading for every sociologist and sociologically oriented historian, apart from constituting a living part of the heritage of sociological theory.

The pages which follow contain Spencer's main ideas of sociological relevance. As (in contrast to many recent writers on social systems) he always illustrates his general propositions with a wealth of concrete and vivid examples, the reader will acquaint himself with a good sample of the factual data which Spencer used to substantiate his theories. However, given the limited scope of an introductory volume, any more extensive analyses of separate institutions have had to be omitted; for despite their great interest they must give precedence to the basic ideas. The most valuable parts of his treatment of institutions can be found in the abridged edition of *Principles of Sociology* recently published by Macmillan, London.

It was necessary, on the other hand, to include some exposition of his social philosophy because Spencer believed that ethics ought to rest upon biology and sociology which alone can reveal the goal of social evolution; and that the value of individual as well as collective practices can be assessed by ascertaining whether they subserve or impede the attainment of this goal. This view naturally assumes an unproven premise that the general direction of the march of mankind must be good; and Spencer advances no arguments to invalidate Hume's objection to jumping from what is to what ought to be. Nonetheless, Spencer's evolutionary ethics provide some guidance for judging what is good and bad, whereas the linguistic philosophers' discussions of how people talk about ethics do not. In any case, whether Spencer was right or wrong, he always employed his tremendous powers of reasoning to deal with issues of enduring importance, and launched ideas with which we may disagree but which we can ignore only at the price of deplorably narrowing our intellectual horizon.

Part One
A Science of Society

(A) Nature of the Social Science[1]

KINDS OF AGGREGATES[2]

Out of bricks, well burnt, hard, and sharp-angled, lying in heaps by his side, the bricklayer builds, even without mortar, a wall of some height that has considerable stability. With bricks made of bad materials, irregularly burnt, warped, cracked, and many of them broken, he cannot build a dry wall of the same height and stability. The dockyard-labourer, piling cannon-shot, is totally unable to make these spherical masses stand at all as the bricks stand. There are, indeed, certain definite shapes into which they may be piled—that of a tetrahedron, or that of a pyramid having a square base, or that of an elongated wedge allied to the pyramid. In any of these forms they may be put together symmetrically and stably; but not in forms with vertical sides or highly-inclined sides. Once more, if, instead of equal spherical shot, the masses to be piled are boulders, partially but irregularly rounded and of various sizes, no definite stable form is possible. A loose heap, indefinite in its surface and angles, is all the labourer can make of them. Putting which several facts together, and asking what is the most general truth they imply, we see it to be this—that the character of the aggregate is determined by the characters of the units.

If we pass from units of these visible, tangible kinds, to the units contemplated by chemists and physicists as making up masses of matter, the same truth meets us. Each so-called element, each combination of elements, each re-combination of the compounds, has a form of crystallization. Though its crystals differ

---

[1] From *The Study of Sociology*, 1889.
[2] The paragraph numbers with which Spencer characteristically divided his sections have been removed since they would not have the same consecutive relevance in selected passages. In their place, small subtitles have been introduced throughout, in order to 'signpost' and make as clear as possible the order and flow of his argument. (R.F.)

in their sizes, and are liable to be modified by truncations of angles and apices, as well as by partial mergings into one another, yet the type of structure, as shown by cleavage, is constant: particular kinds of molecules severally have particular shapes into which they settle themselves as they aggregate. And though in some cases it happens that a substance, simple or compound, has two or even more forms of aggregation, yet the recognized interpretation is, that these different forms are the forms assumed by molecules made different in their structures by allotropic or isomeric changes. In brief, it may be unhesitatingly affirmed, as an outcome of physics and chemistry, that throughout all phenomena presented by dead matter, the qualities of the units necessitate certain traits in the aggregates.

This truth is again exemplified by aggregates of living matter. The substance of each plant or animal has a proclivity towards the structure which that plant or animal presents—a proclivity clearly shown where the conditions to the maintenance of life are sufficiently simple, and where the tissue has not become too much organized to permit rearrangement. The perpetually-cited case of the polype, each part of which, when it is cut into several, presently puts on the polype-shape, and gains structures and powers like those of the original whole, illustrates this truth among animals. Among plants it is well exemplified by the begonias. Here a complete plant grows from a fragment of a leaf stuck in the ground; and, in *Begonia phyllomaniaca*, complete plants grow even out of scales that fall from the leaves and the stem—a fact showing, like the fact which the polype furnishes, that the units everywhere present, tend to aggregate in a form like that of the organism they belong to; and reminding us of the universal fact that the units composing every germ, animal or vegetal, tend towards the parental type of aggregation.

Thus, given the natures of the units, and the nature of the aggregate they compose is pre-determined. I say the *nature*, meaning, of course, the essential traits, and not including the incidental. By the characters of the units are necessitated certain limits within which the characters of the aggregate must fall. The circumstances attending aggregation greatly modify the results; but the truth here to be recognized is, that these circumstances, in some cases perhaps preventing aggregation altogether, in other cases impeding it, in other cases facilitating it more or less, can never give to the aggregate characters that do not consist with the characters of the units. No favouring conditions will enable the labourer to pile cannon-shot into a vertical wall; no favouring conditions will make it possible for common salt, which crystallizes on the regular system, to crystallize, like sulphate of soda, on the oblique prismatic system; no favouring conditions will empower the fragment of a polype to take on the structure of a mollusk.

Among such social aggregates as inferior creatures fall into, the same truth holds. Whether they live in a mere assemblage, or whether they live in something like an organized union with division of labour among its members, as happens in many cases, is unquestionably determined by the properties of the units. Given the structures and instincts of the individuals as we find them, and the community they form will inevitably present certain traits; and no community having such traits can be formed out of individuals having other structures and instincts.

SOCIETIES AS AGGREGATES

Those who have been brought up in the belief that there is one law for the rest of the Universe and another law for Mankind, will doubtless be astonished by the proposal to include aggregates of men in this generalization. And yet that the properties of ultimate parts determine the properties of the whole they make up, evidently holds of societies as of other things. A general survey of tribes and nations, past and present, shows clearly that it is so; and a brief consideration of the conditions shows, with no less clearness, that it must be so.

Ignoring for the moment the peculiar traits of races and individuals, observe the traits common to members of the species at large; and consider how these must affect their relations when associated.

They have all needs for food, and have corresponding desires. To all of them exertion is a physiological expense; must bring a certain return in nutriment, if it is not to be detrimental; and is accompanied by repugnance when pushed to excess, or even before reaching excess. All of them are liable to bodily injuries, with accompanying pains, from various extreme physical actions. They are in common liable to emotional pains, of positive and negative

kinds, from one another's actions; and from one another's actions
of particular classes they receive emotional pleasures.

Conspicuous, however, as is this possession of certain fundamental qualities by all individuals, there is no due recognition of the
truths that from these individual qualities must result certain
qualities in an assemblage of individuals; that if the individuals
forming one assemblage are like in nature to the individuals
forming another assemblage, the two assemblages will have
likenesses; and that the assemblages will differ in their characters
in proportion as the component individuals of the one differ in
their characters from those of the other. Yet when this, which is
almost a truism, has been admitted, it cannot be denied that in
every community there is a group of phenomena growing out of
the phenomena presented by its members—a set of properties in
the aggregate determined by the sets of properties in the units;
and that the relations of the two sets form the subject-matter of a
science. It needs but to ask what would happen if men avoided
one another, as various inferior creatures do, to see that the very
possibility of a society depends on a certain emotional attribute in
the individual. It needs but to ask what would happen if each man
liked best the man who gave him most pain, to perceive that social
relations, supposing them to be possible, would be utterly unlike
the social relations resulting from the greater liking which men
individually have for others who give them pleasure. It needs but to
ask what would happen if, instead of ordinarily preferring the
easiest ways of achieving their ends, men preferred to achieve
their ends in the most troublesome ways, to infer that then a
society, if one could exist, would be a widely-different society from
any we know. And if, as these extreme cases show us, cardinal
traits in societies arise from cardinal traits in men, it cannot be
questioned that less-marked traits in societies arise from less-
marked traits in men; and that there must everywhere be a
consensus between the special structures and actions of the one and
the special structures and actions of the other.

A SCIENCE OF THE SOCIAL AGGREGATE REQUIRED

Setting out, then, with this general principle, that the properties
of its members determine the properties of the mass, we conclude

that there must be a social science expressing the relations between the two. Beginning with types of men who form but small and incoherent social aggregates, such a science has to show in what ways the individual qualities, intellectual and emotional, negative further aggregation. It has to explain how modifications of individual nature, arising under modified conditions of life, make larger aggregates possible. It has to trace, in societies of some size, the genesis of the social relations, regulative and operative, into which the members fall. It has to exhibit the stronger and more prolonged influences which, by further modifying the characters of citizens, facilitate wider and closer unions with consequent further complexities of structure. Among societies of all orders and sizes, from the smallest and rudest up to the largest and most civilized, it has to ascertain what traits there are in common, determined by the common traits of human beings; what less general traits, distinguishing certain groups of societies, result from traits distinguishing certain races of men; and what peculiarities in each society are traceable to the peculiarities of its members. In every case *its object is to interpret the growth, development, structure, and functions, of the social aggregate, as brought about by the mutual actions of individuals whose natures are partly like those of all men, partly like those of kindred races, partly distinctive.*[1]

These phenomena have, of course, to be explained with due reference to the conditions each society is placed in—the conditions furnished by its locality and by its relations to neighbouring societies. Noting this merely to prevent misapprehensions, the general fact which here concerns us, is that, given men having certain properties, and an aggregate of such men must have certain derivative properties which form the subject-matter of a science.

STRUCTURES AND FUNCTIONS, THEIR ORIGIN, DEVELOPMENT AND DECLINE

The kind of relation which an account of a man's sayings and doings throughout life, bears to an account of his bodily and mental evolution, structural and functional, is like the kind of relation borne by that narrative of a nation's actions and fortunes its historian gives us, to a description of its organization, and the

[1] The italics are mine. S. A.

ways in which the structures and functions of its parts have gradually established themselves. And if it is an error to say that there is no science of man, because the events of a man's life cannot be foreseen, it is equally an error to say that there is no science of society, because there can be no prevision of the occurrences which make up ordinary history.

Of course, I do not say that the parallel between an individual organism and a social organism is so close, that the distinction to be clearly drawn in the one case may be drawn with like clearness in the other. The structures and functions of a social organism are obviously far less specific, far more modifiable, far more dependent on conditions that are never twice alike. All I mean is that, as in the one case so in the other, there lie underneath the incidents of conduct, not forming subject-matter for science, certain vital phenomena, which do form subject-matter for science. Just as in the man there are structures and functions which make possible the doings his biographer tells of, so in the nation there are structures and functions which make possible the doings its historian tells of; and in both cases it is with these structures and functions, in their origin, development and decline, that science is concerned.

To make better the parallel, and further to explain the nature of the social science, we must say that the morphology and physiology of society, instead of corresponding to the morphology and physiology of man, correspond rather to morphology and physiology in general. Social organisms, like individual organisms, are to be arranged into classes and sub-classes; though not, of course, into classes and sub-classes having anything like the same definiteness or the same constancy. But they exhibit likenesses and differences which justify the putting of them into major groups most-markedly contrasted, and, within these, arranging them in minor groups less-markedly contrasted. And just as biology discovers certain general traits of development, structure, and function, holding throughout all organisms, others holding throughout certain great groups, others throughout certain sub-groups these contain; so sociology has to recognize truths of social development, structure, and function, that are some of them universal, some of them general, some of them special.

SOME TRUTHS ABOUT SOCIAL SYSTEMS:
A CLEAR IDEA OF SOCIOLOGY

And now to make definite the conception of a social science thus shadowed forth in a general way, let me set down a few truths of the kind indicated. Some that I propose to name are familiar; and others I add, not because of their interest or importance, but because they are easy of exposition. The aim is simply to convey a clear idea of sociology.

Take, first, the uniform fact that along with social aggregation there always goes some kind of organization. In the lowest stages, where the groups are very small and very incoherent, there is no established subordination—no centre of control. Chieftainships of settled kinds come only along with larger and more coherent groups. The evolution of a governmental structure having some strength and permanence, is the condition under which alone any considerable growth of a society can take place. A differentiation of the originally-homogeneous mass of units into a co-ordinating part and a co-ordinated part, is the indispensable first step.

Evolution of societies in size is ever accompanied by evolution of their regulative centres; which, having become permanent, presently become more or less complex. In small tribes, chieftain-ship, generally wanting in stability, is quite simple; but as tribes enlarge by growth, or by reduction of other tribes to subjection, the governing agency begins to develop by the addition of sub-ordinate governing agencies.

Simple and familiar as are these facts, we are not, therefore, to overlook their significance. That men rise into the state of social aggregation only on condition that they lapse into relations of inequality in respect of power, and are made to co-operate as a whole only by the help of a structure securing obedience, is none the less a fact in science because it is a trite fact. This is a primary common trait in social aggregates derived from a common trait in their units. It is a truth in sociology comparable to the bio-logical truth, that the first step in the production of any living organism, high or low, is a differentiation whereby a central portion becomes distinguished from a peripheral portion. And such exceptions to this biological truth as we find in those minute non-nucleated portions of protoplasm that are the very lowest living things, are paralleled by those exceptions to the sociological truth, seen in the small incoherent assemblages of men forming the very lowest types of societies.

Differentiation of the regulating part from the regulated part, is, in primitive groups of men, not only imperfectly established but vague. The chief does not at first become unlike his fellow-savages in his functions, otherwise than by exercising greater sway. He hunts, makes weapons, works, and manages his private affairs, in just the same ways as the rest; while in war he differs from other warriors only by his predominant influence, not by ceasing to be a private soldier. And along with this slight separation from the body of the tribe in military functions and industrial functions, there is only a slight separation politically: judicial action is but feebly represented by exercise of his personal authority in keeping order.

At a higher stage, the power of the chief being well established, he no longer supports himself. Still he remains undistinguished industrially from other members of the dominant class, which has grown up while chieftainship has been getting settled; for he simply gets work done by deputy, as they do. Nor is further extension of his power accompanied by complete separation of the political from the industrial functions; for he habitually remains a regulator of production, and in many cases a regulator of trade, presiding over acts of exchange. Of his several controlling activities, this last is, however, the one which he first ceases personally to carry on. Industry early shows a tendency towards self-control, apart from the control which the chief exercises as political and military head. The primary social differentiation which we have noted between the regulative part and the operative part, is presently followed by a distinction, which eventually becomes very marked, between the internal arrangements of the two parts: the operative part evolving within itself agencies by which processes of production, distribution, and exchange are co-ordinated, while co-ordination of the non-operative part continues on its original footing.

Along with differentiations which make conspicuous the contrast between the operative and regulative structures, there go differentiations within the regulative structures themselves. The head man, at first uniting the characters of king, judge, captain, and often priest, has his functions more and more specialized as the evolution of the society advances. Though continuing to be supreme judge, he does most of his judging by deputy; though remaining nominally head of his army, the actual leading of it falls gradually into the hands of subordinates; though still retaining ecclesiastical supremacy, his priestly functions almost cease; though in theory the maker of the law, the actual making of it is slowly assumed by another instrumentality. So that out of the original co-ordinating agent having various functions, there eventually develop several co-ordinating agencies which divide these functions among them.

Each of these agencies, too, follows the same law. Originally simple, it step by step subdivides into many parts, and becomes an organization, administrative, judicial, ecclesiastical, or military, having within itself graduated classes, and a more or less distinct form of government.

I will not complicate this statement by doing more than recognizing the variations that occur in cases where supreme power does not lapse into the hands of one man (which, however, in early stages of social evolution is an unstable modification). And I must explain that the above propositions are to be taken with the understanding that differences of detail are passed over to gain brevity and clearness. Add to which that it is beside the purpose of the argument to carry the description beyond these first stages. But bearing in mind that without here elaborating a science of sociology, nothing more than a rude outline of cardinal truths can be given, enough has been said to show that in the development of social structures, there may be recognized certain most-general facts, certain less-general facts, and certain facts successively more special; just as there may be recognized general and special facts of evolution in individual organisms.

THE RELATION BETWEEN STRUCTURE AND GROWTH

To extend, as well as to make clearer, this conception of the social science, let me here set down a question which comes within its sphere. What is the relation in a society between structure and growth? Up to what point is structure necessary for growth? after what point does it retard growth? at what point does it arrest growth?

There exists in the individual organism a duplex relation between growth and structure which it is difficult adequately to express. Excluding the cases of a few low organisms living under special conditions, we may properly say that great growth is not possible without high structure. The whole animal kingdom, throughout its invertebrate and vertebrate classes, may be cited in evidence. On the other hand, among the superior organisms, and especially among those leading active lives, there is a marked tendency for completion of structure to go along with arrest of growth. While an animal of elevated type is growing, its parts continue imperfectly organized—the bones remain partially cartilaginous, the muscles are soft, the brain lacks definiteness; and the details of structure throughout all its members are finished only after growth has ceased. Why these relations are as we find them, it is not difficult to see. That a young animal may grow, it must digest, circulate blood, breathe, excrete waste products, and so forth; to do which it must have tolerably complete viscera, vascular system, etc. That it may eventually become able to get its own food, it has to develop gradually the needful appliances and aptitudes; to which end it must begin with limbs, and senses, and nervous system, that have considerable degrees of efficiency. But along with every increment of growth achieved by the help of these partially-developed structures, there has to go an alteration of the structures themselves. If they were rightly adjusted to the preceding smaller size, they are wrongly adjusted to the succeeding larger size. Hence they must be re-moulded—un-built and re-built. Manifestly, therefore, in proportion as the previous building has been complete, is the greatness of the obstacle in the shape of un-building and re-building. The bones show us how this difficulty is met. In the thigh-bone of a boy, for instance, there exists between the head and the cylindrical part of the bone, a place where the original cartilaginous state continues; and where, by the addition of new cartilage in which new osseous matter is deposited, the shaft of the bone is lengthened: the like going on in an answering place at the other end of the shaft. Complete ossification at these two places occurs only when the bone has ceased to increase in length; and, on considering what would have happened had the bone been ossified from end to end before its lengthening was complete, it will be seen what an insuperable obstacle is thus escaped. In like manner throughout the organism:

though structure up to a certain point is requisite for growth, structure beyond that point impedes growth. How necessary is this law we shall equally see in a more complex case—say, the growth of an entire limb. There is a certain size and proportion of parts, which a limb ordinarily has in relation to the rest of the body. Throw upon that limb extra function, and within moderate limits it will increase in strength and bulk. If the extra function begins early in life, the limb may be rendered considerably more massive than usual; but if the extra function begins much later, the deviation is less: in neither case, however, being great. If we consider how increase of the limb is effected, we shall see why this is so. More active function brings a greater local supply of blood; and, for a time, new tissue is formed in excess of waste. But the local supply of blood is limited by the sizes of the arteries which bring it; and though, up to a certain point, increase of flow is gained by temporary dilatation of them, yet, beyond that point, increase can be gained only by un-building and re-building them. Such alterations of arteries slowly take place—less slowly in the smaller peripheral ones, more slowly in the larger ones out of which they branch; since these have to be altered all the way back to their points of divergence from the great central blood-vessels. Simultaneously, the channels for carrying off waste products must be re-modelled, both locally and centrally. The nerve-trunks, too, and also the centres from which they come, must be adjusted to the greater demands on them. Nay, more; with a given visceral system, a large extra quantity of blood cannot be habitually sent to one part of the body, without decreasing the quantities sent to other parts; and, therefore, structural changes have to be made by which the drafting-off of blood to these other parts is diminished. Hence the great resistance to increase in the size of a limb beyond a certain moderate amount. Such increase cannot be effected without un-building and re-building not only the parts that directly minister to the limb but, eventually, all remoter parts. So that the bringing of structures into perfect fitness for certain requirements, immensely hinders the adaptation of them to other requirements—re-adjustments become difficult in proportion as adjustments are made complete.

How far does this law hold in the social organism? To what extent does it happen here, too, that the multiplying and elaborating of institutions, and the perfecting of arrangements for gaining immediate ends, raise impediments to the development of better institutions and to the future gaining of higher ends? Socially, as well as individually, organization is indispensable to growth: beyond a certain point there cannot be further growth without further organization. Yet there is good reason to suspect that beyond this point organization is indirectly repressive—increases the obstacles to those re-adjustments required for larger growth and more perfect structure. Doubtless the aggregate we call a society is much more plastic than an individual living aggregate to which it is here compared—its type is far less fixed. Nevertheless, there is evidence that its type tends continually to become fixed, and that each addition to its arrangements is a step towards the fixation. A few instances will show how this is true alike of the material structures a society develops and of its institutions, political or other.

Cases, insignificant perhaps, but quite to the point, are furnished by our appliances for locomotion. Not to dwell on the minor ones within cities which, however, show us that existing arrangements are impediments to better arrangements, let us pass to railways. Observe how the inconveniently narrow gauge (which, taken from that of stage-coach wheels, was itself inherited from an antecedent system of locomotion), has become an insuperable obstacle to a better gauge. Observe, also, how the kind of carriage, which was derived from the body of a stage-coach (some of the early first-class carriages bearing the words *tria juncta in uno*), having become established, it is difficult now to replace it by the more convenient kind later established in America, where they profited by our experience but were not hampered by our adopted plans. The enormous capital invested in our stock of carriages cannot be sacrificed. Gradually to introduce carriages of the American kind, by running them along with those of our own kind, is inconvenient, because of our many partings and joinings of trains. And thus we are obliged to go on with a kind that is inferior.

Take, again, our system of drainage. Urged on as it was some thirty years ago as a panacea for sundry sanitary evils, and spread as it has been by force of law through all our great towns, this system cannot now be replaced by a better system without extreme difficulty. Though, by necessitating decomposition where oxygen cannot get, and so generating chemical compounds that are unstable and poisonous, it has in many cases produced the very mischiefs it was to have prevented; though, by delivering the morbid products from fever-patients, etc., into a branching tube which communicates with all houses, it conveys to them infecting gases that are kept out only so long as stink-traps are in good order; yet it has become almost impossible now to adopt those methods by which the excreta of towns may be got rid of at once innocuously and usefully. Nay, worse—one part of our sanitary administration having insisted on a sewage-system by which Oxford, Reading, Maidenhead, Windsor, etc., pollute the water London has to drink, another part of our sanitary administration makes loud protests against the impurity of the water, which it charges with causing disease, not remarking, however, that law-enforced arrangements have produced the impurity. And now there must be a reorganization, which will be immensely impeded by the existing premature organization, before we can have either pure air or pure water.

Instances of another class are supplied by our educational institutions. Richly endowed, strengthened by their prestige, and by the bias given to those they have brought up, our colleges, public schools, and kindred schools early founded, useful as they once were, have long been great impediments to a higher education. By subsidizing the old they have starved the new. Even now they are retarding a culture better in matter and manner; both by occupying the field, and by partially incapacitating those who pass through them for seeing what a better culture is. Evidence of allied kind is offered by the educational organization established for dealing with the masses. The struggle going on between secularism and denominationalism in teaching, might alone show to anyone who seeks for the wider meanings of facts, that a structure which has ramified throughout a society, acquired an army of salaried officials looking for personal welfare and promotion, backed by classes, ecclesiastical and political, whose ideas and interests they further, is a structure which, if not unalterable, is difficult to alter in proportion as it is highly developed.

These few examples, which might be supported by others from the military organization, the ecclesiastical organization, the legal organization, will make comprehensible the analogy I have indicated; while they make clearer the nature of the social science, by bringing into view one of its questions. That with social organisms, as with individual organisms, structure up to a certain point facilitates growth, is obvious. That in the one case, as in the other, continued growth implies un-building and re-building, and that pre-existing structure therefore becomes in so far an impediment, seems also obvious. Whether it is true in the one case, as in the other, that completion of structure involves arrest of growth, and fixes the society to the type it has then reached, is a question to be considered. Without saying anything more by way of answer, it is, I think, manifest that this is one belonging to an order of questions entirely overlooked by historians and readers of history; and one pertaining to that social science which they say does not exist.

THE USE OF SOCIOLOGY

Are there any who utter the cui bono criticism? Probably not a few. I think I hear from some whose mental attitude is familiar to me, the doubt whether it is worth while to ask what happens among savage tribes; in what way chiefs and medicine-men arise; how the industrial functions become separated from the political; what are the original relations of the regulative classes to one another; how far the social structure is determined by the emotional natures of individuals, how far by their ideas, how far by their environment. Busied as men of this stamp are with what they call 'practical legislation' (by which they mean legislation that recognizes proximate causes and effects and ignores remote ones), they doubt whether conclusions of the kind social science proposes to draw, are good for much when drawn.

Something may, however, be said in defence of the study which they thus estimate. Of course, it is not to be put on the same level with their historical studies. The supreme value of knowledge respecting the genealogies of kings, and the fates of dynasties, and the quarrels of courts, is beyond question. Whether or not the plot for the murder of Amy Robsart was contrived by Leicester himself, with Queen Elizabeth as an accomplice, and whether or not the account of the Gowrie Conspiracy, as given by King James, was true, are obviously doubts to be decided before there can be formed any rational conclusions respecting the development of our political institutions. That Friedrich I of Prussia quarrelled with his stepmother, suspected her of trying to poison him, fled to his aunt, and when he succeeded to the Electorate, intrigued and bribed to obtain his kingship; that half-an-hour after his death his son Friedrich Wilhelm gave his courtiers notice to quit, commenced economizing his revenues, recruited and drilled his army, and presently began to hate and bully his son—these, and facts like these about all royal families in all ages, are facts without which civilization would evidently be incomprehensible. Nor can one dispense with full knowledge of events like those of Napoleon's wars—his Italian conquests and exactions, and perfidious treatment of Venice; his expedition to Egypt, successes and massacres there, failure at Acre, and eventual retreat; his various campaigns in Germany, Spain, Russia, etc.; for how, in the absence of such information, is it possible to judge what institutions should be advocated, and what legislative changes should be opposed?

Still, after due attention has been paid to these indispensable matters, a little time might, perhaps, with advantage be devoted to the natural history of societies. Some guidance for political conduct would possibly be reached by asking: what is the normal course of social evolution, and how will it be affected by this or that policy? It may turn out that legislative action of no kind can be taken that is not either favourable to, or at variance with, the processes of national growth and development as naturally going on; and that its desirableness is to be judged by this ultimate standard rather than by proximate standards. Without claiming too much, we may at any rate expect that, if there does exist an order among those structural and functional changes which societies pass through, knowledge of that order can scarcely fail to affect our judgments as to what is progressive and what retrograde —what is desirable, what is practicable, what is Utopian.

Part Two

Evolution

(A) Evolution and Dissolution[1]

An entire history of anything must include its appearance out of the imperceptible and its disappearance into the imperceptible. Be it a single object or the whole universe, any account which begins with it in a concrete form, or leaves off with it in a concrete form, is incomplete; since there remains an era of its knowable existence undescribed and unexplained. Admitting, or rather asserting, that knowledge is limited to the phenomenal, we have, by implication, asserted that the sphere of knowledge is co-extensive with the phenomenal—co-extensive with all modes of the unknowable that can affect consciousness. Hence, wherever we now find being so conditioned as to act on our senses, there arise the questions—how came it thus conditioned? and how will it cease to be thus conditioned? Unless on the assumption that it acquired a sensible form at the moment of perception, and lost its sensible form the moment after perception, it must have had an antecedent existence under this sensible form, and will have a subsequent existence under this sensible form. These preceding and succeeding existences under sensible forms, are possible subjects of knowledge; and knowledge has obviously not reached its limits until it has united the past, present, and future histories into a whole.

The sayings and doings of daily life imply more or less such knowledge, actual or potential, of states which have gone before and of states which will come after; and, indeed, the greater part of our knowledge involves these elements. Knowing any man personally, implies having before seen him under a shape much the same as his present shape; and knowing him simply as a man, implies the inferred antecedent states of infancy, childhood, and youth. Though the man's future is not known specifically, it is known generally: the facts that he will die and that his body will

[1] From *First Principles*, 1893.

decay are facts which complete in outline the changes to be hereafter gone through by him. So with all the objects around. The pre-existence under concrete forms of the woollens, silks, and cottons we wear, we can trace some distance back. We are certain that our furniture consists of matter which was aggregated by trees within these few generations. Even of the stones composing the walls of the house, we are able to say that years or centuries ago they formed parts of some stratum embedded in the earth. Moreover, respecting the hereafter of the wearable fabrics, the furniture, and the walls, we can assert thus much, that they are all in process of decay, and in periods of various lengths will lose their present coherent shapes. This general information which all men gain concerning the past and future careers of surrounding things, science has extended, and continues unceasingly to extend. To the biography of the individual man, it adds an intra-uterine biography beginning with him as a microscopic germ; and it follows out his ultimate changes until it finds his body resolved into the gaseous products of decomposition. Not stopping short at the sheep's back and the caterpillar's cocoon, it identifies in wool and silk the nitrogenous matters absorbed by the sheep and the caterpillar from plants. The substance of a plant's leaves, in common with the wood from which furniture is made, it again traces back to the vegetal assimilation of gases from the air and of certain minerals from the soil. And inquiring whence came the stratum of stone that was quarried to build the house, it finds that this was once a loose sediment deposited in an estuary or on the sea bottom.

If, then, the past and the future of each object, is a sphere of possible knowledge; and if intellectual progress consists largely, if not mainly, in widening our acquaintance with this past and this future; it is obvious that we have not acquired all the information within the grasp of our intelligence until we can, in some way or other, express the whole past and the whole future of each object and the aggregate of objects. Usually able, as we are, to say of any visible tangible thing how it came to have its present shape and consistence, we are fully possessed with the conviction that, setting out abruptly as we do with some substance which already had a concrete form, our history is incomplete: the thing had a history preceding the state with which we started. Hence our theory of things, considered individually or in their totality, is confessedly imperfect so long as any past or future portions of their sensible existences are unaccounted for.

May it not be inferred that philosophy has to formulate this passage from the imperceptible into the perceptible, and again from the perceptible into the imperceptible? Is it not clear that this general law of the redistribution of matter and motion, which we lately saw is required to unify the various kinds of changes, must also be one that unifies the successive changes which sensible existences, separately and together, pass through? Only by some formula combining these characters can knowledge be reduced to a coherent whole.

A FORMULA OF EVOLUTION

Already in the foregoing paragraphs the outline of such a formula is foreshadowed. Already in recognizing the fact that science, tracing back the genealogies of various objects, finds their components were once in diffused states, and pursuing their histories forwards, finds diffused states will be again assumed by them, we have recognized the fact that the formula must be one comprehending the two opposite processes of concentration and diffusion. And already in thus describing the general nature of the formula we have approached a specific expression of it. The change from a diffused, imperceptible state to a concentrated, perceptible state is an integration of matter and concomitant dissipation of motion; and the change from a concentrated, perceptible state to a diffused, imperceptible state is an absorption of motion and concomitant disintegration of matter. These are truisms. Constituent parts cannot aggregate without losing some of their relative motion; and they cannot separate without more relative motion being given to them. We are not concerned here with any motion which the components of a mass have with respect to other masses: we are concerned only with the motion they have with respect to one another. Confining our attention to this internal motion, and to the matter possessing it, the axiom which we have to recognize is that a progressing consolidation involves a decrease of internal motion; and that increase of internal motion involves a progressing unconsolidation.

When taken together, the two opposite processes thus formulated constitute the history of every sensible existence, under its simplest form. Loss of motion and consequent integration, eventually followed by gain of motion and consequent disintegration—see here a statement comprehensive of the entire series of changes passed through: comprehensive in an extremely general way, as any statement which holds of sensible existences at large must be; but still, comprehensive in the sense that all the changes gone through fall within it. This will probably be thought too sweeping an assertion; but we shall quickly find it justified.

For here we have to note the further all-important fact, that every change undergone by every sensible existence is a change in one or other of these two opposite directions. Apparently an aggregate which has passed out of some originally discrete state into a concrete state, thereafter remains for an indefinite period without undergoing further integration and without beginning to disintegrate. But this is untrue. All things are growing or decaying, accumulating matter or wearing away, integrating or disintegrating. All things are varying in their temperatures, contracting or expanding, integrating or disintegrating. Both the quantity of matter contained in an aggregate and the quantity of motion contained in it, increase or decrease; and increase or decrease of either is an advance towards greater diffusion or greater concentration. Continued losses or gains of substance, however slow, imply ultimate disappearance of indefinite enlargement; and losses or gains of the insensible motion we call heat will, if continued, produce complete integration or complete disintegration. The sun's rays falling on a cold mass, augmenting the molecular motions throughout it, and causing it to occupy more space, are beginning a process which if carried far will disintegrate the mass into liquid, and if carried farther will disintegrate the liquid into gas; and the diminution of bulk which a volume of gas undergoes as it parts with some of its molecular motion, is a diminution which, if the loss of molecular motion proceeds, will presently be followed by liquefaction and eventually by solidification. And since there is no such thing as an absolutely constant temperature, the necessary inference is that every aggregate is at every moment progressing towards either greater concentration or greater diffusion.

Not only does all change consisting in the addition or subtraction of matter come under this head; and not only does this head include all change called thermal expansion or contraction; but it is also, in a general way, comprehensive of all change distinguished as transposition. Every internal redistribution which leaves the component molecules or the constituent portions of a mass differently placed with respect to one another, is sure to be at the same time a progress towards integration or towards disintegration—is sure to have altered in some degree the total space occupied. For when the parts have been moved relatively to one another, the chances are infinity to one that their average distances from the common centre of the aggregate are no longer the same. Hence whatever be the special character of the redistribution—be it that of superficial accretion or detachment, be it that of general expansion or contraction, be it that of rearrangement, it is always an advance in integration or disintegration. It is always this, though it may at the same time be something further.

A general idea of these universal actions under their simplest aspects having been obtained, we may now consider them under certain relatively complex aspects. Changes towards greater concentration or greater diffusion, nearly always proceed after a manner much more involved than that above described. Thus far we have supposed one or other of the two opposite processes to go on alone—we have supposed an aggregate to be either losing motion and integrating or gaining motion and disintegrating. But though it is true that every change furthers one or other of these processes, it is not true that either process is ever wholly unqualified by the other. For each aggregate is at all times both gaining motion and losing motion.

Every mass from a grain of sand to a planet radiates heat to other masses, and absorbs heat radiated by other masses; and in so far as it does the one it becomes integrated, while in so far as it does the other it becomes disintegrated. Ordinarily in inorganic objects this double process works but unobtrusive effects. Only in a few cases, among which that of a cloud is the most familiar, does the conflict produce rapid and marked transformations. One of these floating bodies of vapour expands and dissipates if the amount of molecular motion it receives from the sun and earth exceeds that which it loses by radiation into space and towards adjacent surfaces; while, contrariwise, if, drifting over cold mountain tops it radiates to them much more heat than it receives,

C

the loss of molecular motion is followed by increasing integration of the vapour, ending in the aggregation of it into liquid and the fall of rain. Here as elsewhere the integration or the disintegration is a differential result.

In living aggregates and more especially those classed as animals, these conflicting processes go on with great activity under several forms. There is not merely what we may call the passive integration of matter, that results in inanimate objects from simple molecular attractions; but there is an active integration of it under the form of food. In addition to that passive superficial disintegration which inanimate objects suffer from external agents, animals produce in themselves active internal disintegration by absorbing such agents into their substance. While, like inorganic aggregates, they passively give off and receive motion, they are also active absorbers of motion latent in food, and active expenders of that motion. But notwithstanding this complication of the two processes, and the immense exaltation of the conflict between them, it remains true that there is always a differential progress towards either integration or disintegration. During the earlier part of the cycle of changes, the integration predominates—there goes on what we call growth. The middle part of the cycle is usually characterized, not by equilibrium between the integrating and disintegrating processes, but by alternate excesses of them. And the cycle closes with a period in which the disintegration, beginning to predominate, eventually puts a stop to integration, and undoes what integration had originally done. At no moment are assimilation and waste so balanced that no increase or decrease of mass is going on. Even in cases where one part is growing while other parts are dwindling, and even in cases where different parts are differently exposed to external sources of motion so that some are expanding while others are contracting, the truth still holds. For the chances are infinity to one against these opposite changes balancing one another; and if they do not balance one another, the aggregate as a whole is integrating or disintegrating.

Everywhere and to the last, therefore, the change at any moment going on forms a part of one or other of the two processes. While the general history of every aggregate is definable as a change from a diffused imperceptible state to a concentrated perceptible state, and again to a diffused imperceptible state;

every detail of the history is definable as a part of either the one change or the other. This, then, must be that universal law of redistribution of matter and motion, which serves at once to unify the seemingly diverse groups of changes, as well as the entire course of each group.

The processes thus everywhere in antagonism, and everywhere gaining now a temporary and now a more or less permanent triumph the one over the other, we call evolution and dissolution. *Evolution under its simplest and most general aspect is the integration of matter and concomitant dissipation of motion; while dissolution is the absorption of motion and concomitant disintegration of matter.*[1]

These titles are by no means all that is desirable; or rather we may say that while the last answers its purpose tolerably well, the first is open to grave objections. Evolution has other meanings, some of which are incongruous with, and some even directly opposed to, the meaning here given to it. The evolution of a gas is literally an absorption of motion and disintegration of matter, which is exactly the reverse of that which we here call evolution—is that which we here call dissolution. As ordinarily understood, to evolve is to unfold, to open and expand, to throw out, to emit; whereas as we understand it, the act of evolving, though it implies increase of a concrete aggregate, and in so far an expansion of it, implies that its component matter has passed from a more diffused to a more concentrated state—has contracted. The antithetical word involution would much more truly express the nature of the process; and would indeed describe better the secondary characters of the process which we shall have to deal with presently. We are obliged, however, notwithstanding the liabilities to confusion that must result from these unlike and even contradictory meanings, to use evolution as antithetical to dissolution. The word is now so widely recognized as signifying, not, indeed, the general process above described, but sundry of the most conspicuous varieties of it, and certain of its secondary but most remarkable accompaniments, that we cannot now substitute another word. All we can do is carefully to define the interpretation to be given to it.

While, then, we shall by dissolution everywhere mean the

---

[1] The italics are mine. The process which Spencer calls evolution is more or less equivalent to what the cyberneticians call an 'increase in negative entropy'. S. A.

process tacitly implied by its ordinary meaning—the absorption of motion and disintegration of matter; we shall everywhere mean by evolution, the process which is always an integration of matter and dissipation of motion, but which, as we shall now see, is in most cases much more than this.

(B) The Law of Evolution[1]

All sensible existences *must* in some way or other and at some time or other reach their concrete shapes through processes of concentration; and such facts as have been named have been named merely to clarify the perception of this necessity. But we cannot be said to have arrived at that unified knowledge constituting philosophy, until we have seen how existences of all orders *do* exhibit a progressive integration of matter and concomitant loss of motion. Tracing, so far as we may by observation and inference, the objects dealt with by the astronomer and the geologist, as well as those which biology, psychology and sociology treat of, we have to consider what direct proof there is that the cosmos, in general and in detail, conforms to this law.

In doing this, manifestations of the law more involved than those hitherto indicated, will chiefly occupy us. Throughout the classes of facts successively contemplated, our attention will be directed not so much to the truth that every aggregate has undergone, or is undergoing, integration, as to the further truth that in every more or less separate part of every aggregate, integration has been, or is, in progress. Instead of simple wholes and wholes of which the complexity has been ignored, we have here to deal with wholes as they actually exist—mostly made up of many members combined in many ways. And in them we shall have to trace the transformation as displayed under several forms—a passage of the total mass from a more diffused to a more consolidated state; a concurrent similar passage in every portion of it that comes to have a distinguishable individuality; and a simultaneous increase of combination among such individuated portions.

[1] From *First Principles*, 1893.

ASTRONOMIC EVOLUTION

Our sidereal system by its general form, by its clusters of stars of all degrees of closeness, and by its nebulae in all stages of condensation, gives us grounds to suspect that, generally and locally, concentration is going on. Assume that its matter has been, and still is being, drawn together by gravitation, and we have an explanation of all its leading traits of structure—from its solidified masses up to its collections of attenuated flocculi barely discernible by the most powerful telescopes, from its double stars up to such complex aggregates as the nubeculae. Without dwelling on this evidence, however, let us pass to the case of the solar system.

The belief, for which there are so many reasons, that this has had a nebular genesis, is the belief that it has arisen by the integration of matter and concomitant loss of motion. Evolution, under its primary aspect, is illustrated most simply and clearly by this passage of the solar system from a widely diffused incoherent state to a consolidated coherent state. While, according to the nebular hypothesis, there has been going on this gradual concentration of the solar system as an aggregate, there has been a simultaneous concentration of each partially-independent member. The substance of every planet in passing through its stages of nebulous ring, gaseous spheroid, liquid spheroid, and spheroid externally solidified, has in essentials paralleled the changes gone through by the general mass; and every satellite has done the like. Moreover, at the same time that the matter of the whole as well as the matter of each partially-independent part, has been thus integrating, there has been the further integration implied by increasing combination among the parts. The satellites of each planet are linked with their primary into a balanced cluster; while the planets and their satellites form with the sun a compound group of which the members are more strongly bound up with one another than were the far-spread portions of the nebulous medium out of which they arose.

Even apart from the nebular hypothesis, the solar system furnishes evidence having a like general meaning. Not to make much of the meteoric matter perpetually being added to the mass of the earth, and probably to the masses of other planets, as well as, in larger quantities, to the mass of the sun, it will suffice to name two generally-admitted instances. The one is the appreciable retardation of comets by the ethereal medium, and the inferred retardation of planets—a process which, in time, must bring comets, and eventually planets, into the sun. The other is the sun's still-continued loss of motion in the shape of radiated heat; accompanying the still-continued integration of his mass.

GEOLOGIC EVOLUTION

To geologic evolution we pass without break from the evolution which, for convenience, we separate as astronomic. The history of the earth, as traced out from the structure of its crust, carries us back to that molten state which the nebular hypothesis implies; and the changes classed as igneous are the accompaniments of the progressing consolidation of the earth's substance and accompanying loss of its contained motion. Both the general and the local effects may be briefly exemplified.

Leaving behind the period when the more volatile elements now existing as solids were kept by the high temperature in a gaseous form, we may begin with the fact that until the earth's surface had cooled down below red heat, the vast mass of water at present covering three-fifths of it, must have existed as vapour. This enormous volume of disintegrated liquid became integrated as fast as the dissipation of the earth's contained motion allowed; leaving, at length, a comparatively small portion unintegrated, which would be far smaller but for the unceasing absorption of molecular motion from the sun. In the formation of the earth's crust we have a similar change similarly caused. The passage from a thin solid film, everywhere fissured and movable on the subjacent molten matter, to a crust so thick and strong as to be but now and then very slightly dislocated by disturbing forces, illustrates the process. And while, in this superficial solidification, we see under one form how concentration accompanies loss of contained motion, we see it under another form in that diminution of the earth's bulk implied by superficial corrugation.

Local or secondary integrations have advanced along with this general integration. A molten spheroid merely skinned over with solid matter, could have presented nothing beyond small patches of land and water. Differences of elevation great enough to form islands of considerable size, imply a crust of some rigidity; and only as the crust grew thick could the land be united into continents divided by oceans. So, too, with the more striking elevations. The collapse of a thin crust round its cooling and contracting contents, would throw it into low ridges: it must have acquired a relatively great depth and strength before extensive mountain systems of vast elevation became possible. In sedimentary changes, also, a like progress is inferable. Denudation acting on the small surfaces exposed during early stages, would produce but small local deposits. The collection of detritus into strata of great extent, and the union of such strata into extensive 'systems', imply wide surfaces of land and water, as well as subsidences great, in both area and depth; whence it follows that integrations of this order must have grown more pronounced as the earth's crust thickened.

ORGANIC EVOLUTION

Already we have recognized the fact that organic evolution is primarily the formation of an aggregate, by the continued incorporation of matter previously spread through a wider space. Merely reminding the reader that every plant grows by concentrating in itself elements that were before diffused as gases, and that every animal grows by re-concentrating these elements previously dispersed in surrounding plants and animals, it will be here proper to complete the conception by pointing out that the early history of a plant or animal, still more clearly than its later history, shows us this fundamental process. For the microscopic germ of each organism undergoes, for a long time, no other change than that implied by absorption of nutriment. Cells embedded in the stroma of an ovarium, become ova by little else than continued growth at the expense of adjacent materials. And when, after fertilization, a more active evolution commences, its most conspicuous trait is the drawing-in, to a germinal centre, of the substance which the ovum contains.

Here, however, our attention must be directed mainly to the secondary integrations which habitually accompany the primary integration. We have to observe how, along with the formation of a larger mass of matter, there goes on a drawing together and consolidation of the matter into parts, as well as an increasingly-intimate combination of parts. In the mammalian embryo the heart, at first a long pulsating blood-vessel, by and by twists upon itself and integrates. The bile-cells constituting the rudimentary liver, do not simply become different from the wall of the intestine in which they at first lie; but, as they accumulate, they simultaneously diverge from it and consolidate into an organ. The anterior segments of the cerebro-spinal axis, which are at first continuous with the rest, and distinguished only by their larger size, undergo a gradual union, and at the same time the resulting head folds into a mass clearly marked off from the rest of the vertebral column. The like process, variously exemplified in other organs, is meanwhile exhibited by the body as a whole, which becomes integrated somewhat in the same way that an outspread handkerchief and its contents become integrated when its edges are drawn in and fastened to make a bundle. Analogous changes go on long after birth, and continue even up to old age. In man that solidification of the bony framework which during childhood is seen in the coalescence of portions of the same bone ossified from different centres, is afterwards seen in the coalescence of bones that were originally distinct. The appendages of the vertebrae unite with the vertebral centres to which they belong—a change not completed until towards thirty. At the same time the epiphyses, formed separately from the main bodies of their respective bones, have their cartilaginous connections turned into osseous ones—are fused to the masses beneath them. The component vertebrae of the sacrum, which remain separate till about the sixteenth year, then begin to unite; and in ten or a dozen years more their union is complete. Still later occurs the coalescence of the coccygeal vertebrae; and there are some other bony unions which remain unfinished unless advanced age is reached. To which add that the increase of density and toughness, going on throughout the tissues in general during life, is the formation of a more highly integrated substance.

The species of change thus illustrated under several aspects in the unfolding human body, may be traced in all animals. That mode of it which consists in the union of similar parts originally separate, has been described by Milne-Edwards and others, as exhibited in various of the invertebrata, though it does not seem to have been included by them as an essential peculiarity in the process of organic development. We shall, however, see clearly that local integration is an all-important part of this process, when we find it displayed not only in the successive stages passed through by every embryo, but also in ascending from the lower creatures to the higher. As manifested in either way, it goes on both longitudinally and transversely, under which different forms we may, indeed, most conveniently consider it. Of longitudinal integration, the sub-kingdom Annulosa supplies abundant examples. Its lower members, such as worms and myriapods, are mostly characterized by the great number of segments composing them; reaching in some cases to several hundreds. But in the higher divisions—crustaceans, insects and spiders—we find this number reduced down to twenty-two, thirteen, or even fewer; while, accompanying the reduction, there is a shortening or integration of the whole body, reaching its extreme in the crab and the spider. The significance of these contrasts, as bearing on the general doctrine of evolution, will be seen when it is pointed out that they are parallel to those which arise during the development of individual annulose animals. In the lobster, the head and thorax form one compact box, made by the union of a number of segments which in the embryo were separable. Similarly the butterfly shows us segments so much more closely united than they were in the caterpillar, as to be, some of them, no longer distinguishable from one another. The vertebrata again, through-out their successively higher classes, furnish like instances of longitudinal union. In most fishes, and in reptiles that have no limbs, none of the vertebrae coalesce. In most mammals and in birds, a variable number of vertebrae become fused together to form the sacrum; and in the higher apes and in man, the caudal vertebrae also lose their separate individualities in a single *os coccygis*. That which we may distinguish as transverse integration, is well illustrated among the Annulosa in the development of the nervous system. Leaving out those most degraded forms which do not present distinct ganglia, it is to be observed that the lower annulose animals, in common with the larvae of the higher, are severally characterized by a double chain of ganglia running from end to end of the body; while in the more perfectly-formed annulose animals, this double chain becomes united into a single chain. Mr Newport has described the course of this concentration as exhibited in insects; and by Rathke it has been traced in crustaceans. During the early stages of the Astacus fluviatilis, or common cray-fish, there is a pair of separate ganglia to each ring. Of the fourteen pairs belonging to the head and thorax, the three pairs in advance of the mouth consolidate into one mass to form the brain, or cephalic ganglion. Meanwhile, out of the remainder, the first six pairs severally unite in the median line, while the rest remain more or less separate. Of these six double ganglia thus formed, the anterior four coalesce into one mass; the remaining two coalesce into another mass; and then these two masses coalesce into one. Here we see longitudinal and transverse integration going on simultaneously; and in the highest crustaceans they are both carried still further. The vertebrata clearly exhibit transverse integration in the development of the generative system. The lowest mammals—the Monotremata—in common with birds, to which they are in many respects allied, have oviducts which towards their lower extremities are dilated into cavities, severally performing in an imperfect way the function of a uterus. 'In the Marsupialia there is a closer approximation of the two lateral sets of organs on the median line; for the oviducts converge towards one another and meet (without coalescing) on the median line; so that their uterine dilatations are in contact with each other, forming a true "double uterus". . . . As we ascend the series of "placental" mammals, we find the lateral coalescence becoming more and more complete. . . . In many of the Rodentia the uterus still remains completely divided into two lateral halves; whilst in others these coalesce at their lower portions, forming a rudiment of the true "body" of the uterus in the human subject. This part increases at the expense of the lateral "cornua" in the higher herbivora and carnivora; but even in the lower quadrumana the uterus is somewhat cleft at its summit.'[1]

Under the head of organic integrations there remain to be noted some which do not occur within the limits of one organism, and which only in an indirect way involve concentration of matter and dissipation of motion. These are the integrations by which organisms are made dependent on one another. We may set down two kinds of them—those which occur within the same species, and those which occur among different species. More or less of the gregarious tendency is general in animals, and when it is

[1] Carpenter's *Prin. of Comp. Phys.*, p. 617. (Spencer's footnote.)

marked there is, in addition to simple aggregation, a certain degree of combination. Creatures that hunt in packs, or that have sentinels, or that are governed by leaders, form bodies partially united by co-operation. Among polygamous mammals and birds this mutual dependence is closer; and the social insects show us assemblages of individuals of a still more consolidated character: some of them having carried the consolidation so far that the individuals cannot exist if separated. How organisms in general are mutually dependent, and in that sense integrated, we shall see on remembering—first, that while all animals live directly or indirectly on plants, plants live on the carbonic acid excreted by animals; second, that among animals the flesh-eaters cannot exist without the plant-eaters; third, that a large proportion of plants can continue their respective races only by the help of insects, and that in many cases particular plants need particular insects. Without detailing the more complex connections, which Mr Darwin has so beautifully illustrated, it will suffice to say that the flora and fauna in each habitat, constitute an aggregate so far integrated that many of its species die out if placed amid the plants and animals of another habitat. And it is to be remarked that this integration, too, increases as organic evolution progresses.

SUPER-ORGANIC (SOCIAL) EVOLUTION

The phenomena set down in the foregoing paragraph are introductory to others of a higher order, with which they ought, perhaps, in strictness, to be grouped—phenomena which, for want of a better word, we may term super-organic. Inorganic bodies present us with certain facts. Certain other facts, mostly of a more involved kind, are presented by organic bodies. There remain yet further facts, not presented by any organic body taken singly, but which result from the actions of aggregated organic bodies on one another and on inorganic bodies. Though phenomena of this order are, as we see, foreshadowed among inferior organisms, they become so extremely conspicuous in mankind as socially united, that practically we may consider them to commence here.

In the social organism integrative changes are clearly and abundantly exemplified. Uncivilized societies display them when wandering families, such as we see among Bushmen, join into tribes of considerable numbers. A further progress of like nature is everywhere manifested in the subjugation of weaker tribes by stronger ones; and in the subordination of their respective chiefs to the conquering chief. The combinations thus resulting, which, among aboriginal races, are being continually formed and continually broken up, become, among superior races, relatively permanent. If we trace the stages through which our own society or any adjacent one has passed, we see this unification from time to time repeated on a larger scale and gaining in stability. The aggregation of juniors and the children of juniors under elders and the children of elders; the consequent establishment of groups of vassals bound to their respective nobles; the subsequent subordination of groups of inferior nobles to dukes or earls; and the still later growth of the kingly power over dukes and earls; are so many instances of increasing consolidation. This process through which petty tenures are aggregated in feuds, feuds into provinces, provinces into kingdoms, and finally contiguous kingdoms into a single one, slowly completes itself by destroying the original lines of demarcation. And it may be further remarked of the European nations as a whole, that in the tendency to form alliances more or less lasting, in the restraining influences exercised by the several governments over one another, in the system, now becoming customary, of settling international disputes by congresses, as well as in the breaking down of commercial barriers and the increasing facilities of communication, we may trace the beginnings of a European federation—a still larger integration than any now established.

But it is not only in these external unions of groups with groups, and of the compound groups with one another, that the general law is exemplified. It is exemplified also in unions that take place internally, as the groups become more highly organized. There are two orders of these, which may be broadly distinguished as regulative and operative. A civilized society is made unlike a barbarous one by the establishment of regulative classes—governmental, administrative, military, ecclesiastical, legal, etc., which, while they have their several special bonds of union constituting them sub-classes, are also held together as a general class by a certain community of privileges, of blood, of education, of intercourse. In some societies, fully developed after their particular types, this consolidation into castes and this union among the upper castes by separation from the lower, eventually grow very decided: to be afterwards rendered less decided, only in cases of social metamorphosis caused by the industrial regime. The integrations that accompany the operative or industrial organization, later in origin, are not merely of this indirect kind, but they are also direct—they show us physical approach. We have integrations consequent on the simple growth of adjacent parts performing like functions; as, for instance, the junction of Manchester with its calico-weaving suburbs. We have other integrations that arise when, out of several places producing a particular commodity, one monopolizing more and more of the business, draws to it masters and workers, and leaves the other places to dwindle; as witness the growth of the Yorkshire cloth districts at the expense of those in the West of England; or the absorption by Staffordshire of the pottery manufacture, and the consequent decay of the establishments that once flourished at Derby and elsewhere. We have those more special integrations that arise within the same city; whence result the concentration of publishers in Paternoster Row, of corn-merchants about Mark Lane, of civil engineers in Great George Street, of bankers in the centre of the City. Industrial combinations that consist, not in the approximation or fusion of parts, but in the establishment of common centres of connection, are exhibited in the bank clearing-house and the railway clearing-house. While of yet another species are those unions which bring into relation, the more or less dispersed citizens who are occupied in like ways; as traders are brought by the exchange, and as are professional men by institutes like those of civil engineers, architects, etc.

At first sight these seem to be the last of our instances. Having followed up the general law to social aggregates, there apparently remain no other aggregates to which it can apply. This however is not true. Among what we have above distinguished as super-organic phenomena, we shall find sundry groups of very remarkable and interesting illustrations. Though evolution of the various products of human activities cannot be said directly to exemplify the integration of matter and dissipation of motion, yet they exemplify it indirectly. For the progress of language, of science and of the arts, industrial and aesthetic, is an objective register of subjective changes. Alterations of structure in human beings, and concomitant alterations of structure in aggregates of human beings jointly produce corresponding alterations of structure in all those things which humanity creates. As in the changed impress on the wax, we read a change in the seal; so in the integrations of advancing language, science and art, we see reflected certain integrations of advancing human structure, individual and social.

INTEGRATION

The integration of groups of like entities and like relations, may be said to constitute the most conspicuous part of scientific progress. A glance at the classificatory sciences, shows us that the confused incoherent aggregations which the vulgar make of natural objects, are gradually rendered complete and compact, and bound up into groups within groups. While, instead of considering all marine creatures as fish, shellfish, and jellyfish, zoology establishes divisions and sub-divisions under the heads vertebrata, Annulosa, mollusca, etc.; and while, in place of the wide and vague assemblage popularly described as 'creeping things', it makes the specific classes Annelida, Myriopoda, Insecta, Arachnida; it simultaneously gives to these an increasing consolidation. The several orders and genera of which each consists, are arranged according to their affinities and tied together under common definitions; at the same time that, by extended observation and rigorous criticism, the previously unknown and undetermined forms are integrated with their respective congeners. Nor is the process less clearly manifested in those sciences which have for their subject-matter, not classified objects but classified relations. Under one of its chief aspects, scientific advance is the advance of generalization; and generalizing is uniting into groups all like co-existencies and sequences among phenomena. The colligation of many concrete relations into a generalization of the lowest order, exemplifies this principle in its simplest form; and it is again exemplified in a more complex form by the colligation of these lowest generalizations into higher ones, and these into still higher ones. Year by year are established certain connections among orders of phenomena that appear unallied; and these connections, multiplying and strengthening, gradually bring the seemingly unallied orders under a common bond. When, for example, Humboldt quotes the saying of the Swiss—'it is going to rain because we hear the murmur of the torrents nearer'—when he remarks the relation between this and an observation of his own, that the cataracts of the Orinoco are heard at a greater distance by night than by day—when he notes the essential parallelism existing between these facts and the fact that the unusual visibility of remote objects is also an indication of coming rain—and when he points out that the common cause of these variations is the smaller hindrance offered to the passage of both light and sound, by media which are comparatively homogeneous, either in temperature or hygrometric state; he helps in bringing under one generalization the phenomena of light and those of sound. Experiment having shown that these conform to like laws of reflection and refraction, the conclusion that they are both produced by undulations gains probability: there is an incipient integration of two great orders of phenomena, between which no connection was suspected in times past. A still more decided integration has been of late taking place between the once independent sub-sciences of electricity, magnetism, and light.

Nor do the industrial and aesthetic arts fail to supply us with equally conclusive evidence. The progress from rude, small and simple tools to perfect, complex, and large machines, is a progress in integration. Among what are classed as the mechanical powers, the advance from the lever to the wheel-and-axle is an advance from a simple agent to an agent made up of several simple ones. On comparing the wheel-and-axle, or any of the machines used in early times with those used now, we see that in each of our machines several of the primitive machines are united into one. A modern apparatus for spinning or weaving, for making stockings or lace, contains not simply a lever, an inclined plane, a screw, a wheel-and-axle, joined together; but several of each integrated into one whole. Again, in early ages, when horse-power and man-power were alone employed, the motive agent was not bound up with the tool moved; but the two have now become in many cases fused together. The fire-box and boiler of a locomotive are combined with the machinery which the steam works. A still more extensive integration is exhibited in every factory. Here we find a large number of complicated machines, all connected by driving shafts with the same steam engine—all united with it into one vast apparatus.

Contrast the mural decorations of the Egyptians and Assyrians with modern historical paintings, and there becomes manifest a great advance in unity of composition—in the subordination of the parts to the whole. One of these ancient frescoes is, in truth, made up of a number of pictures that have little mutual dependence. The several figures of which each group consists, show very imperfectly by their attitudes, and not at all by their expressions, the relations in which they stand to each other: the respective groups might be separated with but little loss of meaning; and the centre of chief interest, which should link all parts together, is often inconspicuous. The same trait may be noted in the tapestries of medieval days. Representing perhaps a hunting scene, one of these contains men, horses, dogs, beasts, birds, trees, and flowers, miscellaneously dispersed: the living objects being variously occupied, and mostly with no apparent consciousness of each other's proximity. But in the paintings since produced, faulty as many of them are in this respect, there is always a more or less distinct co-ordination of parts—an arrangement of attitudes, expressions, lights and colours, such as to combine the picture into an organic whole; and the success with which unity of effect is educed from variety of components, is a chief test of merit.

In music, progressive integration is displayed in still more numerous ways. The simple cadence embracing but a few notes, which in the chants of savages is monotonously repeated, becomes, among civilized races, a long series of different musical phrases combined into one whole; and so complete is the integration, that the melody cannot be broken off in the middle, nor shorn of its final note, without giving us a painful sense of incompleteness. When to the air, a bass, a tenor, and an alto are added, and when to the harmony of different voice-parts there is added an accompaniment, we see exemplified integrations of another order, which grow gradually more elaborate. And the process is carried a stage higher when these complex solos, concerted pieces, choruses, and orchestral effects, are combined into the vast ensemble of a musical drama; of which, be it remembered, the artistic perfection largely consists in the subordination of the particular effects to the total effect.

Once more the arts of literary delineation, narrative and dramatic, furnish us with parallel illustrations. The tales of primitive times, like those with which the story-tellers of the

East still daily amuse their listeners, are made up of successive occurrences that are not only in themselves unnatural but have no natural connection: they are but so many separate adventures put together without necessary sequence. But in a good modern work of imagination, the events are the proper products of the characters working under given conditions and cannot at will be changed in their order or kind, without injuring or destroying the general effect. Further, the characters themselves, which in early fictions play their respective parts without showing how their minds are modified by one another or by the events, are now presented to us as held together by complex moral relations, and as acting and re-acting upon one another's natures.

Evolution then, under its primary aspect, is a change from a less coherent form to a more coherent form, consequent on the dissipation of motion and integration of matter. This is the universal process through which sensible existences, individually and as a whole, pass during the ascending halves of their histories. This proves to be a character displayed equally in those earliest changes which the universe at large is supposed to have under-gone, and in those latest changes which we trace in society and the products of social life. And throughout, the unification proceeds in several ways simultaneously.

Alike during the evolution of the solar system, of a planet, of an organism, of a nation, there is progressive aggregation of the entire mass. This may be shown by the increasing density of the matter already contained in it; or by the drawing into it of matter that was before separate; or by both. But in any case it implies a loss of relative motion. At the same time, the parts into which the mass has divided, severally consolidate in like manner. We see this in that formation of planets and satellites which has gone on along with the concentration of the nebula out of which the solar system originated; we see it in the growth of separate organs that advances, *pari passu*, with the growth of each organism; we see it in that rise of special industrial centres and special masses of population, which is associated with the rise of each society. Always more or less of local integration accompanies the general integration. And then, beyond the increased closeness of juxta-position among the components of the whole, and among the components of each part, there is increased closeness of combination among the parts, producing mutual dependence of them. Dimly foreshadowed as this mutual dependence is in inorganic existences, both celestial and terrestrial, it becomes distinct in organic and super-organic existences. From the lowest living forms upwards, the degree of development is marked by the degree in which the several parts constitute a co-operative assemblage. The advance from those creatures which live on in each part when cut to pieces, up to those creatures which cannot lose any considerable part without death, nor any inconsiderable part without great constitutional disturbance, is an advance to creatures which, while more integrated in respect to their solidification, are also more integrated as consisting of organs that live for and by each other. The like contrast between undeveloped and developed societies, need not be shown in detail: the ever-increasing co-ordination of parts, is conspicuous to all. And it must suffice just to indicate that the same thing holds true of social products: as, for instance, of science, which has become highly integrated not only in the sense that each division is made up of mutually-dependent propositions, but in the sense that the several divisions are mutually dependent—cannot carry on their respective investigations without aid from one another.

(C) The Law of Evolution Continued[1]

DIFFERENTIATION

Changes great in their amounts and various in their kinds, which accompany those dealt with in the last chapter, have thus far been wholly ignored—or, if tacitly recognized, have not been avowedly recognized. Integration of each whole has been described as taking place simultaneously with integration of each of the parts into which the whole divides itself. But how comes each whole to

---

[1] From *First Principles*, 1893.

divide itself into parts? This is a transformation more remarkable than the passage of the whole from an incoherent to a coherent state; and a formula which says nothing about it omits more than half the phenomena to be formulated.

This larger half of the phenomena we have now to treat. In this chapter we are concerned with those secondary redistributions of matter and motion that go on along with the primary re-distribution. We saw that while in very incoherent aggregates, secondary re-distributions produce but evanescent results, in aggregates that reach and maintain a certain medium state, neither very incoherent nor very coherent, results of a relatively persistent character are produced—structural modifications. And our next inquiry must be—what is the universal expression for these structural modifications?

Already in distinguishing as simple evolution, that integration of matter and dissipation of motion which is unaccompanied by secondary re-distributions, it has been tacitly asserted that where secondary re-distributions occur, complexity arises. Obviously if, while there has gone on a transformation of the incoherent into the coherent, there have gone on other transformations, the mass, instead of remaining uniform, must have become multiform. The proposition is an identical one. To say that the primary re-distribution is accompanied by secondary re-distributions, is to say that along with the change from a diffused to a concentrated state, there goes on a change from a homogeneous state to a heterogeneous state. The components of the mass while they become integrated also become differentiated.[1]

This, then, is the second aspect under which we have to study evolution. As, in the last chapter, we contemplated existences of all orders as displaying progressive integration; so, in this chapter, we have to contemplate them as displaying progressive differentia-tion.

[1] The terms here used must be understood in relative senses. Since we know of no such thing as absolute diffusion or absolute concentration, the change can never be anything but a change from a more diffused to a less diffused state— from smaller coherence to greater coherence; and, similarly, as no concrete existences present us with absolute simplicity—as nothing is perfectly uniform— as we nowhere find complete homogeneity—the transformation is literally always towards greater complexity, or increased multiformity, or further heterogeneity. This qualification the reader must habitually bear in mind.

IN ORGANISMS

The clearest, most numerous, and most varied illustrations of the advance in multiformity that accompanies the advance in integration, are furnished by living organic bodies. Distinguished as we found these to be by the great quantity of their contained motion, they exhibit in an extreme degree the secondary re-distributions which contained motion facilitates. The history of every plant and every animal, while it is a history of increasing bulk, is also a history of simultaneously-increasing differences among the parts. This transformation has several aspects.

The chemical composition which is almost uniform throughout the substance of a germ, vegetable or animal, gradually ceases to be uniform. The several compounds, nitrogenous and non-nitrogenous, which were homogeneously mixed, segregate by degrees, become diversely proportioned in diverse places, and produce new compounds by transformation or modification. In plants the albuminous and amylaceous matters which form the substance of the embryo, give origin here to a preponderance of chlorophyll and there to a preponderance of cellulose. Over the parts that are becoming leaf-surfaces, certain of the materials are metamorphosed into wax. In this place starch passes into one of its isomeric equivalents, sugar; and in that place into another of its isomeric equivalents, gum. By secondary change some of the cellulose is modified into wood; while some of it is modified into the allied substance which, in large masses, we distinguish as cork. And the more numerous compounds thus gradually arising, initiate further unlikenesses by mingling in unlike ratios. An animal-ovum, the components of which are at first evenly diffused among one another, chemically transforms itself in like manner. Its protein, its fats, its salts, become dissimilarly proportioned in different localities; and multiplication of isomeric forms leads to further mixtures and combinations that constitute many minor distinctions of parts. Here a mass darkening by accumulation of hematine, presently dissolves into blood. There fatty and albuminous matters uniting, compose nerve-tissue. At this spot the nitrogenous substance takes on the character of cartilage; and at that, calcareous salts, gathering together in the cartilage, lay the foundation of bone. All these chemical differentiations slowly and insensibly become more marked and more multiplied.

Simultaneously there arise contrasts of minute structure. Distinct tissues take the place of matter that had previously no recognizable unlikenesses of parts; and each of the tissues first produced undergoes secondary modifications, causing sub-species of tissues. The granular protoplasm of the vegetal germ, equally with that which forms the unfolding point of every shoot, gives origin to cells that are at first alike. Some of these, as they grow, flatten and unite by their edges to form the outer layer. Others elongate greatly, and at the same time join together in bundles to lay the foundation of woody-fibre. Before they begin to elongate, certain of these cells show a breaking-up of the lining deposit, which, during elongation, becomes a spiral thread, or a reticulated framework, or a series of rings; and by the longitudinal union of cells so lined, vessels are formed. Meanwhile each of these differentiated tissues is re-differentiated: instance that which constitutes the essential part of the leaf, the upper stratum of which is composed of chlorophyll-cells that remain closely packed, while the lower stratum becomes spongey. Of the same general character are the transformations undergone by the fertilized ovum which, at first a cluster of similar cells, quickly reaches a stage in which these cells have become dissimilar. More frequently recurring fission of the superficial cells, a resulting smaller size of them, and subsequent union of them into an outer layer, constitute the first differentiation; and the middle area of this layer is rendered unlike the rest by still more active processes of like kind. By such modifications upon modifications, too multitudinous to enumerate here, arise the classes and sub-classes of tissues which, variously involved one with another, compose organs.

Equally conforming to the law are the changes of general shape and of the shapes of organs. All germs are at first spheres and all organs are at first buds or mere rounded lumps. From this primordial uniformity and simplicity there takes place divergence, both of the wholes and the leading parts, towards multiformity of contour and towards complexity of contour. Cut away the compactly-folded young leaves that terminate every shoot, and the nucleus is found to be a central knob bearing lateral knobs, one of which may grow into either a leaf, a sepal, a petal, a stamen, a carpel, all these eventually-unlike parts being at first alike. The shoots themselves also depart from their primitive unity of form;

and while each branch becomes more or less different from the rest, the whole exposed part of the plant becomes different from the imbedded part. So, too, is it with the organs of animals. One of the Articulata, for instance, has limbs that are originally indistinguishable from one another—compose a homogeneous series; but by continuous divergences there arise among them unlikenesses of size and form, such as we see in the crab and the lobster. Vertebrate creatures equally exemplify this truth. The wings and legs of a bird are of similar shapes when they bud out from the sides of the embryo.

Thus in every plant and animal, conspicuous secondary re-distributions accompany the primary re-distribution. A first difference between two parts; in each of these parts other differences that presently become as marked as the first; and a like multiplication of differences in geometrical progression, until there is reached that complex combination constituting the adult. This is the history of all living things whatever. Pursuing an idea which Harvey set afloat, it has been shown by Wolff and Von Baer, that during its evolution each organism passes from a state of homogeneity to a state of heterogeneity. For a generation this truth has been accepted by biologists.

IN SOCIETIES

The change from the homogeneous to the heterogeneous is displayed equally in the progress of civilization as a whole, and in the progress of every tribe or nation; and is still going on with increasing rapidity.

As we see in existing barbarous tribes, society in its first and lowest form is a homogeneous aggregation of individuals having like powers and like functions: the only marked difference of function being that which accompanies difference of sex. Every man is warrior, hunter, fisherman, tool-maker, builder; every woman performs the same drudgeries; every family is self-sufficing, and, save for purposes of aggression and defence, might as well live apart from the rest. Very early, however, in the process of social evolution, we find an incipient differentiation between the governing and the governed. Some kind of chieftainship seems coeval with the first advance from the state of separate wandering

families to that of a nomadic tribe. The authority of the strongest
makes itself felt among a body of savages, as in a herd of animals,
or a posse of schoolboys. At first, however, it is indefinite, uncertain; is shared by others of scarcely inferior power; and is
unaccompanied by any difference in occupation or style of living.
The first ruler kills his own game, makes his own weapons,
builds his own hut and, economically considered, does not differ
from others of his tribe. Gradually, as the tribe progresses, the
contrast between the governing and the governed grows more
decided. Supreme power becomes hereditary in one family, the
head of that family, ceasing to provide for his own wants, is served
by others, and he begins to assume the sole office of ruling. At
the same time there has been arising a co-ordinate species of
government—that of religion. As all ancient records and traditions
prove, the earliest rulers are regarded as divine personages. The
maxims and commands they uttered during their lives are held
sacred after their deaths, and are enforced by their divinely-
descended successors; who in their turns are promoted to the
pantheon of the race, there to be worshipped and propitiated
along with their predecessors, the most ancient of whom is the
supreme god, and the rest subordinate gods. For a long time these
connate forms of government—civil and religious—continue
closely associated. For many generations the king continues to
be the chief priest, and the priesthood to be members of the royal
race. For many ages religious law continues to contain more or
less of civil regulation, and civil law to possess more or less of
religious sanction; and even among the most advanced nations
these two controlling agencies are by no means completely
differentiated from each other. Having a common root with these,
and gradually diverging from them, we find yet another controlling
agency—that of manners or ceremonial usages. All titles of honour
are originally the names of the god-king; afterwards of God and
the king; still later of persons of high rank; and finally come,
some of them, to be used between man and man. All forms of
complimentary address were at first the expression of submission
from prisoners to their conqueror, or from subjects to their ruler,
either human or divine—expressions that were afterwards used to
propitiate subordinate authorities, and slowly descended into
ordinary intercourse. All models of salutation were once obeisances
made before the monarch and used in worship of him after his

death. Presently others of the god-descended race were similarly saluted; and by degrees some of the salutations have become the due of all.[1] Thus, no sooner does the originally homogeneous social mass differentiate into the governed and the governing parts, than this last exhibits an incipient differentiation into religious and secular—Church and State; while at the same time there begins to be differentiated from both, that less definite species of government which rules our daily intercourse—a species of government which, as we may see in herald's colleges, in books of the peerage, in masters of ceremonies, is not without a certain embodiment of its own. Each of these kinds of government is itself subject to successive differentiations. In the course of ages there arises, as among ourselves, a highly complex political organization of monarch, ministers, lords and commons, with their subordinate administrative departments, courts of justice, revenue offices, etc., supplemented in the provinces by municipal governments, county governments, parish or union governments—all of them more or less elaborated. By its side there grows up a highly complex religious organization, with its various grades of officials from archbishops down to sextons, its colleges, convocations, ecclesiastical courts, etc.; to all which must be added the ever-multiplying independent sects, each with its general and local authorities. And at the same time there is developed a highly complex aggregation of customs, manners, and temporary fashions, enforced by society at large, and serving to control those minor transactions between man and man which are not regulated by civil and religious law. Moreover, it is to be observed that this ever-increasing heterogeneity in the governmental appliances of each nation, has been accompanied by an increasing heterogeneity in the governmental appliances of different nations, all of which are more or less unlike in their political systems and legislation, in their creeds and religious institutions, in their customs and ceremonial usages.

Simultaneously there has been going on a second differentiation of a more familiar kind; that, namely, by which the mass of the community has been segregated into distinct classes and orders of workers. While the governing part has undergone the complex development above detailed, the governed part has undergone an equally complex development; which has resulted in that minute

[1] For detailed proof of these assertions see essay on *Manners and Fashion.*

division of labour characterizing advanced nations. It is needless to trace out this progress from its first stages, up through the caste divisions of the East and the incorporated guilds of Europe, to the elaborate producing and distributing organization existing among ourselves. Political economists have long since indicated the evolution which, beginning with a tribe whose members severally perform the same actions, each for himself ends with a civilized community whose members severally perform different actions for each other; and they have further pointed out the changes through which the solitary producer of any one commodity is transformed into a combination of producers who, united under a master, take separate parts in the manufacture of such commodity. But there are yet other and higher phases of this advance from the homogeneous to the heterogeneous in the industrial organization of society. Long after considerable progress has been made in the division of labour among the different classes of workers, there is still little or no division of labour among the widely separated parts of the community: the nation continues comparatively homogeneous in the respect that in each district the same occupations are pursued. But when roads and other means of transit become numerous and good, the different districts begin to assume different functions, and to become mutually dependent. The calico-manufacture locates itself in this county, the woollen-manufacture in that; silks are produced here, lace there; stockings in one place, shoes in another; pottery, hardware, cutlery, come to have their special towns; and ultimately every locality grows more or less distinguished from the rest by the leading occupation carried on in it. Nay, more, this subdivision of functions shows itself not only among the different parts of the same nation, but among different nations. That exchange of commodities which free trade promises so greatly to increase, will ultimately have the effect of specializing, in a greater or less degree, the industry of each people. So that beginning with a barbarous tribe, almost if not quite homogeneous in the functions of its members, the progress has been, and still is, towards an economic aggregation of the whole human race; growing ever more heterogeneous in respect of the separate functions assumed by separate nations, the separate functions assumed by the local sections of each nation, the separate functions assumed by the many kinds of makers and traders in each town, and the separate functions assumed by the workers united in producing each commodity.

IN ASPECTS OF SOCIETY: LANGUAGE

Not only is the law thus clearly exemplified in the evolution of the social organism, but it is exemplified with equal clearness in the evolution of all products of human thought and action; whether concrete or abstract, real or ideal. Let us take language as our first illustration.

The lowest form of language is the exclamation, by which an entire idea is vaguely conveyed through a single sound; as among the lower animals. That human language ever consisted solely of exclamations, and so was strictly homogeneous in respect of its part of speech, we have no evidence. But that language can be traced down to a form in which nouns and verbs are its only elements, is an established fact. In the gradual multiplication of parts of speech out of these primary ones—in the differentiation of verbs into active and passive, of nouns into abstract and concrete—in the rise of distinctions of mood, tense, person, of number and case—in the formation of auxiliary verbs, of adjectives, adverbs, pronouns, prepositions, articles—in the divergence of those orders, genera, species, and varieties of parts of speech by which civilized races express minute modifications of meaning— we see a change from the homogeneous to the heterogeneous.

On passing from spoken to written language, we come upon several classes of facts, all having similar implications. Written language is connate with painting and sculpture; and at first all three are appendages of architecture, and have a direct connection with the primary form of all government—the theocratic. Merely noting by the way the fact that sundry wild races, as for example the Australians and the tribes of South Africa, are given to depicting personages and events upon the walls of caves, which are probably regarded as sacred places, let us pass to the case of the Egyptians. Among them, as also among the Assyrians, we find mural paintings used to decorate the temple of the god and the palace of the king (which were, indeed, originally identical); and as such they were governmental appliances in the same sense that state-pageants and religious feasts were. Further, they were governmental appliances in virtue of representing the worship of the god, the triumphs of the god-king, the submission of his subjects, and the punishment of the rebellious. And yet again they were governmental, as being the products of an art reverenced by the people as a sacred mystery. From the habitual use of this pictorial representation, there naturally grew up the but slightly-modified practice of picture-writing—a practice which was found still extant among the Mexicans at the time they were discovered. By abbreviations analogous to those still going on in our own written and spoken language, the most familiar of these pictured figures were successively simplified; and ultimately there grew up a system of symbols, most of which had but a distant resemblance to the things for which they stood. The inference that the hiero-glyphics of the Egyptians were thus produced, is confirmed by the fact that the picture-writing of the Mexicans was found to have given birth to a like family of ideographic forms; and among them, as among the Egyptians, these had been partially differ-entiated into the kuriological or imitative, and the tropical or symbolic: which were, however, used together in the same record. In Egypt, written language underwent a further differentiation; whence resulted the hieratic and the epistolographic or enchorial, both of which are derived from the original hieroglyphic. At the same time we find that for the expression of proper names, which could not be otherwise conveyed, phonetic symbols were employed; and though it is alleged that the Egyptians never actually achieved complete alphabetic writing, yet it can scarcely be doubted that these phonetic symbols occasionally used in aid of their ideo-graphic ones, were the germs out of which alphabetic writing grew. Once having become separate from hieroglyphics, alpha-betic writing itself underwent numerous differentiations—multi-plied alphabets were produced, between most of which, however, more or less connection can still be traced. And in each civilized nation there has now grown up, for the representation of one set of sounds, several sets of written signs, used for distinct purposes. Finally, through a yet more important differentiation came printing; which, uniform in kind as it was at first has since become multiform.

IN PAINTING AND SCULPTURE

While written language was passing through its earlier stages of development, the mural decoration which formed its root was being differentiated into painting and sculpture. The gods, kings, men, and animals represented, were originally marked by indented outlines and coloured. In most cases these outlines were of such depth, and the object they circumscribed so far rounded and marked out in its leading parts, as to form a species of work intermediate between intaglio and bas-relief. In other cases we see an advance upon this: the raised spaces between the figures being chiselled off, and the figures themselves appropriately tinted, a painted bas-relief was produced. The restored Assyrian architecture at Sydenham exhibits this style of art carried to greater perfection—the persons and things represented, though still barbarously coloured, are carved out with more truth and in greater detail; and in the winged lions and bulls used for the angles of gateways we may see a considerable advance towards a completely sculptured figure, which, nevertheless, is still coloured, and still forms part of the building. But while in Assyria the production of a statue proper seems to have been little, if at all, attempted, we may trace in Egyptian art the gradual separation of the sculptured figure from the wall. A walk through the collection in the British Museum will clearly show this; while it will at the same time afford an opportunity of observing the evident traces which the independent statues bear of their derivation from bas-relief: seeing that nearly all of them not only display that union of the limbs with the body which is the characteristic of bas-relief, but have the back of the statue united from head to foot with a block which stands in place of the original wall. Greece repeated the leading stages of this progress. As in Egypt and Assyria, these twin arts were at first united with each other and with their parent, architecture, and were the aids of religion and government. On the friezes of Greek temples, we see coloured bas-reliefs representing sacrifices, battles, processions, games—all in some sort religious. On the pediments we see painted sculptures more or less united with the tympanum and having for subjects the triumphs of gods or heroes. Even when we come to statues that are definitely separated from the buildings to which they pertain, we still find them coloured; and only in the later periods of Greek civilization does the differentiation of sculpture from painting appear to have become complete. In Christian art we may clearly trace a parallel re-genesis. All early paintings and sculptures throughout Europe, were religious in subject—represented Christs, crucifixions, virgins, holy families, apostles, saints. They formed integral parts of church architecture, and were among the means of exciting worship: as in Roman Catholic countries they still are. Moreover, the early sculptures of Christ on the cross, of virgins, of saints, were coloured; and it needs but to call to mind the painted madonnas and crucifixes still abundant in continental churches and highways to perceive the significant fact that painting and sculpture continued in closest connection with each other, where they continue in closest connection with their parent. Even when Christian sculpture was pretty clearly differentiated from painting, it was still religious and governmental in its subjects—was used for tombs in churches and statues of kings; while, at the same time, painting, where not purely ecclesiastical, was applied to the decoration of palaces, and besides representing royal personages, was almost wholly devoted to sacred legends. Only in quite recent times have painting and sculpture become entirely secular arts. Only within these few centuries has painting been divided into historical, landscape, marine, architectural, genre, animal, still-life, etc., and sculpture grown heterogeneous in respect of the variety of real and ideal subjects with which it occupies itself.

Strange as it seems then, we find it no less true that all forms of written language, of painting, and of sculpture, have a common root in the politico-religious decorations of ancient temples and palaces. Little resemblance as they now have, the bust that stands on the console, the landscape that hangs against the wall, and the copy of the *Times* lying upon the table, are remotely akin, not only in nature, but by extraction. The brazen face of the knocker which the postman has just lifted, is related not only to the woodcuts of the *Illustrated London News* which he is delivering, but to the characters of the billet-doux which accompanies it. Between the painted window, the prayer-book on which its light falls, and the adjacent monument, there is consanguinity. The effigies on our coins, the signs over shops, the figures that fill every ledger, the coat of arms outside the carriage-panel, and the placards inside the omnibus are, in common with dolls, blue-books and paper-hangings, lineally descended from the rude sculpture-paintings in which the Egyptians represented the triumphs and worship of their god-kings. Perhaps no example can be given which more vividly illustrates the multiplicity and heterogeneity of the products that in course of time may arise by successive differentiations from a common stock.

Before passing to other classes of facts, it should be observed that the evolution of the homogeneous into the heterogeneous is displayed not only in the separation of painting and sculpture from architecture and from each other, and in the greater variety of subjects they embody, but it is further shown in the structure of each work. A modern picture or statue is of far more heterogeneous nature than an ancient one. An Egyptian sculpture-fresco represents all its figures as on one plane—that is, at the same distance from the eye; and so is less heterogeneous than a painting that represents them as at various distances from the eye. It exhibits all objects as exposed to the same degree of light; and so is less heterogeneous than a painting which exhibits different objects, and different parts of each object, as in different degrees of light. It uses scarcely any but the primary colours, and these in their full intensity, and so is less heterogeneous than a painting which, introducing the primary colours but sparingly, employs an endless variety of intermediate tints, each of heterogeneous composition, and differing from the rest not only in quality but in intensity. Moreover, we see in these earliest works a great uniformity of conception. The same arrangement of figures is perpetually reproduced—the same actions, attitudes, faces, dresses. In Egypt the modes of representation were so fixed that it was sacrilege to introduce a novelty; and indeed it could have been only in consequence of a fixed mode of representation that a system of hieroglyphics became possible. The Assyrian bas-reliefs display parallel characters. Deities, kings, attendants, winged-figures and animals, are severally depicted in like positions, holding like implements, doing like things, and with like expression or non-expression of face. If a palm-grove is introduced, all the trees are of the same height, have the same number of leaves, and are equidistant. When water is imitated, each wave is a counterpart of the rest; and the fish, almost always of one kind, are evenly distributed over the surface. The beards of the kings, the gods, and the winged-figures, are everywhere similar; as are the manes of the lions, and equally so those of the horses. Hair is represented throughout by one form of curl. The king's beard is quite architecturally built up of compound tiers of uniform curls, alternating with twisted tiers placed in a transverse direction, and arranged with perfect regularity; and the terminal tufts of the bulls' tails are represented in exactly the same manner. Without tracing out analogous facts in early Christian art, in which, though less striking, they are still visible, the advance in heterogeneity will be sufficiently manifest on remembering that in the pictures of our own day the composition is endlessly varied; the attitudes, faces, expressions, unlike; the subordinate objects different in size, form, position, texture; and more or less of contrast even in the smallest details. Or, if we compare an Egyptian statue seated bolt upright on a block, with hands on knees, fingers outspread and parallel, eyes looking straight forward and the two sides perfectly symmetrical in every particular, with a statue of the advanced Greek or the modern school, which is asymmetrical in respect of the position of the head, the body, the limbs, the arrangement of the hair, dress, appendages, and in its relations to neighbouring objects, we shall see the change from the homogeneous to the heterogeneous clearly manifested.

IN POETRY, MUSIC AND DANCING

In the co-ordinate origin and gradual differentiation of poetry, music, and dancing, we have another series of illustrations. Rhythm in speech, rhythm in sound, and rhythm in motion were in the beginning parts of the same thing, and have only in process of time become separate things. Among various existing barbarous tribes we find them still united. The dances of savages are accompanied by some kind of monotonous chant, the clapping of hands, the striking of rude instruments: there are measured movements, measured words, and measured tones; and the whole ceremony, usually having reference to war or sacrifice, is of governmental character. In the early records of the historic races we similarly find these three forms of metrical action united in religious festivals. In the Hebrew writings we read that the triumphal ode composed by Moses on the defeat of the Egyptians, was sung to an accompaniment of dancing and timbrels. The Israelites danced and sung 'at the inauguration of the golden calf. And as it is generally agreed that this representation of the Deity was borrowed from the mysteries of Apis, it is probable that the dancing was copied from that of the Egyptians on those occasions'. There was an annual dance in Shiloh on the sacred festival, and David danced before the ark. Again, in Greece the like relation is every-where seen, the original type being there, as probably in other cases, a simultaneous chanting and mimetic representation of the life and adventures of the god. The Spartan dances were accom-panied by hymns and songs; and in general the Greeks had 'no festivals or religious assemblies but what were accompanied with songs and dances'—both of them being forms of worship used before altars. Among the Romans, too, there were sacred dances, the Salian and Lupercalian being named as of that kind. And even in Christian countries, as at Limoges in comparatively recent times, the people have danced in the choir in honour of a saint. The incipient separation of these once united arts from each other and from religion, was early visible in Greece. Probably diverging from dances partly religious, partly warlike, as the Corybantian, came the war-dances proper, of which there were various kinds; and from these resulted secular dances. Meanwhile music and poetry, though still united, came to have an existence separate from dancing. The aboriginal Greek poems, religious in subject, were not recited but chanted; and though at first the chant of the poet was accompanied by the dance of the chorus, it ultimately grew into independence. Later still, when the poem had been differentiated into epic and lyric—when it became the custom to sing the lyric and recite the epic—poetry was born. As during the same period musical instruments were being multiplied, we may presume that music came to have an existence apart from words. And both of them were beginning to assume other forms besides the religious. Facts having like implications might be cited from the histories of later times and peoples; as the practices of our own early minstrels, who sang to the harp heroic narratives versified by themselves to music of their own composition, thus uniting the now separate offices of poet, composer, vocalist, and instrumentalist. But, without further illustration, the common origin and gradual differentiation of dancing, poetry, and music will be sufficiently manifest.

The advance from the homogeneous to the heterogeneous is displayed not only in the separation of these arts from each other and from religion, but also in the multiplied differentiations which each of them afterwards undergoes. Not to dwell upon the numberless kinds of dancing that have, in course of time, come into use; and not to occupy space in detailing the progress of poetry, as seen in the development of the various forms of metre, of rhyme, and of general organization; let us confine our attention to music as a type of the group. As argued by Dr Burney, and as implied by the customs of still extant barbarous races, the first musical instruments were, without doubt, percussive—sticks, calabashes, tom-toms—and were used simply to mark the time of the dance; and in this constant repetition of the same ground, we see music in its most homogeneous form. The Egyptians had a lyre with three strings. The early lyre of the Greeks had four, constituting their tetrachord. In course of some centuries lyres of seven and eight strings were employed. And, by the expiration of a thousand years, they had advanced to their 'great system' of the double octave. Through all which changes there of course arose a greater heterogeneity of melody. Simultaneously there came into use the different modes—Dorian, Ionian, Phrygian, Æolian, and Lydian—answering to our keys: and of these there were ultimately fifteen. As yet, however, there was but little heterogeneity in the time of their music. Instrumental music during this period being merely the accompaniment of vocal music, and vocal music being completely subordinated to words—the singer being also the poet, chanting his own compositions and making the lengths of his notes agree with the feet of his verses; there unavoidably arose a tiresome uniformity of measure, which, as Dr Burney says, 'no resources of melody could disguise'. Lacking the complex rhythm obtained by our equal bars and unequal notes, the only rhythm was that produced by the quantity of the syllables, and was of necessity comparatively monotonous. And further, it may be observed that the chant thus resulting, being like recitative, was much less clearly differentiated from ordinary speech than is our modern song. Nevertheless, considering the extended range of notes in use, the variety of modes, the occasional variations of time consequent on changes of metre, and the multiplication of instruments, we see that music had, towards the close of Greek civilization, attained to considerable heterogeneity: not indeed as compared with our music, but as compared with that which preceded it. As yet, however, there existed nothing but melody: harmony was unknown. It was not until Christian church-music had reached some development,

D

that music in parts was evolved; and then it came into existence
through a very unobtrusive differentiation. Difficult as it may be
to conceive, *a priori*, how the advance from melody to harmony
could take place without a sudden leap, it is none the less true
that it did so. The circumstance which prepared the way for it,
was the employment of two choirs singing alternately the same air.
Afterwards it became the practice (very possibly first suggested
by a mistake) for the second choir to commence before the first
had ceased, thus producing a fugue. With the simple airs then in
use, a partially harmonious fugue might not improbably thus
result; and a very partially harmonious fugue satisfied the ears of
that age, as we know from still preserved examples. The idea
having once been given, the composing of airs productive of fugal
harmony would naturally grow up, as in some way it *did* grow
up out of this alternate choir-singing. And from the fugue to
concerted music of two, three, four, and more parts, the transition
was easy. Without pointing out in detail the increasing complexity
that resulted from introducing notes of various lengths, from the
multiplication of keys, from the use of accidentals, from varieties
of time, from modulations and so forth, it needs but to contrast
music as it is, with music as it was, to see how immense is the
increase of heterogeneity. We see this if, looking at music in its
ensemble, we enumerate its many different genera and species—if
we consider the divisions into vocal, instrumental, and mixed, and
their subdivisions into music for different voices and different
instruments—if we observe the many forms of sacred music,
from the simple hymn, the chant, the canon, motet, anthem, etc.,
up to the oratorio; and the still more numerous forms of secular
music, from the ballad up to the serenata, from the instrumental
solo up to the symphony. Again, the same truth is seen on comparing any one sample of aboriginal music with a sample of modern
music—even an ordinary song for the piano; which we find to be
relatively highly heterogeneous, not only in respect of the varieties
in the pitch and in the length of the notes, the number of different
notes sounding at the same instant in company with the voice, and
the variations of strength with which they are sounded and sung,
but in respect of the changes of key, the changes of time, the
changes of timbre of the voice and the many other modifications
of expression. While between the old monotonous dance-chant
and a grand opera of our own day, with its endless orchestral

complexities and vocal combinations, the contrast in heterogeneity is so extreme that it seems scarcely credible that the one should have been the ancestor of the other.

Were they needed, many further illustrations might be cited. Going back to the early time when the deeds of the god-king, chanted and mimetically represented in dances round his altar, were further narrated in picture-writings on the walls of temples and palaces, and so constituted a rude literature, we might trace the development of literature through phases in which, as in the Hebrew Scriptures, it presents in one work, theology, cosmology, history, biography, civil law, ethics, poetry; through other phases in which, as in the *Iliad*, the religious, martial, historical, the epic, dramatic, and lyric elements are similarly commingled, down to its present heterogeneous development, in which its divisions and subdivisions are so numerous and varied as to defy complete classification. Or we might track the evolution of science, beginning with the era in which it was not yet differentiated from art, and was, in union with art, the handmaid of religion; passing through the era in which the sciences were so few and rudimentary, as to be simultaneously cultivated by the same philosophers; and ending with the era in which the genera and species are so numerous that few can enumerate them, and no one can adequately grasp even one genus. Or we might do the like with architecture, with the drama, with dress. But doubtless the reader is already weary of illustrations, and my promise has been amply fulfilled. I believe it has been shown beyond question, that that which the German physiologists have found to be a law of organic development, is a law of all development. The advance from the simple to the complex, through a process of successive differentiations, is seen alike in the earliest changes of the universe to which we can reason our way back, and in the earliest changes which we can inductively establish; it is seen in the geologic and climatic evolution of the earth, and of every single organism on its surface; it is seen in the evolution of humanity, whether contemplated in the civilized individual, or in the aggregations of races; it is seen in the evolution of society, in respect alike of its political, its religious, and its economical organization; and it is seen in the evolution of all those endless concrete and abstract products of human activity, which constitute the environment of our daily life. From the remotest past which science can fathom, up to the novelties of yesterday, an essential trait of evolution has been the transformation of the homogeneous into the heterogeneous.

Evolution, under its primary aspect, is a change from a less coherent form to a more coherent form, consequent on the dissipation of motion and integration of matter, but this is by no means the whole truth. Along with a passage from the coherent to the incoherent, there goes on a passage from the uniform to the multiform. Such, at least, is the fact wherever evolution is compound; which it is in the immense majority of cases. While there is a progressing concentration of the aggregate, either by the closer approach of the matter within its limits, or by the drawing in of further matter, or by both; and while the more or less distinct parts into which the aggregate divides and sub-divides are severally concentrating, these parts are also becoming unlike—unlike in size or in form or in texture or in composition or in several or all of these. The same process is exhibited by the whole and by its members. The entire mass in integrating, and simultaneously differentiating from other masses; and each member of it is also integrating and simultaneously differentiating from other members.

As we now understand it, evolution is definable as a change from an incoherent homogeneity to a coherent heterogeneity, accompanying the dissipation of motion and integration of matter.

(D) The Law of Evolution Continued[1]

FROM THE INDEFINITE TO THE DEFINITE

Changes from the less heterogeneous to the more heterogeneous, which do not come within what we call evolution, occur in every local disease. A portion of the body in which there arises a morbid growth, displays a new differentiation. Whether this morbid

[1] From *First Principles*, 1893.

growth be or be not more heterogeneous than the tissues in which it is seated, is not the question. The question is, whether the organism as a whole is, or is not, rendered more heterogeneous by the addition of a part unlike every pre-existing part, in form, or composition, or both. And to this question there can be none but an affirmative answer. Again, it may be contended that the earlier stages of decomposition in a dead body involve increase of heterogeneity. Supposing the chemical changes to commence in some parts sooner than in other parts, as they commonly do, and to affect different tissues in different ways, as they must, it seems to be a necessary admission that the entire body, made up of undecomposed parts and parts decomposed in various modes and degrees, has become more heterogeneous than it was. Though greater homogeneity will be the eventual result, the immediate result is the opposite. And yet this immediate result is certainly not evolution. Other instances are furnished by social disorders and disasters. A rebellion which, while leaving some provinces undisturbed, develops itself here in secret societies, there in public demonstrations, and elsewhere in actual conflicts, necessarily renders the society, as a whole, more heterogeneous. Or when a dearth causes commercial derangement with its entailed bank-ruptcies, closed factories, discharged operatives, food-riots, incendiarisms; it is manifest that, as a large part of the community retains its ordinary organization displaying the usual phenomena, these new phenomena must be regarded as adding to the complexity previously existing. But such changes, so far from constituting further evolution, are steps towards dissolution.

Clearly, then, the definition arrived at in the last chapter is an imperfect one. The changes above instanced as coming within the formula as it now stands, are so obviously unlike the rest, that the inclusion of them implies some distinction hitherto overlooked. Such further distinction we have now to supply.

At the same time that evolution is a change from the homogeneous to the heterogeneous, it is a change from the indefinite to the definite. Along with an advance from simplicity to complexity, there is an advance from confusion to order—from undetermined arrangement to determined arrangement. Development, no matter of what kind, exhibits not only a multiplication of unlike parts, but an increase in the distinctness with which these parts are marked off from one another. And this is the distinction sought. For proof, it needs only to reconsider the instances given above. The changes constituting disease have no such definiteness, either in locality, extent or outline, as the changes constituting development. Though certain morbid growths are more common in some parts of the body than in others (as warts on the hands, cancer on the breasts, tubercle in the lungs), yet they are not confined to these parts; nor, when found on them, are they anything like so precise in their relative positions as are the normal parts around them. Their sizes are extremely variable: they bear no such constant proportions to the body as organs do. Their forms, too, are far less specific than organic forms. And they are extremely confused in their internal structures. That is, they are in all respects comparatively indefinite. The like peculiarity may be traced in decomposition. That total indefiniteness to which a dead body is finally reduced is a state towards which the putrefactive changes tend from their commencement. The advancing destruction of the organic compounds blurs the minute structure—diminishes its distinctness. From the portions that have undergone most decay, there is a gradual transition to the less decayed portions. And step by step the lines of organization, once so precise, disappear. Similarly with social changes of an abnormal kind. The disaffection which initiates a political outbreak, implies a loosening of those ties by which citizens are bound up into distinct classes and sub-classes. Agitation, growing into revolutionary meetings, fuses ranks that are usually separated. Acts of insubordination break through the ordained limits to individual conduct, and tend to obliterate the lines previously existing between those in authority and those beneath them. At the same time, by the arrest of trade, artisans and others lose their occupations; and in ceasing to be functionally distinguished, merge into an indefinite mass. And when at last there comes positive insurrection, all magisterial and official powers, all class distinctions, and all industrial differences, cease: organized society lapses into an unorganized aggregation of social units. Similarly, in so far as famines and pestilences cause changes from order towards disorder, they cause changes from definite arrangements to indefinite arrangements.

Thus, then, is that increase of heterogeneity which constitutes evolution, distinguished from that increase of heterogeneity which does not do so. Though in disease and death, individual or social, the earliest modifications are additions to the pre-existing hetero-geneity, they are not additions to the pre-existing definiteness. They begin from the very outset to destroy this definiteness; and gradually produce a heterogeneity that is indeterminate instead of determinate. As a city, already multiform in its variously-arranged structures of various architecture, may be made more multiform by an earthquake, which leaves part of it standing and overthrows other parts in different ways and degrees, but is at the same time reduced from orderly arrangement to disorderly arrangement; so may organized bodies be made for a time more multiform by changes which are nevertheless disorganizing changes. And in the one case as in another, it is the absence of definiteness which distinguishes the multiformity of regression from the multi-formity of progression.

If advance from the indefinite to the definite is an essential characteristic of evolution, we shall of course find it everywhere displayed; as in the last chapter we found the advance from the homogeneous to the heterogeneous. With a view of seeing whether it is so, let us now re-consider the same classes of facts.

IN ORGANISMS

The first change which the ovum of a mammal undergoes after continued segmentation has reduced its yolk to a mulberry-like mass, is the appearance of a greater definiteness in the peripheral cells of this mass, each of which acquires a distinct enveloping membrane. These peripheral cells, vaguely distinguished from the internal ones by their minuter sub-division as well as by their greater completeness, coalesce to form the blastoderm or germinal membrane. Presently, one portion of this membrane is rendered unlike the rest by the accumulation of cells still more sub-divided, which, together, form an opaque roundish spot. This *area germinativa*, as it is called, shades off gradually into the surrounding parts of the blastoderm; and the *area pellucida*, subsequently formed in the midst of it, is similarly without precise margin. The 'primitive trace', which makes its appearance in the centre of the *area pellucida*, and is the rudiment of that vertebrate axis which is to be the fundamental characteristic of the mature animal, is shown by its name to be at first indefinite—a mere trace.

Beginning as a shallow groove, it becomes slowly more pronounced: its sides grow higher, their summits overlap and at last unite, and so the indefinite groove passes into a definite tube, forming the vertebral canal. In this vertebral canal the leading divisions of the brain are at first discernible only as slight bulgings, while the vertebræ commence as indistinct modifications of the tissue bounding the canal. Simultaneously, the outer surface of the blastoderm has been differentiating from the inner surface: there has arisen a division into the serous and mucous layers—a division at the outset indistinct, and traceable only about the germinal area, but which insensibly spreads throughout nearly the whole germinal membrane, and becomes definite. From the mucous layer, the development of the alimentary canal proceeds as that of the vertebral canal does from the serous layer. Originally a simple channel along the under surface of the embryonic mass, the intestine is rendered distinct by the bending down, on each side, of ridges which finally join to form a tube—the permanent absorbing surface is by degrees cut off from that temporary absorbing surface with which it was continuous and uniform. And in an analogous manner the entire embryo, which at first lies outspread on the yolk-sack, gradually rises up from it, and by the infolding of its ventral region, becomes a separate mass connected with the yolk-sack only by a narrow duct.

These changes through which the general structure is marked out with slowly-increasing precision, are paralleled in the evolution of each organ. The heart begins as a mere aggregation of cells, of which the inner liquefy to form blood, while the outer are transformed into the walls; and when thus sketched out, the heart is indefinite not only as being unlined by limiting membrane, but also as being little more than a dilatation of the central blood-vessel. By and by the receiving portion of the cavity becomes distinct from the propelling portion. Afterwards there begins to grow across the ventricle, a septum, which is, however, some time before it shuts off the two halves from each other; while the later-formed septum of the auricle remains incomplete during the whole of fœtal life. Again, the liver commences by multiplication of certain cells in the wall of the intestine. The thickening produced by this multiplication 'increases so as to form a projection upon the exterior of the canal', and at the same time that the organ grows and becomes distinct from the intestine, the channels running through it are transformed into ducts having clearly marked walls. Similarly, certain cells of the external coat of the alimentary canal at its upper portion accumulate into lumps or buds from which the lungs are developed; and these, in their general outlines and detailed structure, acquire distinctness step by step.

Changes of this order continue long after birth; and, in the human being, some of them are not completed till middle life. During youth, most of the articular surfaces of the bones remain rough and fissured—the calcareous deposit ending irregularly in the surrounding cartilage. But between puberty and the age of thirty, these articular surfaces are finished off into smooth, hard, sharply-cut 'epiphyses'. Generally, indeed, we may say that increase of definiteness continues when there has ceased to be any appreciable increase of heterogeneity. And there is reason to think that those modifications which take place after maturity, bringing about old age and death, are modifications of this nature; since they cause rigidity of structure, a consequent restriction of movement and of functional pliability, a gradual narrowing of the limits within which the vital processes go on, ending in an organic adjustment too precise—too narrow in its margin of possible variation to permit the requisite adaptation to changes of external conditions.

IN SOCIETIES

The successive phases through which societies pass, very obviously display the progress from indeterminate arrangement to determinate arrangement. A wandering tribe of savages, being fixed neither in its locality nor in its internal distribution, is far less definite in the relative positions of its parts than a nation. In such a tribe the social relations are similarly confused and unsettled. Political authority is neither well established nor precise. Distinctions of rank are neither clearly marked nor impassable. And save in the different occupations of men and women, there are no complete industrial divisions. Only in tribes of considerable size, which have enslaved other tribes, is the economical differentiation decided.

Any one of these primitive societies, however, that evolves, becomes step by step more specific. Increasing in size, consequently ceasing to be so nomadic, and restricted in its range by neighbouring societies, it acquires, after prolonged border warfare, a settled territorial boundary. The distinction between the royal race and the people, eventually amounts in the popular apprehension to a difference of nature. The warrior-class attains a perfect separation from classes devoted to the cultivation of the soil, or other occupations regarded as servile. And there arises a priesthood that is defined in its rank, its functions, its privileges. This sharpness of definition, growing both greater and more variously exemplified as societies advance to maturity, is extremest in those that have reached their full development or are declining. Of ancient Egypt we read that its social divisions were precise and its customs rigid. Recent investigations make it more than ever clear that among the Assyrians and surrounding peoples not only were the laws unalterable, but even the minor habits, down to those of domestic routine, possessed a sacredness which insured their permanence. In India at the present day, the unchangeable distinctions of caste, not less than the constancy in modes of dress, industrial processes, and religious observances, show us how fixed are the arrangments where the antiquity is great. Nor does China, with its long-settled political organization, its elaborate and precise conventions, and its unprogressive literature, fail to exemplify the same truth.

The successive phases of our own and adjacent societies, furnish facts somewhat different in kind but similar in meaning. Originally, monarchical authority was more baronial, and baronial authority more monarchical, than afterwards. Between modern priests and the priests of old times, who while officially teachers of religion were also warriors, judges, architects, there is a marked difference in definiteness of function. And among the people engaged in productive occupations, the like contrasts would be found to hold: the industrial class has become more distinct from the military; and its various divisions from one another. A history of our constitution, reminding us how the powers of king, lords and commons, have been gradually settled, would clearly exhibit analogous changes. Countless facts bearing the like construction, would meet us were we to trace the development of legislation, in the successive stages of which we should find statutes gradually rendered more specific in their applications to particular cases.

Even now we see that each new law, beginning as a vague proposition, is, in the course of enactment, elaborated into specific clauses; and further that only after its interpretation has been established by judges' decisions in courts of justice, does it reach its final definiteness. From the annals of minor institutions like evidence may be gathered. Religious, charitable, literary, and all other societies, starting with ends and methods roughly sketched out and easily modifiable, show us how, by the accumulation of rules and precedents, the purposes become more distinct and the modes of action more restricted; until at last decay follows a fixity which admits of no adaptation to new conditions. Should it be objected that among civilized nations there are examples of decreasing definiteness (instance the breaking down of limits between ranks), the reply is that such apparent exceptions are the accompaniments of a social metamorphosis—a change from the military or predatory type of social structure, to the industrial or mercantile type, during which the old lines of organization are disappearing and the new ones becoming more marked.

IN ASPECTS OF SOCIETY: LANGUAGE

All organized results of social action—all super-organic structures, pass through parallel phases. Being, as they are, objective products of subjective processes, they must display corresponding changes; and that they do this, the cases of language, of science, of art, clearly prove.

Strike out from our sentences everything but nouns and verbs, and there stands displayed the vagueness characterizing undeveloped tongues. When we note how each inflection of a verb, or addition by which the case of a noun is marked, serves to limit the conditions of action or of existence, we see that these constituents of speech enable men to communicate their thoughts more precisely. That the application of an objective to a noun or an adverb to a verb, narrows the class of things or changes indicated, implies that the additional word serves to make the proposition more distinct. And similarly with other parts of speech.

The like effect results from the multiplication of words of each order. When the names for objects and acts and qualities are but few, the range of each is proportionately wide, and its meaning therefore unspecific. The similes and metaphors so much used by aboriginal races, indirectly and imperfectly suggest ideas which they cannot express directly and perfectly from lack of words. Or to take a case from ordinary life, if we compare the speech of the peasant who, out of his limited vocabulary, can describe the contents of the bottle he carries, only as 'doctor's stuff' which he has got for his 'sick' wife, with the speech of the physician, who tells those educated like himself the particular composition of the medicine and the particular disorder for which he has prescribed it, we have vividly brought home to us the precision which language gains by the multiplication of terms.

Again, in the course of its evolution, each tongue acquires a further accuracy through processes which fix the meaning of each word. Intellectual intercourse slowly diminishes laxity of expression. By and by dictionaries give definitions. And eventually, among the most cultivated, indefiniteness is not tolerated either in the terms used or in their grammatical combinations.

Once more, languages considered as wholes become gradually more sharply marked off from one another, and from their common parent: as witness in early times the divergence from the same root of two languages so unlike as Greek and Latin, and in later times the development of three Latin dialects into Italian, French, and Spanish.

THE SCIENCES

In his *History of the Inductive Sciences*, Dr Whewell says that the Greeks failed in physical philosophy because their 'ideas were not distinct, and appropriate to the facts'. I do not quote this remark for its luminousness, since it would be equally proper to ascribe the indistinctness and inappropriateness of their ideas to the imperfection of their physical philosophy; but I quote it because it serves as good evidence of the indefiniteness of primitive science. The same work and its fellow on *The Philosophy of the Inductive Sciences*, supply other evidences equally good, because equally independent of any such hypothesis as is here to be established. Respecting mathematics, we have the fact that geometrical theorems grew out of empirical methods; and that these theorems, at first isolated, did not acquire the clearness which complete demonstration gives, until they were arranged by Euclid into a series of dependent propositions. At a later period, the same general truth was exemplified in the progress from the 'method of exhaustions' and the 'method of indivisibles' to the 'method of limits', which is the central idea of the infinitesimal calculus. In early mechanics, too, may be traced a dim perception that action and re-action are equal and opposite; though, for ages after, this truth remained unformulated. And similarly, the property of inertia, though not distinctly comprehended until Kepler lived, was vaguely recognized long previously. 'The conception of statical force', 'was never presented in a distinct form till the works of Archimedes appeared'; and 'the conception of accelerating force was confused in the mind of Kepler and his contemporaries, and did not become clear enough for purposes of sound scientific reasoning before the succeeding century'. To which specific assertions may be added the general remark, that 'terms which originally, and before the laws of motion were fully known, were used in a very vague and fluctuating sense, were afterwards limited and rendered precise'. When we turn from abstract scientific conceptions to the concrete provisions of science, of which astronomy furnishes numerous examples, a like contrast is visible. The times at which celestial phenomena will occur have been predicted with ever-increasing accuracy. Errors once amounting to days are now diminished to seconds. The correspondence between the real and supposed forms of orbits, has been gradually rendered more precise. Originally thought circular, then epicyclical, then elliptical, orbits are now ascertained to be curves which always deviate from perfect ellipses, and are ever undergoing changes.

But the general advance of science in definiteness, is best shown by the contrast between its qualitative stage, and its quantitative stage. At first the facts ascertained were that between such and such phenomena some connection existed —that the appearances a and b always occurred together or in succession; but it was known neither what was the nature of the relation between a and b, nor how much of a accompanied so much of b. The development of science has in part been the reduction of these vague connections to distinct ones. Most relations have been classed as mechanical, chemical, thermal, electric, magnetic, etc.; and we have learnt to infer the amounts of the antecedents and consequents from each other with exactness. Of illustrations, some furnished by physics have been given, and from other sciences plenty may be added. We have positively ascertained the constituents of numerous compounds which our ancestors could not analyse, and of a far greater number which they never even saw; and the combining equivalents of these elements are accurately calculated. Physiology shows advance from qualitative to quantitative prevision in the weighing and measuring of organic products, and of the materials consumed; as well as in measurement of functions by the spirometer and the sphygmograph. By pathology it is displayed in the use of the statistical method of determining the sources of diseases, and the effects of treatment. In botany and zoology, the numerical comparisons of floras and faunas, leading to specific conclusions respecting their sources and distributions, illustrate it. And in sociology, questionable as are the conclusions usually drawn from the classified sum-totals of the census, from Board-of-Trade tables, and from criminal returns, it must be admitted that these imply a progress towards more accurate conceptions of social phenomena.

That an essential characteristic of advancing science is increase in definiteness, appears indeed almost a truism when we remember that science may be described as definite knowledge, in contradistinction to that indefinite knowledge possessed by the uncultured. And if, as we cannot question, science has, in the course of ages, been evolved out of this indefinite knowledge of the uncultured, then the gradual acquirement of that great definiteness which now distinguishes it must have been a leading trait in its evolution.

THE ARTS

The arts, industrial and æsthetic, supply illustrations perhaps still more striking. Flint implements of the kind recently found in certain of the later geologic deposits, show the extreme want of precision in men's first handiworks. Though a great advance on these is seen in the tools and weapons of existing savage tribes, yet an inexactness in forms and fittings distinguishes such tools and weapons from those of civilized races. In a smaller degree, the productions of the less-advanced nations are characterized by like defects. A Chinese junk, with all its contained furniture and appliances, nowhere presents a line that is quite straight, a uniform curve, or a true surface. Nor do the utensils and machines of our ancestors fail to exhibit a similar inferiority to our own. An antique chair, an old fireplace, a lock of the last century, or almost any article of household use that has been preserved for a few generations, proves by contrast how greatly the industrial products of our time excel those of the past in their accuracy. Since planing machines have been invented, it has become possible to produce absolutely straight lines, and surfaces so truly level as to be air-tight when applied to each other. While in the dividing-engine of Troughton, in the micrometer of Whitworth, and in microscopes that show fifty thousand divisions to the inch, we have an exactness as far exceeding that reached in the works of our great-grandfathers, as theirs exceeded that of the aboriginal celt-makers.

In the fine arts there has been a parallel progress. From the rudely-carved and painted idols of savages, through the early sculptures characterized by limbs without muscular detail, wooden-looking drapery and faces devoid of individuality, up to the later statues of the Greeks or some of those now produced, the increased accuracy of representation is conspicuous. Compare the mural paintings of the Egyptians with the paintings of mediæval Europe, or these with modern paintings, and the more precise rendering of the appearances of objects is manifest. It is the same with fiction and the drama. In the marvellous tales current among Eastern nations, in the romantic legends of feudal Europe, as well as in the mystery-plays and those immediately succeeding them, we see great want of correspondence to the realities of life; alike in the predominance of supernatural events, in the extremely improbable coincidences, and in the vaguely-indicated personages. Along with social advance, there has been a progressive diminution of unnaturalness—an approach to truth of representation. And now, novels and plays are applauded in proportion to the fidelity with which they exhibit individual characters; improbabilities, like the impossibilities which preceded them, are disallowed; and there is even an incipient abandonment of those elaborate plots which life rarely if ever furnishes.

It would be easy to accumulate evidences of other kinds. The progress from myths and legends, extreme in their misrepresentations, to a history that has slowly become and is still becoming more accurate; the establishment of settled systematic methods of doing things, instead of the indeterminate ways at first pursued— these might be enlarged upon in further exemplification of the general law. But the basis of induction is already wide enough. Proof that all evolution is from the indefinite to the definite we find to be not less abundant than proof that all evolution is from the homogeneous to the heterogeneous.

Part Three
Society: Structure and Function:
Classification and Comparison:
Change and Evolution

(A) What is a Society?[1]

This question has to be asked and answered at the outset. Until we have decided whether or not to regard a society as an entity, and until we have decided whether, if regarded as an entity, a society is to be classed as absolutely unlike all other entities or as like some others, our conception of the subject-matter before us remains vague.

It may be said that a society is but a collective name for a number of individuals. Carrying the controversy between nominalism and realism into another sphere, a nominalist might affirm that just as there exist only the members of a species, while the species considered apart from them has no existence; so the units of a society alone exist, while the existence of the society is but verbal. Instancing a lecturer's audience as an aggregate which by disappearing at the close of the lecture, proves itself to be not a thing but only a certain arrangement of persons, he might argue that the like holds of the citizens forming a nation.

But without disputing the other steps of his argument, the last step may be denied. The arrangement, temporary in the one case, is permanent in the other; and it is the permanence of the relations among component parts which constitutes the individuality of a whole as distinguished from the individualities of its parts. A mass broken into fragments ceases to be a thing; while, conversely, the stones, bricks and wood, previously separate, become the thing called a house if connected in fixed ways.

Thus we consistently regard a society as an entity because, though formed of discrete units, a certain concreteness in the aggregate of them is implied by the general persistence of the arrangements among them throughout the area occupied. And it is this trait which yields our idea of a society. For, withholding the name from an ever-changing cluster such as primitive men

[1] From *The Principles of Sociology*, Vol. I, 1876.

107

form, we apply it only where some constancy in the distribution of parts has resulted from settled life.

But now, regarding a society as a thing, what kind of thing must we call it? It seems totally unlike every object with which our senses acquaint us. Any likeness it may possibly have to other objects, cannot be manifest to perception, but can be discerned only by reason. If the constant relations among its parts make it an entity, the question arises whether these constant relations among its parts are akin to the constant relations among the parts of other entities. Between a society and anything else, the only conceivable resemblance must be one due to *parallelism of principle in the arrangement of components*.

There are two great classes of aggregates with which the social aggregate may be compared—the inorganic and the organic. Are the attributes of a society in any way like those of a not-living body? or are they in any way like those of a living body? or are they entirely unlike those of both?

The first of these questions needs only to be asked to be answered in the negative. A whole of which the parts are alive, cannot, in its general characters, be like lifeless wholes. The second question, not to be thus promptly answered, is to be answered in the affirmative. The reasons for asserting that the permanent relations among the parts of a society, are analogous to the permanent relations among the parts of a living body, we have now to consider.

(B) A Society is an Organism[1]

GROWTH

When we say that growth is common to social aggregates and organic aggregates, we do not thus entirely exclude community with inorganic aggregates. Some of these, as crystals, grow in a visible manner; and all of them, on the hypothesis of evolution, have arisen by integration at some time or other. Nevertheless, compared with things we call inanimate, living bodies and societies

[1] From *The Principles of Sociology*, Vol. I, 1876.

so conspicuously exhibit augmentation of mass, that we may fairly regard this as characterizing them both. Many organisms grow throughout their lives; and the rest grow throughout considerable parts of their lives. Social growth usually continues either up to times when the societies divide, or up to times when they are overwhelmed.

Here, then, is the first trait by which societies ally themselves with the organic world and substantially distinguish themselves from the inorganic world.

DIFFERENTIATION IN STRUCTURE

It is also a character of social bodies, as of living bodies, that while they increase in size they increase in structure. Like a low animal, the embryo of a high one has few distinguishable parts; but while it is acquiring greater mass, its parts multiply and differentiate. It is thus with a society. At first the unlikenesses among its groups of units are inconspicuous in number and degree; but as population augments, divisions and sub-divisions become more numerous and more decided. Further, in the social organism as in the individual organism, differentiations cease only with that completion of the type which marks maturity and precedes decay.

Though in inorganic aggregates also, as in the entire solar system and in each of its members, structural differentiations accompany the integrations; yet these are so relatively slow, and so relatively simple, that they may be disregarded. The multiplication of contrasted parts in bodies politic and in living bodies is so great that it substantially constitutes another common character which marks them off from inorganic bodies.

DIFFERENTIATION OF FUNCTIONS

This community will be more fully appreciated on observing that progressive differentiation of structures is accompanied by progressive differentiation of functions.

The divisions, primary, secondary and tertiary, which arise in a developing animal, do not assume their major and minor unlikenesses to no purpose. Along with diversities in their shapes and compositions go diversities in the actions they perform: they grow into unlike organs having unlike duties. Assuming the entire function of absorbing nutriment at the same time that it takes on its structural characters, the alimentary system becomes gradually marked off into contrasted portions, each of which has a special function forming part of the general function. A limb, instrumental to locomotion or prehension, acquires divisions and subdivisions which perform their leading and their subsidiary shares in this office. So is it with the parts into which a society divides. A dominant class arising does not simply become unlike the rest, but assumes control over the rest, and when this class separates into the more and the less dominant, these again begin to discharge distinct parts of the entire control. With the classes whose actions are controlled it is the same. The various groups into which they fall have various occupations, each of such groups also, within itself, acquiring minor contrasts of parts along with minor contrasts of duties.

And here we see more clearly how the two classes of things we are comparing distinguish themselves from things of other classes; for such differences of structure as slowly arise in inorganic aggregates, are not accompanied by what we can fairly call differences of function.

MUTUALITY OR INTERDEPENDENCE OF PARTS

Why in a body politic and in a living body these unlike actions of unlike parts are properly regarded by us as functions, while we cannot so regard the unlike actions of unlike parts in an inorganic body, we shall perceive on turning to the next and most distinctive common trait.

Evolution establishes in them both, not differences simply, but definitely-connected differences—differences such that each makes the others possible. The parts of an inorganic aggregate are so related that one may change greatly without appreciably affecting the rest. It is otherwise with the parts of an organic aggregate or of a social aggregate. In either of these the changes in the parts are mutually determined, and the changed actions of the parts are mutually dependent. In both, too, this mutuality increases as the evolution advances. The lowest type of animal is all stomach, all respiratory surface, all limb. Development of a type having appendages by which to move about or lay hold of food can take place only if these appendages, losing power to absorb nutriment directly from surrounding bodies, are supplied with nutriment by parts which retain the power of absorption. A respiratory surface to which the circulating fluids are brought to be aerated, can be formed only on condition that the concomitant loss of ability to supply itself with materials for repair and growth, is made good by the development of a structure bringing these materials. Similarly in a society. What we call with perfect propriety its organization, necessarily implies traits of the same kind. While rudimentary, a society is all warrior, all hunter, all hut-builder, all tool-maker: every part fulfils for itself all needs. Progress to a stage characterized by a permanent army, can go on only as there arise arrangements for supplying that army with food, clothes, and munitions of war by the rest. If here the population occupies itself solely with agriculture and there with mining—if these manufacture goods while those distribute them, it must be on condition that in exchange for a special kind of service rendered by each part to other parts, these other parts severally give due proportions of their services.

This division of labour, first dwelt on by political economists as a social phenomenon, and thereupon recognized by biologists as a phenomenon of living bodies, which they called the 'physiological division of labour', is that which in the society, as in the animal, makes it a living whole. Scarcely can I emphasize enough the truth that in respect of this fundamental trait, a social organism and an individual organism are entirely alike. When we see that in a mammal, arresting the lungs quickly brings the heart to a stand; that if the stomach fails absolutely in its office all other parts by-and-by cease to act; that paralysis of its limbs entails on the body at large death from want of food, or inability to escape; that loss of even such small organs as the eyes deprives the rest of a service essential to their preservation; we cannot but admit that mutual dependence of parts is an essential characteristic. And when, in a society, we see that the workers in iron stop if the miners do not supply materials; that makers of clothes cannot carry on their business in the absence of those who spin and weave textile fabrics; that the manufacturing community will cease to act unless the food-producing and food-distributing agencies are acting; that the controlling powers, governments, bureaux, judicial officers, police, must fail to keep order when the necessaries of life are not supplied to them by the parts kept in order; we are obliged to say that this mutual dependence of parts is similarly rigorous. Unlike as the two kinds of aggregates otherwise are, they are alike in respect of this fundamental character, and the characters implied by it.

EVEN ORGANISMS ARE 'SOCIETIES' OF NUMEROUS PARTS

How the combined actions of mutually-dependent parts constitute life of the whole, and how there hence results a parallelism between social life and animal life, we see still more clearly on learning that the life of every visible organism is constituted by the lives of units too minute to be seen by the unaided eye.

An undeniable illustration is furnished by the strange order *Myxomycetes*. The spores or germs produced by one of these forms become ciliated monads which after a time of active locomotion change into shapes like those of amœbæ, move about, take in nutriment, grow, multiply by fission. Then these amœba-form individuals swarm together, begin to coalesce into groups, and these groups to coalesce with one another: making a mass sometimes barely visible, sometimes as big as the hand. This *plasmodium*, irregular, mostly reticulated and in substance gelatinous, itself exhibits movements of its parts like those of a gigantic rhizopod creeping slowly over surfaces of decaying matters, and even up the stems of plants. Here, then, union of many minute living individuals to form a relatively vast aggregate in which their individualities are apparently lost, but the life of which results from combination of their lives, is demonstrable.

In other cases, instead of units which, originally discrete, lose their individualities by aggregation, we have units which, arising by multiplication from the same germ, do not part company, but nevertheless display their separate lives very clearly. A growing sponge has its horny fibres clothed with a gelatinous substance; and the microscope shows this to consist of moving monads. We cannot deny life to the sponge as a whole, for it shows us some corporate actions. The outer amœba-form units partially lose their individualities by fusion into a protective layer or skin; the supporting framework of fibres is produced by the joint agency of the monads; and from their joint agency also result those currents of water which are drawn in through the smaller orifices and expelled through the larger. But while there is thus shown a feeble aggregate life, the lives of the myriads of component units are very little subordinated: these units form as it were a nation having scarcely any sub-division of functions. Or, in the words of Professor Huxley: 'the sponge represents a kind of sub-aqueous city, where the people are arranged about the streets and roads, in such a manner, that each can easily appropriate his food from the water as it passes along.' Again, in the hydroid polype *Myriothela*, 'pseudopodial processes are being constantly projected from the walls of the alimentary canal into its cavity', and these Dr Allman regards as processes from the cells forming the walls, which lay hold of alimentary matter just as those of an amœba do. The like may be seen in certain planarian worms.

Even in the highest animals there remains traceable this relation between the aggregate life and the lives of components. Blood is a liquid in which, along with nutritive matters, circulate innumerable living units—the blood corpuscles. These have severally their life-histories. During its first stage each of them, then known as a white corpuscle, makes independent movements like those of an amœba; it 'may be fed with coloured food, which will then be seen to have accumulated in the interior', 'and in some cases the colourless blood-corpuscles have actually been seen to devour their more diminutive companions, the red ones'. Nor is this individual life of the units provable only where flotation in a liquid allows its signs to be readily seen. Sundry mucous surfaces, as those of the air passages, are covered with what is called ciliated epithelium—a layer of minute elongated cells packed side by side, and each bearing on its exposed end several cilia continually in motion. The wavings of these cilia are essentially like those of the monads which live in the passages running through a sponge; and just as the joint action of these ciliated sponge-monads propels the current of water, so does the joint action of the ciliated epithelium-cells move forward the mucous secretion covering them. If there needs further proof that these epithelium-cells have independent lives, we have it in the fact that when detached and placed in a fit menstruum, they 'move about with considerable rapidity for some time, by the continued vibrations of the cilia with which they are furnished'.

On thus seeing that an ordinary living organism may be regarded as a nation of units which live individually, and have many of them considerable degrees of independence, we shall have the less difficulty in regarding a nation of human beings as an organism.

THE WHOLE HAS AN ONGOING UNITY AND NATURE, THOUGH THE UNITS CHANGE

The relation between the lives of the units and the life of the aggregate has a further character common to the two cases. By a catastrophe the life of the aggregate may be destroyed without immediately destroying the lives of all its units; while, on the other hand, if no catastrophe abridges it, the life of the aggregate is far longer than the lives of its units.

In a cold-blooded animal, ciliated cells perform their motions with perfect regularity long after the creature they are part of has become motionless. Muscular fibres retain their power of contracting under stimulation. The cells of secreting organs go on pouring out their product if blood is artificially supplied to them. And the components of an entire organ, as the heart, continue their co-operation for many hours after its detachment. Similarly, arrest of those commercial activities, governmental co-ordinations, etc., which constitute the corporate life of a nation, may be caused, say by an inroad of barbarians, without immediately stopping the actions of all the units. Certain classes of these, especially the widely-diffused ones engaged in food-production, may long survive and carry on their individual occupations.

On the other hand, the minute living elements composing a developed animal, severally evolve, play their parts, decay, and are replaced, while the animal as a whole continues. In the deep layer of the skin, cells are formed by fission which, as they enlarge, are thrust outwards, and, becoming flattened to form the epidermis, eventually exfoliate, while the younger ones beneath take their places. Liver-cells, growing by imbibition of matters from which they separate the bile, presently die, and their vacant seats are occupied by another generation. Even bone, though so dense and seemingly inert, is permeated by blood-vessels carrying materials to replace old components by new ones. And the replacement, rapid in some tissues and in others slow, goes on at such rate that during the continued existence of the entire body each portion of it has been many times over produced and destroyed. Thus it is also with a society and its units. Integrity of the whole as of each large division is perennially maintained, notwithstanding the deaths of component citizens. The fabric of living persons which, in a manufacturing town, produces some commodity for national use, remains after a century as large a fabric, though all the masters and workers who a century ago composed it have long since disappeared. Even with minor parts of this industrial structure the like holds. A firm that dates from past generations, still carrying on business in the name of its founder, has had all its members and employees changed one by one, perhaps several times over; while the firm has continued to occupy the same place and to maintain like relations with buyers and sellers. Throughout we find this. Governing bodies, general and local, ecclesiastical corporations, armies, institutions of all orders down to guilds, clubs, philanthropic associations, etc., show us a continuity of life exceeding that of the persons constituting them. Nay, more. As part of the same law, we see that the existence of the society at large exceeds in duration that of some of these compound parts. Private unions, local public bodies, secondary national institutions, towns carrying on special industries, may decay, while the nation, maintaining its integrity, evolves in mass and structure.

In both cases, too, the mutually-dependent functions of the various divisions, being severally made up of the actions of many units, it results that these units dying one by one are replaced without the function in which they share being sensibly affected. In a muscle each sarcous element wearing out in its turn is removed and a substitution made while the rest carry on their combined contractions as usual; and the retirement of a public official or death of a shopman, perturbs inappreciably the business of the department, or activity of the industry, in which he had a share.

Hence arises in the social organism, as in the individual organism, a life of the whole quite unlike the lives of the units, though it is a life produced by them.

DIFFERENCES: A SOCIETY NOT A CONCRETE WHOLE

From these likenesses between the social organism and the individual organism, we must now turn to an extreme unlikeness. The parts of an animal form a concrete whole, but the parts of a society form a whole which is discrete. While the living units composing the one are bound together in close contact, the living units composing the other are free, are not in contact, and are more or less widely dispersed. How, then, can there be any parallelism?

Though this difference is fundamental and apparently puts comparison out of the question, yet examination proves it to be less than it seems. Presently I shall have to point out that complete admission of it consists with maintenance of the alleged analogy, but we will first observe how one who thought it needful might argue that even in this respect there is a smaller contrast than a cursory glance shows.

He might urge that the physically-coherent body of an animal is not composed all through of living units, but that it consists in large measure of differentiated parts which the vitally active parts have formed, and which thereafter become semi-vital and in some cases un-vital. Taking as an example the protoplasmic layer underlying the skin, he might say that while this consists of truly living units, the cells produced in it, changing into epithelium scales, become inert, protective structures; and pointing to the insensitive nails, hair, horns, etc., arising from this layer, he might show that such parts, though components of the organism, are hardly living components. Carrying out the argument, he would contend that elsewhere in the body there exist such protoplasmic layers, from which grow the tissues composing the various organs—layers which alone remain fully alive, while the structures evolved from them lose their vitality in proportion as they are specialized: instancing cartilage, tendon, and connective tissue, as showing this in conspicuous ways. From all which he would draw the inference that though the body forms a coherent whole, its essential units, taken by themselves, form a whole which is coherent only throughout the protoplasmic layers.

And then would follow the facts showing that the social

organism, rightly conceived, is much less discontinuous than it seems. He would contend that as, in the individual organism, we include with the fully living parts, the less living and not living parts which co-operate in the total activities, so in the social organism we must include not only those most highly vitalized units, the human beings, who chiefly determine its phenomena, but also the various kinds of domestic animals, lower in the scale of life, which, under the control of man, co-operate with him, and even those far inferior structures, the plants which, propagated by human agency, supply materials for animal and human activities. In defence of this view he would point out how largely these lower classes of organisms, co-existing with men in societies, affect the structures and activities of the societies—how the traits of the pastoral type depend on the natures of the creatures reared, and how in settled societies the plants producing food, materials for textile fabrics, etc., determine certain kinds of social arrangements and actions. After which he might insist that since the physical characters, mental natures, and daily doings, of the human units, are, in part, moulded by relations to these animals and vegetals, which, living by their aid and aiding them to live, enter so much into social life as even to be cared for by legislation, these lower forms cannot rightly be excluded from the conception of the social organism. Hence would come his conclusion that when, with human beings, are incorporated the less vitalized beings, animals and vegetal, covering the surface occupied by the society, there results an aggregate having a continuity of parts more nearly approaching to that of an individual organism; and which is also like it in being composed of local aggregations of highly vitalized units, embedded in a vast aggregation of units of various lower degrees of vitality, which are, in a sense, produced by, modified by, and arranged by, the higher units.

But without accepting this view, and admitting that the discreteness of the social organism stands in marked contrast with the concreteness of the individual organism, the objection may still be adequately met.

BUT A LIVING WHOLE NONETHELESS

Though coherence among its parts is a prerequisite to that co-operation by which the life of an individual organism is carried on; and though the members of a social organism, not forming a concrete whole, cannot maintain co-operation by means of physical influences directly propagated from part to part, yet they can and do maintain co-operation by another agency. Not in contact, they nevertheless affect one another through intervening spaces both by emotional language and by the language, oral and written, of the intellect. For carrying on mutually-dependent actions, it is requisite that impulses, adjusted in their kinds, amounts and times, shall be conveyed from part to part. This requisite is fulfilled in living bodies by molecular waves, that are indefinitely diffused in low types, and in high types are carried along definite channels (the function of which has been significantly called internuncial). It is fulfilled in societies by the signs of feelings and thoughts, conveyed from person to person, at first in vague ways and only through short distances, but afterwards more definitely and through greater distances. That is to say, the internuncial function, not achievable by stimuli physically transferred, is nevertheless achieved by language—emotional and intellectual.

That mutual dependence of parts which constitutes organization is thus effectually established. Though discrete instead of concrete, the social aggregate is rendered a living whole.

IN A SOCIETY NO ONE PART IS THE SEAT OF AN ENTIRE FUNCTION

But now, on pursuing the course of thought opened by this objection and the answer to it, we arrive at an implied contrast of great significance—a contrast fundamentally affecting our idea of the ends to be achieved by social life.

Though the discreteness of a social organism does not prevent sub-division of functions and mutual dependence of parts, yet it does prevent that differentiation by which one part becomes an organ of feeling and thought while other parts become insensitive. High animals of whatever class are distinguished from low ones by complex and well-integrated nervous systems. While in inferior types the minute scattered ganglia may be said to exist for the benefit of other structures, the concentrated ganglia in superior types are the structures for the benefit of which the rest may be said to exist. Though a developed nervous system so directs the actions of the whole body as to preserve its integrity, yet the welfare of the nervous system is the ultimate object of all these actions, damage to any other organ being serious in proportion as it immediately or remotely entails that pain or loss of pleasure which the nervous system suffers. But the discreteness of a society negatives differentiations carried to this extreme. In an individual organism the minute living units, most of them permanently localized, growing up, working, reproducing and dying away in their respective places, are in successive generations moulded to their respective functions, so that some become specially sentient and others entirely insentient. But it is otherwise in a social organism. The units of this, out of contact and much less rigidly held in their relative positions, cannot be so much differentiated as to become feelingless units and units which monopolize feeling. There are, indeed, traces of such a differentiation. Human beings are unlike in the amounts of sensation and emotion producible in them by like causes: here callousness, here susceptibility, is a characteristic. The mechanically-working and hard-living units are less sensitive than the mentally-working and more protected units. But while the regulative structures of the social organism tend, like those of the individual organism, to become specialized as seats of feeling, the tendency is checked by want of that physical cohesion which brings fixity of function; and it is also checked by the continued need for feeling in the mechanically-working units for the due discharge of their functions.

Hence, then, a cardinal difference in the two kinds of organisms. In the one, consciousness is concentrated in a small part of the aggregate. In the other, it is diffused throughout the aggregate: all the units possess the capacities for happiness and misery, if not in equal degrees, still in degrees that approximate. As, then, there is no social sensorium, the welfare of the aggregate, considered apart from that of the units, is not an end to be sought. The society exists for the benefit of its members, not its members for the benefit of the society. It has ever to be remembered that great as may be the efforts made for the prosperity of the body politic, yet the claims of the body politic are nothing in themselves, and become something only in so far as they embody the claims of its component individuals.

From this last consideration, which is a digression rather than a part of the argument, let us now return and sum up the reasons for regarding a society as an organism.

It undergoes continuous growth. As it grows, its parts become unlike: it exhibits increase of structure. The unlike parts simultaneously assume activities of unlike kinds. These activities are not simply different, but their differences are so related as to make one another possible. The reciprocal aid thus given causes mutual dependence of the parts. And the mutually-dependent parts, living by and for one another, form an aggregate constituted on the same general principle as is an individual organism. The analogy of a society to an organism becomes still clearer on learning that every organism of appreciable size is a society; and on further learning that in both, the lives of the units continue for some time if the life of the aggregate is suddenly arrested, while if the aggregate is not destroyed by violence, its life greatly exceeds in duration the lives of its units. Though the two are contrasted as respectively discrete and concrete, and though there results a difference in the ends subserved by the organization, there does not result a difference in the laws of the organization: the required mutual influences of the parts, not transmissible in a direct way being, in a society, transmitted in an indirect way.

Having thus considered in their most general forms the reasons for regarding a society as an organism, we are prepared for following out the comparison in detail.

(C) Social Growth[1]

Societies, like living bodies, begin as germs—originate from masses which are extremely minute in comparison with the masses some of them eventually reach. That out of small wandering hordes have arisen the largest societies, is a conclusion not to be contested. The implements of pre-historic peoples, ruder even than existing

[1] From *The Principles of Sociology*, Vol. I, 1876.

savages use, imply absence of those arts by which alone great aggregations of men are made possible. Religious ceremonies that survived among ancient historic races, pointed back to a time when the progenitors of those races had flint knives, and got fire by rubbing together pieces of wood, and must have lived in such small clusters as are alone possible before the rise of agriculture.

The implication is that by integrations, direct and indirect, there have in course of time been produced social aggregates a million times in size the aggregates which alone existed in the remote past. Here, then, is a growth reminding us, by its degree, of growth in living bodies.

Between this trait of organic evolution and the answering trait of super-organic evolution, there is a further parallelism: the growths in aggregate of different classes are extremely various in their amounts.

Glancing over the entire assemblages of animal types, we see that the members of one large class, the Protozoa, rarely increase beyond that microscopic size with which every higher animal begins. Among the multitudinous kinds of Cœlenterata, the masses range from that of the small Hydra to that of the large Medusa. The annulose and molluscous types, respectively show us immense contrasts between their superior and inferior members. And the vertebrate animals, much larger on the average than the rest, display among themselves enormous differences.

Kindred unlikenesses of size strike us when we contemplate the entire assemblage of human societies. Scattered over many regions there are minute hordes—still extant samples of the primordial type of society. We have Wood-Veddahs living sometimes in pairs, and only now and then assembling; we have Bushmen wandering about in families, and forming larger groups but occasionally; we have Fuegians clustered by the dozen or the score. Tribes of Australians, of Tasmanians, of Andamanese, are variable within the limits of perhaps twenty to fifty. And similarly, if the region is inhospitable, as with the Esquimaux, or if the arts of life are undeveloped, as with the Digger-Indians, or if adjacent higher races are obstacles to growth, as with Indian hill-tribes like the Juangs, this limitation to primitive size continues. Where a fruitful soil affords much food, and where a more settled life, leading to agriculture, again increases the supply of food, we meet with larger social aggregates: instance those in the Polynesian

E

Islands and in many parts of Africa. Here a hundred or two, here several thousands, here many thousands, are held together more or less completely as one mass. And then in the highest societies, instead of partially-aggregated thousands, we have completely-aggregated millions.

The growths of individual and social organisms are allied in another respect. In each case size augments by two processes, which go on sometimes separately, sometimes together. There is increase by simple multiplication of units, causing enlargement of the group; there is increase by union of groups, and again by union of groups of groups. The first parallelism is too simple to need illustration; but the facts which show us the second must be set forth.

ORGANIC GROWTH

Organic integration, treated of at length in the *Principles of Biology*, must be here summarized to make the comparison intelligible.[1] The compounding and re-compounding, as shown us throughout the vegetal kingdom, may be taken first, as most easily followed. Plants of the lowest orders are minute cells, some kinds of which in their myriads colour stagnant waters, and others compose the green films on damp surfaces. By clusterings of such cells are formed small threads, discs, globes, etc.; as well as amorphous masses and laminated masses. One of these last (called a thallus when scarcely at all differentiated, as in a seaweed, and called a frond in cryptogams that have some structure), is an extensive but simple group of the protophytes first named. Temporarily united in certain low cryptogams, fronds become permanently united in higher cryptogams: then forming a series of foliar surfaces joined by a creeping stem. Out of this comes the phænogamic axis—a shoot with its foliar organs or leaves. That is to say, there is now a permanent cluster of clusters. And then, as these axes develop lateral axes, and as these again branch, the compounding advances to higher stages. In the animal kingdom the like happens, though in a less regular and more disguised manner. The smallest animal, like the smallest plant, is essentially

---

[1] The essential features, however, are explained in the chapter on 'The Law of Evolution' included in the present selection.   S.A.

a minute group of living molecules. There are many forms and stages showing us the clustering of such smallest animals. Sometimes, as in the compound Vorticellæ and in the Sponges, their individualities are scarcely at all masked; but as evolution of the composite aggregate advances, the individualities of the component aggregates become less distinct. In some Cœlenterata, though they retain considerable independence, which they show by moving about like Amœbæ when separated, they have their individualities mainly merged in that of the aggregate formed of them: instance the common Hydra. Tertiary aggregates similarly result from the massing of secondary ones. Sundry modes and phases of the process are observable among cœlenterate types. There is the branched hydroid, in which the individual polypes preserve their identities, and the polypidom merely holds them together; and there are forms, such as Velella, in which the polypes have been so modified and fused, that their individualities were long unrecognized. Again, among the Molluscoida we have feebly-united tertiary aggregates in the Salpidæ; while we have, in the Botryllidæ, masses in which the tertiary aggregate, greatly consolidated, obscures the individualities of the secondary aggregates. So, too, is it with certain annuloid types; and, as I have sought to show, with the Annulosa generally. (*Prin. of Biol.*, p. 205.)

SOCIAL GROWTH

Social growth proceeds by an analogous compounding and re-compounding. The primitive social group, like the primitive group of living molecules with which organic evolution begins, never attains any considerable size by simple increase. Where, as among Fuegians, the supplies of wild food yielded by an inclement habitat will not enable more than a score of so to live in the same place—where, as among Andamanese, limited to a strip of shore backed by impenetrable bush, forty is about the number of individuals who can find prey without going too far from their temporary abode—where, as among Bushmen, wandering over barren tracts, small hordes are alone possible, and even families 'are sometimes obliged to separate, since the same spot will not afford sufficient sustenance for all', we have extreme instances of the limitation of simple groups, and the formation of migrating groups when the limit is passed. Even in tolerably productive habitats, fission of the groups is eventually neccessitated in a kindred manner. Spreading as its number increases, a primitive tribe presently reaches a diffusion at which its parts become incoherent; and it then gradually separates into tribes that become distinct as fast as their continually-diverging dialects pass into different languages. Often nothing further happens than repetition of this. Conflicts of tribes, dwindlings or extinctions of some, growths and spontaneous divisions of others, continue. The formation of a larger society results only by the joining of such smaller societies, which occurs without obliterating the divisions previously caused by separations. This process may be seen now going on among uncivilized races, as it once went on among the ancestors of the civilized races. Instead of absolute independence of small hordes, such as the lowest savages show us, more advanced savages show us slight cohesions among larger hordes. In North America each of the three great tribes of Comanches consists of various bands, having such feeble combination only, as results from the personal character of the great chief. So of the Dakotahs there are, according to Burton, seven principal bands, each including minor bands, numbering altogether, according to Catlin, forty-two. And in like manner the five Iroquois nations had severally eight tribes. Closer unions of these slightly-coherent original groups arise under favourable conditions, but they only now and then become permanent. A common form of the process is that described by Mason as occurring among the Karens. 'Each village, with its scant domain, is an independent state, and every chief a prince; but now and then a little Napoleon arises, who subdues a kingdom to himself, and builds up an empire. The dynasties, however, last only with the controlling mind.' The like happens in Africa. Livingstone says: 'Formerly all the Maganja were united under the government of their great Chief, Undi; . . . but after Undi's death it fell to pieces. . . . This has been the inevitable fate of every African Empire from time immemorial.' Only occasionally does there result a compound social aggregate that endures for a considerable period, as Dahomey or as Ashantee, which is 'an assemblage of states owing a kind of feudal obedience to the sovereign'. The histories of Madagascar and of sundry Polynesian islands also display these transitory compound groups, out of which at length come in some cases permanent ones. During the earliest times of the extinct civilized races, like stages were passed through. In the words of Maspero, Egypt was 'divided at first into a great number of tribes, which at several points simultaneously began to establish small independent states, every one of which had its laws and its worship'. The compound groups of Greeks first formed were those minor ones resulting from the subjugation of weaker towns by stronger neighbouring towns. And in northern Europe during pagan days, the numerous German tribes, each with its cantonal divisions, illustrated this second stage of aggregation. After such compound societies are consolidated, repetition of the process on a larger scale produces doubly-compound societies, which, usually cohering but feebly, become in some cases quite coherent. Maspero infers that the Egyptian nomes described above as resulting from integrations of tribes, coalesced into the two great principalities, Upper Egypt and Lower Egypt, which were eventually united, the small states becoming provinces. The boasting records of Mesopotamian kings similarly show us this union of unions going on. So, too, in Greece the integration at first occurring locally, began afterwards to combine the minor societies into two confederacies. During Roman days there arose for defensive purposes federations of tribes, which eventually consolidated; and subsequently these were compounded into still larger aggregates. Before and after the Christian era, the like happened throughout northern Europe. Then after a period of vague and varying combinations there came, in later times, as is well illustrated by French history, a massing of small feudal territories into provinces, and a subsequent massing of these into kingdoms.

So that in both organic and super-organic growths, we see a process of compounding and re-compounding carried to various stages. In both cases, after some consolidation of the smallest aggregates there comes the process of forming larger aggregates by union of them; and in both cases repetition of this process makes secondary aggregates into tertiary ones.

Organic growth and super-organic growth have yet another analogy. As above said, increase by multiplication of individuals in a group, and increase by union of groups, may go on simultaneously, and it does this in both cases.

The original clusters, animal and social, are not only small, but they lack density. Creatures of low types occupy large spaces considering the small quantities of animal substance they contain; and low-type societies spread over areas that are wide relatively to the numbers of their component individuals. But as integration in animals is shown by concentration as well as by increase of bulk, so that social integration which results from the clustering of clusters, is joined with augmentation of the number contained by each cluster. If we contrast the sprinklings in regions inhabited by wild tribes with the crowds filling equal regions in Europe, or if we contrast the density of population in England under the Heptarchy with its present density, we see that besides the growth produced by union of groups there has gone on interstitial growth. Just as the higher animal has become not only larger than the lower but more solid; so, too, has the higher society.

Social growth, then, equally with the growth of a living body, shows us the fundamental trait of evolution under a twofold aspect. Integration is displayed both in the formation of a larger mass, and in the progress of such mass towards that coherence due to closeness of parts.

It is proper to add, however, that there is a mode of social growth to which organic growth affords no parallel—that caused by the migration of units from one society to another. Among many primitive groups and a few developed ones, this is a considerable factor; but, generally, its effect bears so small a ratio to the effects of growth by increase of population and coalescence of groups, that it does not much qualify the analogy.

(D) Social Structures[1]

In societies, as in living bodies, increase of mass is habitually accompanied by increase of structure. Along with that integration which is the primary trait of evolution, both exhibit in high degrees the secondary trait, differentiation.

The association of these two characters in animals was described in the *Principles of Biology*. Excluding certain low kinds of them whose activities are little above those of plants, we recognized the

[1] From *The Principles of Sociology* Vol. I, 1876

general law that large aggregates have high organizations. The qualifications of this law which go along with differences of medium, of habitat, of type, are numerous; but when made they leave intact the truth that for carrying on the combined life of an extensive mass, involved arrangements are required. So, too, is it with societies. As we progress from small groups to larger; from simple groups to compound groups; from compound groups to doubly compound ones, the unlikenesses of parts increase. The social aggregate, homogeneous when minute, habitually gains in heterogeneity along with each increment of growth; and to reach great size must acquire great complexity. Let us glance at the leading stages.

Naturally in a state like that of the Cayaguas or Wood-Indians of South America, so little social that 'one family lives at a distance from another', social organization is impossible; and even where there is some slight association of families, organization does not arise while they are few and wandering. Groups of Esquimaux, of Australians, of Bushmen, of Fuegians, are without even that primary contrast of parts implied by settled chieftainship. Their members are subject to no control but such as is temporarily acquired by the stronger, or more cunning, or more experienced: not even a permanent nucleus is present. Habitually where larger simple groups exist, we find some kind of head. Though not a uniform rule (for, as we shall hereafter see, the genesis of a controlling agency depends on the nature of the social activities), this is a general rule. The headless clusters, wholly ungoverned, are incoherent, and separate before they acquire considerable sizes; but along with maintenance of an aggregate approaching to, or exceeding, a hundred, we ordinarily find a simple or compound ruling agency—one or more men claiming and exercising authority that is natural, or supernatural, or both. This is the first social differentiation. Soon after it there frequently comes another, tending to form a division between regulative and operative parts. In the lowest tribes this is rudely represented only by the contrast in *status* between the sexes: the men, having unchecked control, carry on such external activities as the tribe shows us, chiefly in war; while the women are made drudges who perform the less skilled parts of the process of sustentation. But that tribal growth, and establishment of chieftainship, which gives military superiority, presently causes enlargement of the operative part by adding captives to it. This begins unobtrusively. While in battle the men are killed, and often afterwards eaten, the non-combatants are enslaved. Patagonians, for example, make slaves of women and children taken in war. Later, and especially when cannibalism ceases, comes the enslavement of male captives; whence results, in some cases, an operative part clearly marked off from the regulative part. Among the Chinooks, 'slaves do all the laborious work'. We read that the Beluchi, avoiding the hard labour of cultivation, impose it on the Jutts, the ancient inhabitants whom they have subjugated. Beecham says it is usual on the Gold Coast to make the slaves clear the ground for cultivation. And among the Felatahs 'slaves are numerous: the males are employed in weaving, collecting wood or grass, or on any other kind of work; some of the women are engaged in spinning . . . in preparing the yarn for the loom, others in pounding and grinding corn, etc.'.

Along with that increase of mass caused by union of primary social aggregates into a secondary one, a further unlikeness of parts arises. The holding together of the compound cluster implies a head of the whole as well as heads of the parts; and a differentiation analogous to that which originally produced a chief, now produces a chief of chiefs. Sometimes the combination is made for defence against a common foe, and sometimes it results from conquest by one tribe of the rest. In this last case the predominant tribe, in maintaining its supremacy, develops more highly its military character, thus becoming unlike the others.

After such clusters of clusters have been so consolidated that their united powers can be wielded by one governing agency, there come alliances with, or subjugations of, other clusters of clusters, ending from time to time in coalescence. When this happens there results still greater complexity in the governing agency, with its king, local rulers and petty chiefs; and at the same time, there arise more marked divisions of classes—military, priestly, slave, etc. Clearly, then, complication of structure accompanies increase of mass.

DIFFERENTIATION AND DEFINITE DIFFERENCE

This increase of heterogeneity which in both classes of aggregates goes along with growth, presents another trait in common.

Beyond unlikenesses of parts due to development of the co-ordinating agencies, there presently follow unlikenesses among the agencies co-ordinated—the organs of alimentation, etc., in the one case, and the industrial structures in the other.

When animal-aggregates of the lowest order unite to form one of a higher order, and when, again, these secondary aggregates are compounded into tertiary aggregates, each component is at first similar to the other components; but in the course of evolution dissimilarities arise and become more and more decided. Among the Cœlenterata the stages are clearly indicated. From the sides of a common hydra, bud out young ones which, when fully developed, separate from their parent. In the compound hydroids the young polypes produced in like manner, remain permanently attached, and, themselves repeating the process, presently form a branched aggregate. When the members of the compound group lead similar and almost independent lives, as in various rooted genera, they remain similar: save those of them which become reproductive organs. But in the floating and swimming clusters, formed by a kindred process, the differently-conditioned members become different, while assuming different functions. It is thus with the minor social groups combined into a major social group. Each tribe originally had within itself such feebly-marked industrial divisions as sufficed for its low kind of life; and these were like those of each other tribe. But union facilitates exchange of commodities; and if, as mostly happens, the component tribes severally occupy localities favourable to unlike kinds of production, unlike occupations are initiated, and there result unlikenesses of industrial structures. Even between tribes not united, as those of Australia, barter of products furnished by their respective habitats goes on so long as war does not hinder. And evidently when there is reached such a stage of integration as in Madagascar, or as in the chief Negro states of Africa, the internal peace that follows subordination to one government makes commercial intercourse easy. The like parts being permanently held together, mutual dependence becomes possible; and along with growing mutual dependence the parts grow unlike.

SPECIALIZATION

The advance of organization which thus follows the advance of aggregation, alike in individual organisms and in social organisms, conforms in both cases to the same general law: differentiations proceed from the more general to the more special. First broad and simple contrasts of parts; then within each of the parts primarily contrasted, changes which make unlike divisions of them; then within each of these unlike divisions, minor unlikenesses, and so on continually.

The successive stages in the development of a vertebrate column, illustrate this law in animals. At the outset an elongated depression of the blastoderm, called the 'primitive groove', represents the entire cerebro-spinal axis: as yet there are no marks of vertebrae, nor even a contrast between the part which is to become head and the part which is to become backbone. Presently the ridges bounding this groove, growing up and folding over more rapidly at the anterior end, which at the same time widens, begin to make the skull distinguishable from the spine; and the commencement of segmentation in the spinal part, while the cephalic part remains unsegmented, strengthens the contrast. Within each of these main divisions minor divisions soon arise. The rudimentary cranium, bending forward, simultaneously acquires three dilatations indicating the contained nervous centres; while the segmentation of the spinal column, spreading to its ends, produces an almost-uniform series of 'proto-vertebræ'. At first these proto-vertebræ not only differ very little from one another, but each is relatively simple—a quadrate mass. Gradually this almost-uniform series falls into unlike divisions—the cervical group, the dorsal group, the lumbar group; and while the series of vertebræ is thus becoming specialized in its different regions, each vertebra is changing from that general form which it at first had in common with the rest, to the more special form eventually distinguishing it from the rest. Throughout the embryo there are, at the same time, going on kindred processes which, first making each large part unlike all other large parts, then make the parts of that part unlike one another. During social evolution analogous metamorphoses may everywhere be traced. The rise of the structure exercising religious control will serve as an example. In simple tribes, and in clusters of tribes during their early stages of aggregation, we find men who are at once sorcerers priests, diviners, exorcists, doctors—men who deal with supposed supernatural beings in all the various possible ways: propitiating them, seeking knowledge and aid from them, commanding them, subduing them. Along with advance in social integration, there come both differences of function and differences of rank. In Tanna 'there are rain-makers . . . and a host of other "sacred men" '. In Fiji there are not only priests, but seers; among the Sandwich Islanders there are diviners as well as priests; among the New Zealanders, Thomson distinguishes between priests and sorcerers; and among the Kaffirs, besides diviners and rain-makers, there are two classes of doctors who respectively rely on super-natural and on natural agents in curing their patients. More advanced societies, as those of ancient America, show us still greater multiformity of this once-uniform group. In Mexico, for example, the medical class, descending from a class of sorcerers who dealt antagonistically with the supernatural agents supposed to cause disease, were distinct from the priests whose dealings with supernatural agents were propitiatory. Further, the sacerdotal class included several kinds, dividing the religious offices among them—sacrificers, diviners, singers, composers of hymns, in-structors of youth; and then there were also gradations of rank in each. This progress from general to special in priesthoods has, in the higher nations, led to such marked distinctions that the original kinships are forgotten. The priest-astrologers of ancient races were initiators of the scientific class, now variously specialized; from the priest-doctors of old have come the medical class with its chief division and minor divisions; while within the clerical class proper, have arisen not only various ranks from Pope down to acolyte, but various kinds of functionaries—dean, priest, deacon, chorister, as well as others classed as curates and chaplains. Similarly if we trace the genesis of any industrial structure; as that which from primitive blacksmiths who smelt their own iron as well as make implements from it, brings us to our iron-manufacturing districts, where preparation of the metal is separated into smelting, refining, puddling, rolling, and where turning this metal into implements is divided into various businesses.

The transformation here illustrated is, indeed, an aspect of that transformation of the homogeneous into the heterogeneous which everywhere characterizes evolution; but the truth to be noted is that it characterizes the evolution of individual organisms and of social organisms in especially high degrees.

PRINCIPLES OF INTERNAL DIFFERENTIATION

Closer study of the facts shows us another striking parallelism. Organs in animals and organs in societies have internal arrangements framed on the same principle.

Differing from one another as the viscera of a living creature do in many respects, they have several traits in common. Each viscus contains appliances for conveying nutriment to its parts, for bringing it materials on which to operate, for carrying away the product, for draining off waste matters; as also for regulating its activity. Though liver and kidneys are unlike in their general appearances and minute structures, as well as in the offices they fulfil, the one as much as the other has a system of arteries, a system of veins, a system of lymphatics—has branched channels through which its excretions escape, and nerves for exciting and checking it. In large measure the like is true of those higher organs which, instead of elaborating and purifying and distributing the blood, aid the general life by carrying on external actions—the nervous and muscular organs. These, too, have their ducts for bringing prepared materials, ducts for drafting off vitiated materials, ducts for carrying away effete matters; as also their controlling nerve-cells and fibres. So that, along with the many marked differences of structure, there are these marked communities of structure.

It is the same in a society. The clustered citizens forming an organ which produces some commodity for national use, or which otherwise satisfies national wants, has within it subservient structures substantially like those of each other organ carrying on each other function. Be it a cotton-weaving district or a district where cutlery is made, it has a set of agencies which bring the raw material and a set of agencies which collect and send away the manufactured articles; it has an apparatus of major and minor channels through which the necessaries of life are drafted out of the general stocks circulating through the kingdom, and brought home to the local workers and those who direct them; it has appliances, postal and other, for bringing those impulses by which the industry of the place is excited or checked; it has local controlling powers, political and ecclesiastical, by which order is maintained and healthful action furthered. So, too, when, from a district which secretes certain goods, we turn to a sea-port which absorbs and sends out goods, we find the distributing and restraining agencies are mostly the same. Even where the social organ, instead of carrying on a material activity, has, like a university, the office of preparing certain classes of units for social functions of particular kinds, this general type of structure is repeated: the appliances for local sustentation and regulation, differing in some respects, are similar in essentials—there are like classes of distributors, like classes for civil control, and a specially-developed class for ecclesiastical control.

On observing that this community of structure among social organs, like the community of structure among organs in a living body, necessarily accompanies mutual dependence, we shall see even more clearly than hitherto how great is the likeness of nature between individual organization and social organization.

PRIMARY, SECONDARY AND TERTIARY FORMATION OF PARTS

One more structural analogy must be named. The formation of organs in a living body proceeds in ways which we may distinguish as primary, secondary, and tertiary; and, paralleling them, there are primary, secondary and tertiary ways in which social organs are formed. We will look at each of the three parallelisms by itself.

In animals of low types, bile is secreted, not by a liver, but by separate cells imbedded in the wall of the intestine at one part. These cells individually perform their function of separating certain matters from the blood, and individually pour out what they separate. No organ, strictly so-called, exists; but only a number of units not yet aggregated into an organ. This is analogous to the incipient form of an industrial structure in a society. At first each worker carries on his occupation alone, and himself disposes of the product to consumers. The arrangement still extant in our villages, where the cobbler at his own fireside makes and sells boots, and where the blacksmith single-handed does what iron-work is needed by his neighbours, exemplifies the primitive type of every producing structure. Among savages slight differentiations arise from individual aptitudes. Even of the degraded Fuegians, Fitzroy tells us that 'one becomes an adept with the spear; another with the sling; another with a bow and arrows'. As like differences of skill among members of primitive tribes cause some to become makers of special things, it results that necessarily the industrial organ begins as a social unit. Where, as among the Shasta Indians of California, 'arrow-making is a distinct profession', it is clear that manipulative superiority being the cause of the differentiation, the worker is at first single. And during subsequent periods of growth, even in small settled communities, this type continues. The statement that among the Coast Negroes, 'the most ingenious man in the village is usually the blacksmith, joiner, architect, and weaver', while it shows us artisan-functions in an undifferentiated stage, also shows us how completely individual is the artisan-structure: the implication being that as the society grows, it is by the addition of more such individuals, severally carrying on their occupations independently, that the additional demand is met.

By two simultaneous changes, an incipient secreting organ in an animal reaches that higher structure with which our next comparison may be made. The cells pass from a scattered cluster into a compact cluster; and they severally become compound. In place of a single cell elaborating and emitting its special product, we now have a small elongated sac containing a family of cells; and this, through an opening at one end, gives exit to their products. At the same time there is formed an integrated group of such follicles, each containing secreting units and having its separate orifice of discharge. To this type of individual organ we find, in semi-civilized societies a type of social organ closely corresponding. In one of these settled and growing communities, the demands upon individual workers, now more specialized in their occupations, have become unceasing; and each worker, occasionally pressed by work, makes helpers of his children. This practice, beginning incidentally, establishes itself; and eventually it grows into an imperative custom that each man shall bring up his boys to his own trade. Illustrations of this stage are numerous. Skilled occupations, 'like every other calling and office in Peru, always descended from father to son. The division of castes, in this particular, was as precise as that which existed in Egypt or Hindostan.' In Mexico, too, 'the sons in general learned the trades of their fathers, and embraced their professions'. The like was true of the industrial structures of European nations in early times. By the Theodosian code, a Roman youth 'was compelled to follow the employment of his father . . . and the suitor who sought the hand of the daughter could only obtain his bride by becoming wedded to the calling of her family'. In medieval France handicrafts were inherited; and the old English periods were characterized by a like usage. Branching of the family through generations into a number of kindred families carrying on the same occupation, produced the germ of the guild, and the related families who monopolized each industry formed a cluster habitually occupying the same quarter. Hence the still extant names of many streets in English towns— 'Fellmonger, Horsemonger, and Fleshmonger, Shoewright and Shieldwright, Turner and Salter Streets': a segregation like that which still persists in Oriental bazaars. And now, on observing how one of these industrial quarters was composed of many allied families, each containing sons working under direction of a father, who while sharing in the work sold the produce, and who, if the family and business were large, became mainly a channel taking in raw material and giving out the manufactured article, we see that there existed an analogy to the kind of glandular organ described above, which consists of a number of adjacent cell-containing follicles having separate mouths.

A third stage of the analogy may be traced. Along with that increase of a glandular organ necessitated by the more active functions of a more developed animal, there goes a change of structure consequent on augmentation of bulk. If the follicles multiply while their ducts have all to be brought to one spot, it results that their orifices, increasingly numerous, occupy a larger area of the wall of the cavity which receives the discharge; and if lateral extension of this area is negatived by the functional requirements, it results that the needful area is gained by formation of a cæcum. Further need of the same kind leads to secondary cæca diverging from this main cæcum, which hence becomes in part a duct. Thus is at length evolved a large viscus, such as a liver, having a single main duct with ramifying branches running throughout its mass. Now we rise from the above-described kind of industrial organ by parallel stages to a higher kind. There is no sudden leap from the household-type to the factory-type, but a gradual transition. The first step is shown us in those rules of trade-guilds under which, to the members of the family, might be added an apprentice (possibly at first a relation), who, as Brentano says, 'became a member of the family of his master, who instructed him in his trade, and who, like a father, had to watch over his morals, as well as his work'; practically, an adopted son. This modification having been established, there followed the employing of apprentices who had changed into journeymen. With development of this modified household-group, the master grew into a seller of goods made, not by his own family only, but by others; and, as his business enlarged, necessarily ceased to be a worker, and became wholly a distributor—a channel through which went out the products, not of a few sons, but of many unrelated artisans. This led the way to establishments in which the employed far outnumbered the members of the family, until at length, with the use of mechanical power, came the factory: a series of rooms, each containing a crowd of producing units, and sending its tributary stream of product to join other streams before reaching the single place of exit. Finally, in greatly-developed industrial organs, we see many factories clustered in the same town, and others in adjacent towns, to and from which, along branching roads, come the raw materials and go the bales of cloth, calico, etc.

There are instances in which a new industry passes through these stages in the course of a few generations, as happened with the stocking-manufacture. In the Midland counties, fifty years ago, the rattle and burr of a solitary stocking-frame came from a road-side cottage every here and there: the single worker made and sold his product. Presently arose workshops in which several such looms might be heard going: there was the father and his sons, with perhaps a journeyman. At length grew up the large building containing many looms driven by a steam-engine; and finally many such large buildings in the same town.

These structural analogies reach a final phase that is still more striking. In both cases there is a contrast between the original mode of development and a substituted later mode.

In the general course of organic evolution from low types to high, there have been passed through by insensible modifications all the stages above described; but now, in the individual evolution of an organism of high type, these stages are greatly abridged, and an organ is produced by a comparatively direct process. Thus the liver of a mammalian embryo is formed by the accumulation of numerous cells, which presently grow into a mass projecting from the wall of the intestine; while simultaneously there dips down into it a cæcum from the intestine. Transformation of this cæcum into the hepatic duct takes place at the same time that within the mass of cells there arise minor ducts, connected with this main duct; and there meanwhile go on other changes, which during evolution of the organ through successively higher types, came one after another. In the formation of industrial organs the like happens. Now that the factory system is well-established— now that it has become ingrained in the social constitution, we see direct assumptions of it in all industries for which its fitness has been shown. If at one place the discovery of ore prompts the setting up of ironworks, or at another a special kind of water facilitates brewing, there is no passing through the early stages of single worker, family, clustered families, and so on; but there is a sudden drafting of materials and men to the spot, followed by formation of a producing structure on the advanced type. Nay, not one large establishment only is thus evolved after the direct manner, but a cluster of large establishments. At Barrow-in-Furness we see a town with its iron-works, its importing and exporting businesses, its extensive docks and means of communication, all in the space of a few years framed after that type which it has taken centuries to develop through successive modifications.

An allied but even more marked change in the evolutionary process, is also common to both cases. Just as in the embryo of a high animal, various organs have their important parts laid down out of their original order, in anticipation, as it were; so, with the body at large, it happens that entire organs which during the serial genesis of the type came comparatively late, come in the evolving individual comparatively soon. This, which Professor Haeckel has called heterochrony, is shown us in the early marking out of the brain in a mammalian embryo, though in the lowest vertebrate animal no brain ever exists; or, again, in the segmentation of the spinal column before any alimentary system is formed, though, in a proto-vertebrate, even when its alimentary system is completed, there are but feeble signs of segmentation. The analogous change of order in social evolution, is shown us by new societies which inherit the confirmed habits of old ones. Instance the United States where a town in the far west, laid down in its streets and plots, has its hotel, church, post office, built while there are but few houses, and where a railway is run through the wilderness in anticipation of settlements. Or instance Australia, where a few years after the huts of gold-diggers begin to cluster round new mines, there is established a printing-office and journal; though, in the mother-country centuries passed before a town of like size developed a like agency.

(E) Social Functions[1]

Changes of structures cannot occur without changes of functions. Much that was said in the last chapter might, therefore, be said here with substituted terms. Indeed, as in societies many changes of structure are more indicated by changes of function than directly seen, it may be said that these last have been already described by implication.

There are, however, certain functional traits not manifestly implied by traits of structure. To these a few pages must be devoted.[2]

SPECIALIZATION AND MUTUAL DEPENDENCE

If organization consists in such a construction of the whole that its parts can carry on mutually-dependent actions, then in proportion as organization is high there must go a dependence of each part upon the rest so great that separation is fatal; and conversely. This truth is equally well shown in the individual organism and in the social organism.

The lowest animal-aggregates are so constituted that each portion, similar to every other in appearance, carries on similar actions, and here spontaneous or artificial separation interferes scarcely at all with the life of either separated portion. When the

[1] From *The Principles of Sociology*, Vol. I, 1876.
[2] It is interesting to compare the following pages with Radcliffe-Brown's analysis of these concepts in *Structure and Function in Primitive Society* (Cohen & West, London, 1652).

faintly-differentiated speck of protoplasm forming a rhizopod is accidentally divided, each division goes on as before. So, too, is it with those aggregates of the second order in which the components remain substantially alike. The ciliated monads clothing the horny fibres of a living sponge, need one another's aid so little that, when the sponge is cut in two, each half carries on its processes without interruption. Even where some unlikeness has arisen among the units, as in the familiar polype, the perturbation caused by division is but temporary: the two or more portions resulting, need only a little time for the units to rearrange themselves into fit forms before resuming their ordinary simple actions. The like happens for the like reason with the lowest social aggregates. A headless wandering group of primitive men divides without any inconvenience. Each man, at once warrior, hunter, and maker of his own weapons, hut etc., with a squaw who has in every case the like drudgeries to carry on, needs concert with his fellows only in war and to some extent in the chase; and, except for fighting, concert with half the tribe is as good as concert with the whole. Even where the slight differentiation implied by chieftainship exists, little inconvenience results from voluntary or enforced separation. Either before or after a part of the tribe migrates, some man becomes head, and such low social life as is possible recommences.

With highly-organized aggregates of either kind it is very different. We cannot cut a mammal in two without causing immediate death. Twisting off the head of a fowl is fatal. Not even a reptile, though it may survive the loss of its tail, can live when its body is divided. And among annulose creatures it similarly happens that though in some inferior genera, bisection does not kill either half, it kills both in an insect, an arachnid, or a crustacean. If in high societies the effect of mutilation is less than in high animals, still it is great. Middlesex separated from its surroundings would in a few days have all its social processes stopped by lack of supplies. Cut off the cotton-district from Liverpool and other ports, and there would come arrest of its industry followed by mortality of its people. Let a division be made between the coal-mining populations and adjacent populations which smelt metals or make broadcloth by machinery, and both, forthwith dying socially by arrest of their actions, would begin to die individually. Though when a civilized society is so divided that part of it is left without a central controlling agency, it may presently evolve one; yet there is meanwhile much risk of dissolution, and before re-organization is efficient, a long period of disorder and weakness must be passed through.

So that the *consensus* of functions becomes closer as evolution advances. In low aggregates, both individual and social, the actions of the parts are but little dependent on one another; whereas in developed aggregates of both kinds, that combination of actions which constitutes the life of the whole, makes possible the component actions which constitute the lives of the parts.

SPECIALIZATION AND SEPARATION OF FUNCTIONS

Another corollary, manifest *a priori* and proved *a posteriori*, must be named. Where parts are little differentiated, they can readily perform one another's functions; but where much differentiated they can perform one another's functions very imperfectly, or not at all.

Again the common polype furnishes a clear illustration. One of these sac-shaped creatures admits of being turned inside out, so that the skin becomes stomach and the stomach becomes skin: each thereupon beginning to do the work of the other. The higher we rise in the scale of organization the less practicable do we find such exchanges. Still, to some extent, substitutions of functions remain possible in highly developed creatures. Even in man the skin shows a trace of its original absorptive power, now mono-polized by the alimentary canal: it takes into the system certain small amounts of matter rubbed on to it. Such vicarious actions are, however, most manifest between parts having functions that are still allied. If, for instance, the bile-excreting function of the liver is impeded, other excretory organs, the kidneys and the skin, become channels through which bile is got rid of. If a cancer in the œsophagus prevents swallowing, the arrested food, dilating the œsophagus, forms a pouch in which imperfect digestion is set up. But these small abilities of the differentiated parts to discharge one another's duties, are not displayed where they have diverged more widely. Though mucous membrane, continuous with skin at various orifices, will, if everted, assume to a considerable extent the characters and powers of skin, yet serous membrane will not; nor can bone or muscle undertake, for any of the viscera, portions of their functions if they fail.

In social organisms, low and high, we find these relatively great and relatively small powers of substitution. Of course, where each member of the tribe repeats every other in his mode of life, there are no unlike functions to be exchanged; and where there has arisen only that small differentiation implied by the barter of weapons for other articles, between one member of the tribe skilled in weapon-making and others less skilled, the destruction of this specially-skilled member entails no great evil, since the rest can severally do for themselves that which he did for them, though not quite so well. Even in settled societies of considerable sizes we find the like holds to a great degree. Of the ancient Mexicans, Zurita says: 'Every Indian knows all handicrafts which do not require great skill or delicate instruments'. And in Peru each man 'was expected to be acquainted with the various handicrafts essential to domestic comfort'. The parts of the societies were so slightly differentiated in their occupations, that assumption of one another's occupations remained practicable. But in societies like our own, specialized industrially and otherwise in high degrees, the actions of one part which fails in its function cannot be assumed by other parts. Even the relatively unskilled farm labourers, were they to strike, would have their duties very inadequately performed by the urban population; and our iron manufactures would be stopped if their trained artisans, refusing to work, had to be replaced by peasants or hands from cotton-factories. Still less could the higher functions, legislative, judicial, etc., be effectually performed by coal-miners and navvies.

Evidently the same reason for this contrast holds in the two cases. In proportion as the units forming any part of an individual organism are limited to one kind of action, as that of absorbing, or secreting, or contracting, or conveying an impulse, and become adapted to that action, they lose adaptation to other actions; and in the social organism the discipline required for effectually discharging a special duty, causes unfitness for discharging special duties widely unlike it.

FURTHER ASPECTS OF FUNCTIONAL DIFFERENTIATION

Beyond these two chief functional analogies between individual organisms and social organisms, that when they are little evolved, division or mutilation causes small inconvenience, but when they are much evolved it causes great perturbation or death, and that in low types of either kind the parts can assume one another's functions, but cannot in high types, sundry consequent functional analogies might be enlarged on did space permit.

There is the truth that in both kinds of organisms the vitality increases as fast as the functions become specialized. In either case, before there exist structures severally adapted for the unlike actions, these are ill-performed; and in the absence of developed appliances for furthering it, the utilization of one another's services is but slight. But along with advance of organization, every part, more limited in its office, performs its office better; the means of exchanging benefits become greater; each aids all, and all aid each with increasing efficiency; and the total activity we call life, individual or national, augments.

Much, too, remains to be said about the parallelism between the changes by which the functions become specialized; but this, along with other parallelisms, will best be seen on following out, as we will now do, the evolution of the several great systems of organs, individual and social, considering their respective structural and functional traits together.

(F) Systems of Organs[1]

The hypothesis of evolution implies a truth which was established independently of it—the truth that all animals, however unlike they finally become, begin their developments in like ways. The first structural changes, once passed through in common by divergent types, are repeated in the early changes undergone by every new individual of each type. Admitting some exceptions, chiefly among parasites, this is recognized as a general law.

[1] From *The Principles of Sociology*, Vol. I, 1876.

This common method of development among individual organisms, we may expect to find paralleled by some common method among social organisms; and our expectation will be verified.

SIMPLE DIFFERENTIATION: OUTER AND INNER SYSTEMS

In *First Principles* and in the *Principles of Biology* were described the primary organic differentiations which arise in correspondence with the primary contrasts of conditions among the parts, as outer and inner. Neglecting earlier stages, let us pass to those which show us the resulting systems of organs in their simple forms.

The aggregated units composing the lowest cœlenterate animal, have become so arranged that there is an outer layer of them directly exposed to the surrounding medium with its inhabitants, and an inner layer lining the digestive cavity directly exposed only to the food. From units of the outer layer are formed those tentacles by which small creatures are caught, and those thread cells, as they are called, whence are ejected minute weapons against invading larger creatures; while by units of the inner layer is poured out the solvent which prepares the food for that absorption afterwards effected by them, both for their own sustentation and for the sustentation of the rest. Here we have in its first stage the fundamental distinction which pervades the animal kingdom, between the external parts which deal with environing existences—earth, air, prey, enemies—and the internal parts which utilize for the benefit of the entire body the nutritious substances which the external parts have secured. Among the higher *Coelenterata* a complication occurs. In place of each single layer of units there is a double layer, and between the two double layers a space. This space, partially separate from the stomach in creatures of this type, becomes completely shut off in types above it. In these last the outer double layer forms the wall of the body; the inner double layer bounds the alimentary cavity; and the space between them, containing absorbed nutriment, is the so-called peri-visceral sac. Though the above-described two simple layers with their intervening protoplasm, are but *analogous to* the outer and inner systems of higher animals, these two double layers, with the intervening cavity, are *homologous with* the outer and inner systems of higher animals. For in the course of evolution the outer double layer gives rise to the skeleton, the nervo-muscular system, the organs of sense, the protecting structures, etc.; while the inner double layer becomes the alimentary canal, with its numerous appended organs which almost monopolize the cavity of the body.

Early stages which are in principle analogous, occur in the evolution of social organisms. When from low tribes entirely undifferentiated, we pass to tribes next above them, we find classes of masters and slaves—masters who, as warriors carry on the offensive and defensive activities and thus especially stand in relations to environing agencies; and slaves who carry on inner activities for the general sustentation, primarily of their masters and secondarily of themselves. Of course this contrast is at first vague. Where the tribe subsists mainly on wild animals, its dominant men, being hunters as well as warriors, take a large share in procuring food; and such few captives as are made by war, become men who discharge the less skilled and more laborious parts of the process of sustentation. But along with establishment of the agricultural state, the differentiation grows more appreciable. Though members of the dominant class, superintending the labour of their slaves in the fields, sometimes join in it, yet the subject-class is habitually the one immediately in contact with the food-supply, and the dominant class, more remote from the food-supply, is becoming directive only, with respect to internal actions, while it is both executive and directive with respect to external actions, offensive and defensive. A society thus composed of two strata in contact, complicates by the rise of grades within each stratum. For small tribes the structure just described suffices; but where there are formed aggregates of tribes, necessarily having more-developed governmental and militant agencies, with accompanying more-developed industrial agencies supporting them, the higher and lower strata severally begin to differentiate internally. The superior class, besides minor distinctions which arise locally, originates everywhere a supplementary class of personal adherents who are mostly also warriors, while the inferior class begins to separate into bond and free. Various of the Malayo-Polynesian societies show us this stage. Among the East Africans, the Congo people, the Coast Negroes, the Inland Negroes, we find the same general sub-division—the king with his relatives, the class of chiefs, the common people, the slaves; of which the first two with their immediate dependents carry on the corporate actions of the society, and the second two those actions of a relatively separate order which yield it all the necessaries of life.

SUBSEQUENT DIFFERENTIATION: THE DISTRIBUTIVE SYSTEM

In both individual and social organisms, after the outer and inner systems have been marked off from one another, there begins to arise a third system, lying between the two and facilitating their co-operation. Mutual dependence of the primarily-contrasted parts, implies intermediation; and in proportion as they develop, the apparatus for exchanging products and influences must develop too. This we find it does.

In the low cœlenterate animal first described, consisting of inner and outer layers with intervening protoplasm, the nutritive matter which members of the inner layer have absorbed from prey caught by members of the outer layer, is transmitted almost directly to these members of the outer layer. Not so, however, in the superior type. Between the double-layered body-wall and the double-layered alimentary cavity, there is now a partially separate peri-visceral sac; and this serves as a reservoir for the digested matters from which the surrounding tissues take up their shares of prepared food. Here we have the rudiment of a distributing system. Higher in the animal series, as in Mollusca, this peri-visceral sac, quite shut off, has ramifications running throughout the body, carrying nutriment to its chief organs; and in the central part of the sac is a contractile tube which by its occasional pulses, causes irregular movements in the nutritive fluid. Further advances are shown by the lengthening and branching of this tube until, dividing and sub-dividing, it becomes a set of blood-vessels, while its central part becomes a heart. As this change progresses, the nutriment taken up by the alimentary structures is better distributed by these vascular structures to the outer and inner organs in proportion to their needs. Evidently this distributing system must arise between the two pre-existing systems; and it necessarily ramifies in proportion as the parts to which it carries materials become more remote, more numerous, and severally more complex.

The like happens in societies. The lowest types have no distributing systems—no roads or traders exist. The two original classes are in contact. Any slaves possessed by a member of the dominant class, stand in such direct relation to him that the transfer of products takes place without intervening persons; and each family being self-sufficing, there need be no agents through whom to effect exchanges of products between families. Even after these two primary divisions become partially subdivided, we find that so long as the social aggregate is a congeries of tribes severally carrying on within themselves the needful productive activities, a distributing system is scarcely traceable: occasional assemblings for barter alone occur. But as fast as consolidation of such tribes makes possible the localization of industries, there begins to show itself an appliance for transferring commodities, consisting now of single hawkers, now of travelling companies of traders, and growing with the formation of roads into an organized system of wholesale and retail distribution which spreads everywhere.

ORDER OF DIFFERENTIATION

There are, then, parallelisms between these three great systems in the two kinds of organisms. Moreover, they arise in the social organism in the same order as in the individual organism, and for the same reasons.

A society lives by appropriating matters from the earth—the mineral matters used for buildings, fuel, etc., the vegetal matters raised on its surface for food and clothing, the animal matters elaborated from these with or without human regulation; and the lowest social stratum is the one through which such matters are taken up and delivered to agents who pass them into the general current of commodities: the higher part of this lowest stratum being that which, in workshops and factories, elaborates some of these materials before they go to consumers. Clearly, then, the classes engaged in manual occupations play the same part in the function of social sustentation, as is played by the components of the alimentary organs in the sustentation of a living body. No less certain is it that the entire class of men engaged in buying and selling commodities of all kinds, on large and small scales, and in sending them along gradually-formed channels to all districts, towns, and individuals, so enabling them to make good the waste caused by action, is, along with those channels, fulfilling an office essentially like that fulfilled in a living body by the vascular system; which, to every structure and every unit of it, brings a current of nutritive matters proportionate to its activity. And it is equally manifest that while in the living body, the brain, the organs of sense and the limbs guided by them, distant in position from the alimentary surfaces, are fed through the tortuous channels of the vascular system, so the controlling parts of a society, most remote from the operative parts, have brought to them through courses of distribution often extremely indirect, the needful supplies of consumable articles.

That the order of evolution is necessarily the same in the two cases, is just as clear. In a creature which is both very small and very inactive, like a hydra, direct passage of nutriment from the inner layer to the outer layer by absorption suffices. But in proportion as the outer structures, becoming more active, expend more, simple absorption from adjacent tissues no longer meets the resulting waste; and in proportion as the mass becomes larger, and the parts which prepare nutriment consequently more remote from the parts which consume it, there arises the need for a means of transfer. Until the two original systems have been marked off from one another, this tertiary system has no function; and when the two original systems arise, they cannot develop far without corresponding development of this tertiary system. In the evolution of the social organism we see the like. Where there exist only a class of masters and a class of slaves, in direct contact, an appliance for transferring products has no place; but a larger society having classes exercising various regulative functions, and localities devoted to different industries, not only affords a place for a transferring system, but can grow and complicate only on condition that this transferring system makes proportionate advances.

(G) Social Types and Constitutions[1]

A glance at the respective antecedents of individual organisms and social organisms, shows why the last admit of no such definite classification as the first. Through a thousand generations a species of plant or animal leads substantially the same kind of life; and its successive members inherit the acquired adaptations. When changed conditions cause divergences of forms once alike, the accumulating differences arising in descendants only superficially disguise the original identity—do not prevent the grouping of the several species into a genus; nor do wider divergences that began earlier, prevent the grouping of genera into orders and orders into classes. It is otherwise with societies. Hordes of primitive men, dividing and subdividing, do, indeed, show us successions of small social aggregates leading like lives, inheriting such low structures as had resulted, and repeating those structures. But higher social aggregates propagate their respective types in much less decided ways. Though colonies tend to grow like their parent societies, yet the parent societies are so comparatively plastic, and the influences of new habitats on the derived societies are so great, that divergences of structure are inevitable. In the absence of definite organizations established during the similar lives of many societies descending one from another, there cannot be the precise distinctions implied by complete classification.

Two cardinal kinds of differences there are, however, of which we may avail ourselves for grouping societies in a natural manner. Primarily we may arrange them according to their degrees of composition, as simple, compound, doubly-compound, trebly-compound; and secondarily, though in a less specific way, we may divide them into the predominantly militant and the predominantly industrial—those in which the organization for offence and defence is most largely developed, and those in which the sustaining organization is most largely developed.

CLASSIFICATION BY DEGREES OF COMPOSITION

We have seen that social evolution begins with small simple aggre-

[1] From *The Principles of Sociology*, Vol. I, 1876.

gates; that it progresses by the clustering of these into larger aggregates; and that after being consolidated, such clusters are united with others like themselves into still larger aggregates. Our classification, then, must begin with societies of the first or simplest order.

We cannot in all cases say with precision what constitutes a simple society; for, in common with products of evolution generally, societies present transitional stages which negative sharp divisions. As the multiplying members of a group spread and diverge gradually, it is not always easy to decide when the groups into which they fall become distinct. Here, inhabiting a barren region, the descendants of common ancestors have to divide while yet the constituent families are near akin; and there, in a more fertile region, the group may hold together until clusters of families remotely akin are formed: clusters which, diffusing slowly, are held by a common bond that slowly weakens. By and by comes the complication arising from the presence of slaves not of the same ancestry, or of an ancestry but distantly allied; and these, though they may not be political units, must be recognized as units sociologically considered. Then there is the kindred complication arising where an invading tribe becomes a dominant class. Our only course is to regard as a simple society, one which forms a single working whole unsubjected to any other, and of which the parts co-operate, with or without a regulating centre, for certain public ends. On page 150 is a table, presenting with as much definiteness as may be, the chief divisions and sub-divisions of such simple societies. On contemplating these uncivilized societies which, though alike as being uncompounded, differ in their sizes and structures, certain generally-associated traits may be noted. Of the groups without political organization, or with but vague traces of it, the lowest are those small wandering ones which live on the wild food sparsely distributed in forests, over barren tracts, or along sea-shores. Where small simple societies remain without chiefs though settled, it is where circumstances allow them to be habitually peaceful. Glancing down the table we find reason for inferring that the changes from the hunting life to the pastoral, and from the pastoral to the agricultural, favour increase of population, the development of political organization, of industrial organization, and of the arts; though these causes do not of themselves produce these results. The second table on page 151 contains societies which have passed to a slight extent, or considerably, or wholly, into a state in which

HEADLESS.	*Nomadic:*—(hunting) Fuegians, some Australians, Wood-Veddahs, Bushmen, Chépángs and Kusúndas of Nepal.	
	Semi-settled:—most Esquimaux.	
	Settled:—Arafuras, Land Dyaks of Upper Sarawak River.	

SIMPLE SOCIETIES

OCCASIONAL HEADSHIP.
Nomadic:—(hunting) some Australians, Tasmanians.
Semi-settled:—some Caribs.
Settled:—some Uaupés of the upper Rio Negro.

VAGUE AND UNSTABLE HEADSHIP.
Nomadic:—(hunting) Andamanese, Abipones, Snakes, Chippewayans (pastoral) some Bedouins.
Semi-settled:—some Esquimaux, Chinooks, Chippewas (at present), some Kamschadales, Village Veddahs, Bodo and Dhimáls.
Settled:—Guiana tribes, Mandans, Coroados, New Guinea people, Tannese, Vateans, Dyaks, Todas, Nagas, Karens, Santals.

STABLE HEADSHIP.
Nomadic:—
Semi-settled:—some Caribs, Patagonians, New Caledonians, Kaffirs.
Settled:—Guaranis, Pueblos.

the simple groups have their respective chiefs under a supreme chief. The stability or instability alleged of the headship in these cases, refers to the headship of the composite group, and not to the headship of the component groups. As might be expected, stability of this compound headship becomes more marked as the original unsettled state passes into the completely settled state, the nomadic life obviously making it difficult to keep the heads of groups subordinate to a general head. Though not in all cases accompanied by considerable organization, this coalescence evidently conduces to organization. The completely-settled compound societies are mostly characterized by division into ranks, four, five, or six, clearly marked off; by established ecclesiastical arrangements; by industrial structures that show advancing division of labour, general and local; by buildings of some permanence clustered into places of some size; and by improved appliances of life generally.

In the table on page 152 are placed societies formed by the re-

COMPOUND SOCIETIES

OCCASIONAL HEADSHIP.

Nomadic:—(pastoral) some Bedouins.
Semi-settled:—Tannese.
Settled:—

UNSTABLE HEADSHIP.

Nomadic:—(hunting) Dacotahs, (hunting and pastoral) Comanches, (pastoral) Kalmucks.
Semi-settled:—Ostyaks, Beluchis, Kookies, Bhils, Congo-people (passing into doubly compound), Teutons before 5th century.
Settled:—Chippewas (in past times), Creeks, Mundrucus, Tupis, Khonds, some New Guinea people, Sumatrans, Malagasy (till recently), Coast Negroes, Inland Negroes, some Abyssinians, Homeric Greeks, Kingdoms of the Heptarchy, Teutons in 5th century, Fiefs of 10th century.

STABLE HEADSHIP.

Nomadic:—(pastoral) Kirghiz.
Semi-settled:—Bechuanas, Zulus.
Settled:—Uaupés, Fijians (when first visited), New Zealanders, Sandwich Islanders (in Cook's time), Javans, Hottentots, Dahomans, Ashantees, some Abyssinians, Ancient Yucatanese, New Granada people, Honduras people, Chibehas, some town Arabs.

compounding of these compound groups, or in which many governments of the types tabulated above have become subject to a still higher government. The first notable fact is that these doubly-compound societies are all completely settled. Along with their greater integration we see in many cases, though not uniformly, a more elaborate and stringent political organization. Where complete stability of political headship over these doubly-compound societies has been established, there is mostly, too, a developed ecclesiastical hierarchy. While becoming more complex by division of labour, the industrial organization has in many cases assumed a caste structure. To a greater or less extent, custom has passed into positive law; and religious observances have grown definite, rigid, and complex. Towns and roads have become general; and considerable progress in knowledge and the arts has taken place.

There remain to be added the great civilized nations which need no tabular form, since they mostly fall under one head—trebly compound. Ancient Mexico, the Assyrian Empire, the Egyptian

DOUBLY COMPOUND SOCIETIES

OCCASIONAL HEADSHIP.
Semi-settled:—
Settled:—Samoans.

UNSTABLE HEADSHIP.
Semi-settled:—
Settled:—Tahitians, Tongans, Javans (occasionally), Fijians (since fire-arms), Malagasy (in recent times), Athenian Confederacy, Spartan Confederacy, Teutonic Kingdoms from 6th to 9th centuries, Greater Fiefs in France of the 13th century.

STABLE HEADSHIP.
Semi-settled:—
Settled:—Iroquois, Araucanians, Sandwich Islanders (since Cook's time), Ancient Vera Paz and Bogota peoples, Guatemalans, Ancient Peruvians, Wahhàbees (Arab), Omán (Arab), Ancient Egyptian Kingdom, England after the 10th century.

Empire, the Roman Empire, Great Britain, France, Germany, Italy, Russia, may severally be regarded as having reached this stage of composition or perhaps, in some cases, a still higher stage. Only in respect of the stabilities of their governments may they possibly require classing apart—not their political stabilities in the ordinary sense, but their stabilities in the sense of continuing to be the supreme centres of these great aggregates. So defining this trait, the ancient trebly-compound societies have mostly to be classed as unstable; and of the modern, the Kingdom of Italy and the German Empire have to be tested by time.

As already indicated, this classification must not be taken as more than an approximation to the truth. In some cases the data furnished by travellers and others are inadequate; in some cases their accounts are conflicting; in some cases the composition is so far transitional that it is difficult to say under which of two heads it should come. Here the gens or the phratry may be distinguished as a local community; and here these groups of near or remote kinsmen are so mingled with other such groups as practically to form parts of one community. Evidently the like combination of several such communities, passing through stages of increasing cohesion, leaves it sometimes doubtful whether they are to be regarded as many or as one. And when, as with the larger social aggregates, there have been successive conquests, resulting unions, subsequent dissolutions, and re-unions otherwise composed, the original lines of structure become so confused or lost that it is difficult to class the ultimate product.

But there emerge certain generalizations which we may safely accept. The stages of compounding and re-compounding have to be passed through in succession. No tribe becomes a nation by simple growth; and no great society is formed by the direct union of the smallest societies. Above the simple group the first stage is a compound group inconsiderable in size. The mutual dependence of parts which constitutes it a working whole, cannot exist without some development of lines of intercourse and appliances for combined action, and this must be achieved over a narrow area before it can be achieved over a wide one. When a compound society has been consolidated by the co-operation of its component groups in war under a single head—when it has simultaneously differentiated somewhat its social ranks and industries, and proportionately developed its arts, which all of them conduce in some way to better co-operation, the compound society becomes practically a single one. Other societies of the same order, each having similarly reached a stage of organization alike required and made possible by this co-ordination of actions throughout a larger mass, now form bodies from which, by conquest or by federation in war, may be formed societies of the doubly-compound type. The consolidation of these has again an accompanying advance of organization distinctive of it—an organization for which it affords the scope and which makes it practicable—an organization having a higher complexity in its regulative, distributive, and industrial systems. And at later stages, by kindred steps, arise still larger aggregates having still more complex structures. In this order has social evolution gone on, and only in this order does it appear to be possible. Whatever imperfections and incongruities the above classification has, do not hide these general facts—that there are societies of these different grades of composition; that those of the same grade have general resemblances in their structures; and that they arise in the order shown.

CLASSIFICATION BY 'TYPES'

We pass now to the classification based on unlikeness between the

F

kinds of social activity which predominate, and on the resulting unlikenesses of organization. The two social types thus essentially constrasted are the militant and the industrial.

It is doubtless true that no definite separation of these can be made. Excluding a few simple groups such as the Esquimaux, inhabiting places where they are safe from invasion, all societies, simple and compound, are occasionally or habitually in antagonism with other societies and, as we have seen, tend to evolve structures for carrying on offensive and defensive actions. At the same time sustentation is necessary and there is always an organization, slight or decided, for achieving it. But while the two systems in social organisms, as in individual organisms, co-exist in all but the rudimentary forms, they vary immensely in the ratios they bear to one another. In some cases the structures carrying on external actions are largely developed; the sustaining system exists solely for their benefit; and the activities are militant. In other cases there is predominance of the structures carrying on sustentation; offensive and defensive structures are maintained only to protect them; and the activities are industrial. At the one extreme we have those warlike tribes which, subsisting mainly by the chase, make the appliances for dealing with enemies serve also for procuring food, and have sustaining systems represented only by their women, who are their slave-classes; while, at the other extreme we have the type, as yet only partially evolved, in which the agricultural, manufacturing and commercial organizations form the chief part of the society and, in the absence of external enemies, the appliances for offence and defence are either rudimentary or absent. Transitional as are nearly all the societies we have to study, we may yet clearly distinguish the constitutional traits of these opposite types, characterized by predominance of the outer and inner systems respectively.

Having glanced at the two thus placed in contrast, it will be most convenient to contemplate each by itself.

THE MILITANT TYPE

As before pointed out, the militant type is one in which the army is the nation mobilized while the nation is the quiescent army, and which, therefore, acquires a structure common to army and nation. We shall most clearly understand its nature by observing in detail this parallelism between the military organization and the social organization at large.[1]

Already we have had ample proof that centralized control is the primary trait acquired by every body of fighting men, be it horde of savages, band of brigands, or mass of soldiers. And this centralized control, necessitated during war, characterizes the government during peace. Among the uncivilized there is a marked tendency for the military chief to become also the political head (the medicine man being his only competitor); and in a conquering race of savages his political headship becomes fixed. In semi-civilized societies the conquering commander and the despotic king are the same, and they remain the same in civilized societies down to late times. The connection is well shown where in the same race, along with a contrast between the habitual activities we find contrasted forms of government. Thus the powers of the patriarchal chiefs of Kaffir tribes are not great, but the Zulus, who have become a conquering division of the Kaffirs, are under an absolute monarch. Of advanced savages the Fijians may be named as well showing this relation between habitual war and despotic rule: the persons and property of subjects are entirely at the king's or chief's disposal. We have seen that it is the same in the warlike African states, Dahomey and Ashantee. The ancient Mexicans, again, whose highest profession was that of arms, and whose eligible prince became king only by feats in war, had an autocratic government, which, according to Clavigero, became more stringent as the territory was enlarged by conquest. Similarly, the unmitigated despotism under which the Peruvians lived, had been established during the spread of the Inca conquests. And that race is not the cause, we are shown by this recurrence in ancient America of a relation so familiar in ancient states of the Old World. The absoluteness of a commander-in-chief goes along with absolute control exercised by his generals over their subordinates, and by their subordinates over the men under them: all are slaves to those above and despots to those below. This structure repeats itself in the accompanying social arrangements. There are precise gradations of rank in the community and complete submission of each rank to the ranks above it. We see this in the society already instanced as

[1] For a modern treatment of the subject which takes Spencer's ideas as the starting point, see S. Andreski, *Military Organization and Society*, 2nd edition, Routledge & Kegan Paul and California University Press, 1968.

showing among advanced savages the development of the militant type. In Fiji six classes are enumerated, from king down to slaves, as sharply marked off. Similarly in Madagascar, where despotism has been in late times established by war, there are several grades and castes. Among the Dahomans, given in so great a degree to bloodshed of all kinds, 'the army, or, what is nearly synonymous, the nation', says Burton, 'is divided, both male and female, into two wings'; and then, of the various ranks enumerated, all are characterized as legally slaves of the king. In Ashantee, too, where his officers are required to die when the king dies, we have a kindred condition. Of old, among the aggressive Persians, grades were strongly marked. So was it in warlike ancient Mexico: besides three classes of nobility, and besides the mercantile classes, there were three agricultural classes down to the serfs—all in precise subordination. In Peru, also, below the Inca there were grades of nobility —lords over lords. Moreover, in each town the inhabitants were registered in decades under a decurion, five of these under a superior, two such under a higher one, five of these centurions under a head, two of these heads under one who thus ruled a thousand men, and for every ten thousand there was a governor of Inca race: the political rule being thus completely regimental. Till lately, another illustration was furnished by Japan. That there were kindred, if less elaborate, structures in ancient militant states of the Old World, scarcely needs saying; and that like structures were repeated in medieval times, when a large nation like France had under the monarch several grades of feudal lords, vassals to those above and suzerains to those below, with serfs under the lowest, again shows us that everywhere the militant type has sharply-marked social gradations as it has sharply-marked military gradations. Along with this natural government there goes a like form of supernatural government. I do not mean merely that in the ideal otherworlds of militant societies, the ranks and powers are conceived as like those of the real world around, though this also is to be noted; but I refer to the militant character of the religion. Ever in antagonism with other societies, the life is a life of enmity and the religion a religion of enmity. The duty of blood-revenge, most sacred of all with the savage, continues to be the dominant duty as the militant type of society evolves. The chief, baulked of his vengeance, dies enjoining his successors to avenge him; his ghost is propitiated by fulfilling his commands; the slaying of his enemies becomes the

highest action; trophies are brought to his grave in token of fulfilment; and, as tradition grows, he becomes the god worshipped
with bloody sacrifices. Everywhere we find evidence. The Fijians
offer the bodies of their victims killed in war to the war-god before
cooking them. In Dahomey, where the militant type is so far
developed that women are warriors, men are almost daily sacrificed
by the monarch to please his dead father; and the ghosts of old
kings are invoked for aid in war by blood sprinkled on their tombs.
The war-god of the Mexicans (originally a conqueror), the most
revered of their gods, had his idol fed with human flesh: wars being
undertaken to supply him with victims. And similarly in Peru,
where there were habitual human sacrifices, men taken captive
were immolated to the father of the Incas, the Sun. How militant
societies of old in the East similarly evolved deities who were
similarly propitiated by bloody rites, needs merely indicating.
Habitually their mythologies represent gods as conquerors; habitually their gods are named 'the strong one', 'the destroyer', 'the
avenger', 'god of battles', 'lord of hosts', 'man of war', and so forth.
As we read in Assyrian inscriptions, wars were commenced by
their alleged will; and, as we read elsewhere, peoples were mas-
sacred wholesale in professed obedience to them. How its theo-
logical government, like its political government, is essentially
military, we see even in late and qualified forms of the militant
type; for down to the present time absolute subordination, like
that of soldier to commander, is the supreme virtue, and disobedience the crime for which eternal torture is threatened. Similarly with the accompanying ecclesiastical organization. Generally
where the militant type is highly developed, the political head and
the ecclesiastical head are identical—the king, chief descendant of
his ancestor who has become a god, is also chief propitiator of him.
It was so in ancient Peru; and in Acolhuacan (Mexico) the high-
priest was the king's second son. The Egyptian wall-paintings show
us kings performing sacrifices; as do also the Assyrian. Babylonian
records harmonize with Hebrew traditions in telling us of priest-
kings. In Lydia it was the same: Crœsus was king and priest. In
Sparta, too, the kings, while military chiefs, were also high priests;
and a trace of the like original relation existed in Rome. A system
of subordination essentially akin to the military, has habitually
characterized the accompanying priesthoods. The Fijians have an
hereditary priesthood forming a hierarchy. In Tahiti, where the

high-priest was often royal, there were grades of hereditary priests belonging to each social rank. In ancient Mexico the priesthoods of different gods had different ranks, and there were three ranks within each priesthood; and in ancient Peru, besides the royal chief priest, there were priests of the conquering race set over various classes of inferior priests. A like type of structure, with subjection of rank to rank, has characterized priesthoods in the ancient and modern belligerent societies of the Old World. A kind of government essentially the same is traceable throughout the sustaining organization also, so long as the social type remains predominantly militant. Beginning with simple societies in which the slave-class furnishes the warrior-class with the necessaries of life, we have already seen that during subsequent stages of evolution the industrial part of the society continues to be essentially a permanent commissariat, existing solely to supply the needs of the governmental-military structures, and having left over for itself only enough for bare maintenance. Hence the development of political regulation over its activities has been in fact the extension throughout it of that military rule which, as a permanent commissariat, it naturally had. An extreme instance is furnished us by the ancient Peruvians, whose political and industrial governments were identical—whose kinds and quantities of labour for every class in every locality, were prescribed by laws enforced by state-officers—who had work legally dictated even for their young children, their blind, and their lame, and who were publicly chastised for idleness, regimental discipline being applied to industry just as our modern advocate of strong government would have it now. The late Japanese system, completely military in origin and nature, similarly permeated industry: great and small things—houses, ships, down even to mats—were prescribed in their structures. In the warlike monarchy of Madagascar the artisan classes are in the employ of government, and no man can change his occupation or locality under pain of death. Without multiplication of cases, these typical ones, reminding the reader of the extent to which even in modern fighting states industrial activities are officially regulated, will sufficiently show the principle. Not industry only, but life at large is, in militant societies, subject to kindred discipline. Before its recent collapse the government of Japan enforced sumptuary laws on each class, mercantile and other, up to the provincial governors, who must rise, dine, go out, give audience and retire to rest at prescribed hours; and the native literature specifies regulations of a scarcely credible minuteness. In ancient Peru, officers 'minutely inspected the houses, to see that the man, as well as his wife, kept the household in proper order, and preserved a due state of discipline among their children'; and householders were rewarded or chastised accordingly. Among the Egyptians of old each person had, at fixed intervals, to report to the local authority his name, abode and mode of living. Sparta, too, yields an example of a society specially organized for offence and defence, in which the private conduct of citizens in all its details was under public control, enforced by spies and censors. Though regulations so stringent have not characterized the militant type in more recent ages, yet we need but recall the laws regulating food and dress, the restraints on locomotion, the prohibitions of some games and dictation of others, to indicate the parallelism of principle. Even now where the military organization has been kept in vigour by military activities, as in France, we are shown by the peremptory control of journals and suppression of meetings, by the regimental uniformity of education, by the official administration of the fine arts, the way in which its characteristic regulating system ramifies everywhere. And then, lastly, is to be noted the theory concerning the relation between the state and the individual, with its accompanying sentiment. This structure, which adapts a society for combined action against other societies, is associated with the belief that its members exist for the benefit of the whole and not the whole for the benefit of its members. As in an army the liberty of the soldier is denied and only his duty as a member of the mass insisted on; as in a permanently encamped army like the Spartan nation, the laws recognize no personal interest, but patriotic ones only; so in the militant type throughout, the claims of the unit are nothing and the claims of the aggregate everything. Absolute subjection to authority is the supreme virtue and resistance to it a crime. Other offences may be condoned, but disloyalty is an unpardonable offence. If we take the sentiments of the sanguinary Fijians, among whom loyalty is so intense that a man stands unbound to be knocked on the head, himself saying that what the king wills must be done; or those of the Dahomans, among whom the highest officials are the king's slaves, and on his decease his women sacrifice one another that they may all follow him; or those of the ancient Peruvians, among whom with a dead Inca, or great

Curaca, were buried alive his favourite attendants and wives that they might go to serve him in the other world; or those of the ancient Persians, among whom a father, seeing his innocent son shot by the king in pure wantonness, 'felicitated' the king 'on the excellence of his archery', and among whom bastinadoed subjects 'declared themselves delighted because his majesty had condescended to recollect them'; we are sufficiently shown that in this social type, the sentiment which prompts assertion of personal rights in opposition to a ruling power, scarcely exists.

Thus the trait characterizing the militant structure throughout, is that its units are coerced into their various combined actions. As the soldier's will is so suspended that he becomes in everything the agent of his officer's will, so is the will of the citizen in all transactions, private and public, overruled by that of the government. The co-operation by which the life of the militant society is maintained, is a *compulsory* co-operation. The social structure adapted for dealing with surrounding hostile societies is under a centralized regulating system to which all the parts are completely subject; just as in the individual organism the outer organs are completely subject to the chief nervous centre.

THE INDUSTRIAL TYPE

The traits of the industrial type have to be generalized from inadequate and entangled data. Antagonism more or less constant with other societies, having been almost everywhere and always the condition of each society, a social structure fitted for offence and defence exists in nearly all cases, and disguises the structure which social sustentation alone otherwise originates. Such conception as may be formed of it has to be formed from what we find in the few simple societies which have been habitually peaceful, and in the advanced compound societies which, though once habitually militant, have become gradually less so.

Already I have referred to the chiefless Arafuras, living in 'peace and brotherly love with one another', of whom we are told that 'they recognize the right of property in the fullest sense of the word, without there being any authority among them than the decisions of their elders, according to the customs of their forefathers'. That is, there has grown up a recognition of mutual claims and personal rights, with voluntary submission to a tacitly-elected representative government formed of the most experienced. Among the Todas 'who lead a peaceful, tranquil life', disputes are 'settled either by arbitration' or by 'a council of five'. The amiable Bodo and Dhimáls, said to be wholly unmilitary, display an essentially free social form. They have nothing but powerless head men, and are without slaves or servants; but they give mutual assistance in clearing ground and housebuilding: there is voluntary exchange of services—giving of equivalents of labour. The Mishmis again, described as quiet, inoffensive, not warlike, and only occasionally uniting in self-defence, have scarcely any political organization. Their village communities under merely nominal chiefs acknowledge no common chief of the tribe, and the rule is democratic: crimes are judged by an assembly. Naturally few, if any, cases occur in which societies of this type have evolved into larger societies without passing into the militant type; for, as we have seen, the consolidation of simple aggregates into a compound aggregate habitually results from war, defensive or offensive, which, if continued, evolves a centralized authority with its coercive institutions. The Pueblos, however, industrious and peaceful agriculturists who, building their unique villages, or compound houses containing 2,000 people, in such ways as to 'wall out black barbarism', fight only when invaded, show us a democratic form of government: 'the governor and his council are elected annually by the people'. The case of Samoa, too, may be named as showing to some extent how, in one of these compound communities where the warlike activity is now not considerable, decline in the rigidity of political control has gone along with some evolution of the industrial type. Chiefs and minor heads, partly hereditary, partly elective, are held responsible for the conduct of affairs: there are village-parliaments and district-parliaments. Along with this we find a considerably-developed sustaining organization separate from the political—masters who have apprentices, employ journeymen, and pay wages; and when payment for work is inadequate, there are even strikes upheld by a tacit trades unionism. Passing to more evolved societies it must be oberved first that the distinctive traits of the industrial type do not become marked, even where the industrial activity is considerable, so long as the industrial government remains identified with the political. In Phœnicia, for example, the foreign wholesale trade seems to have belonged mostly to the State, the kings, and the nobles. Ezekiel describes the King of Tyrus as a prudent commercial prince, who finds out the precious metals in their hidden seats, enriches himself by getting them, and increases these riches by traffic. Clearly, where the political and military heads have thus themselves become the heads of the industrial organization, the traits distinctive of it are prevented from showing themselves. Of ancient societies to be named in connection with the relation between industrial activities and free institutions, Athens will be at once thought of; and, by contrast with other Greek States, it showed this relation as clearly as can be expected. Up to the time of Solon all these communities were under either oligarchies or despots. Those of them in which war continued to be the honoured occupation while industry was despised, retained this political type; but in Athens, where industry was regarded with comparative respect, where it was encouraged by Solon, and where immigrant artisans found a home, there grew up an industrial organization which distinguished the Athenian society from adjacent societies, while it was also distinguished from them by those democratic institutions that simultaneously developed. Turning to later times, the relation between a social régime predominantly industrial and a less coercive form of rule, is shown us by the Hanse Towns, by the towns of the Low Countries out of which the Dutch Republic arose, and in high degrees by ourselves, by the United States, and by our colonies. Along with wars less frequent and these carried on at a distance; and along with an accompanying growth of agriculture, manufactures, and commerce, beyond that of continental states more military in habit, there has gone in England a development of free institutions. As further implying that the two are related as cause and consequence, there may be noted the fact that the regions whence changes towards greater political liberty have come, are the leading industrial regions; and that rural districts, less characterized by constant trading transactions, have retained longer the earlier type with its appropriate sentiments and ideas. In the form of ecclesiastical government we see parallel changes. Where the industrial activities and structures evolve, this branch of the regulating system, no longer as in the militant type a rigid hierarchy, little by little loses strength, while there grows up one of a different kind: sentiments and institutions both relaxing. Right of private judgment in religious matters gradually establishes itself along with establishment

of political rights. In place of a uniform belief imperatively enforced, there come multiform beliefs voluntarily accepted; and the
ever-multiplying bodies espousing these beliefs, instead of being
governed despotically, govern themselves after a manner more or
less representative. Military conformity coercively maintained
gives place to a varied non-conformity maintained by willing union.
The industrial organization itself, which thus as it becomes predominant affects all the rest, of course shows us in an especial degree
this change of structure. From the primitive condition under which
the master maintains slaves to work for him, there is a transition
through stages of increasing freedom to a condition like our own,
in which all who work and employ, buy and sell, are entirely independent; and in which there is an unchanged power of forming
unions that rule themselves on democratic principles. Combinations of workmen and counter-combinations of employers, no less
than political societies and leagues for carrying on this or that agitation, show us the representative mode of government; which characterizes also every joint-stock company, for mining, banking, rail-
way-making, or other commercial enterprise. Further, we see that
as in the militant type the mode of regulation ramifies into all
minor departments of social activity, so here does the industrial
mode of regulation. Multitudinous objects are achieved by spontaneously evolved combinations of citizens governed representa-
tively. The tendency to this kind of organization is so ingrained
that for every proposed end the proposed means is a society ruled
by an elected committee headed by an elected chairman—philanthropic associations of multitudinous kinds, literary institutions,
libraries, clubs, bodies for fostering the various sciences and arts,
etc., etc. Along with all which traits there go sentiments and ideas
concerning the relation between the citizen and the State, opposite
to those accompanying the militant type. In place of the doctrine
that the duty of obedience to the governing agent is unqualified,
there arises the doctrine that the will of the citizens is supreme and
the governing agent exists merely to carry out their will. Thus subordinated in position, the regulating power is also restricted in
range. Instead of having an authority extending over actions of all
kinds, it is shut out from large classes of actions. Its control over
ways of living in respect to food, clothing, amusements, is re-
pudiated; it is not allowed to dictate modes of production nor to
regulate trade. Nor is this all. It becomes a duty to resist irrespon-

sible government and also to resist the excesses of responsible government. There arises a tendency in minorities to disobey even the legislature deputed by the majority, when it interferes in certain ways; and their oppositions to laws they condemn as inequitable, from time to time cause abolitions of them. With which changes of political theory and accompanying sentiment is joined a belief, implied or avowed, that the combined actions of the social aggregate have for their end to maintain the conditions under which individual lives may be satisfactorily carried on; in place of the old belief that individual lives have for their end the maintenance of this aggregate's combined actions.

These pervading traits in which the industrial type differs so widely from the militant type, originate in those relations of individuals implied by industrial activities, which are wholly unlike those implied by militant activities. All trading transactions, whether between masters and workmen, buyers and sellers of commodities, or professional men and those they aid, are effected by free exchange. For some benefit which A's business enables him to give, B willingly yields up an equivalent benefit: if not in the form of something he has produced, then in the form of money gained by his occupation. This relation, in which the mutual rendering of services is unforced and neither individual subordinated, becomes the predominant relation throughout society in proportion as the industrial activities predominate. Daily determining the thoughts and sentiments, daily disciplining all in asserting their own claims while forcing them to recognize the correlative claims of others, it produces social units whose mental structures and habits mould social arrangements into corresponding forms. There results a type characterized throughout by that same individual freedom which every commercial transaction implies. The co-operation by which the multiform activities of the society are carried on, becomes a *voluntary* co-operation. And while the developed sustaining system which gives to a social organism the industrial type, acquires for itself, like the developed sustaining system of an animal, a regulating apparatus of a diffused or uncentralized kind; it tends also to decentralize the primary regulating apparatus, by making it derive from more numerous classes its deputed powers.

The essential traits of these two social types are in most cases obscured, both by the antecedents and by the co-existing circumstances. Every society has been, at each past period, and is at present, conditioned in a way more or less unlike the ways in which others have been and are conditioned. Hence the production of structures characterizing one or other of these opposed types is, in every instance, furthered, or hindered, or modified, in a special manner. Observe the several kinds of causes.

There is, first, the deeply-organized character of the particular race, coming down from those pre-historic times during which the diffusion of mankind and differentiation of the varieties of man, took place. Very difficult to change, this must in every case qualify differently the tendency towards assumption of either type.

There is, next, the effect due to the immediately-preceding mode of life and social type. Nearly always the society we have to study contains decayed institutions and habits belonging to an ancestral society otherwise circumstanced; and these pervert more or less the effects of circumstances subsequently existing.

Again, there are the peculiarities of the habitat in respect of contour, soil, climate, flora, fauna, severally affecting in one mode or other the activities, whether militant or industrial; and severally hindering or aiding, in some special way, the development of either type.

Yet further, there are the complications caused by the particular organizations and practices of surrounding societies. For, supposing the amount of offensive or defensive action to be the same, the nature of it depends in each case on the nature of the antagonist action; and hence its reactive effects on structure vary with the character of the antagonist. Add to this that direct imitation of adjacent societies is a factor of some moment.

There remains to be named an element of complication more potent perhaps than any of these—one which of itself often goes far to determine the type as militant, and which in every case profoundly modifies the social arrangements. I refer to the mixture of races caused by conquest or otherwise. We may properly treat of it separately under the head of social constitution—not, of course, constitution politically understood, but constitution understood as referring to the relative homogeneity or heterogeneity of the units constituting the social aggregate.

THE MIXTURE OF RACES

As the nature of the aggregate, partially determined by environing conditions, is in other respects determined by the natures of its units, where its units are of diverse natures the degrees of contrast between the two or more kinds of them, and the degrees of union among them, must greatly affect the results. Are they of unallied races or of races near akin; and do they remain separate or do they mix?

Clearly where it has happened that a conquering race, continuing to govern a subject race, has developed the militant regulating system throughout the whole social structure, and for ages habituated its units to compulsory co-operation—where it has also happened that the correlative ecclesiastical system with its appropriate cult, has given to absolute subordination the religious sanction—and especially where, as in China, each individual is educated by the governing power and stamped with the appropriate ideas of duty which it is heresy to question, it becomes impossible for any considerable change to be wrought in the social structure by other influences. It is the law of all organization that as it becomes complete it becomes rigid. Only where incompleteness implies a remaining plasticity, is it possible for the type to develop from the original militant form to the form which industrial activity generates. Especially where the two races, contrasted in their natures, do not mix, social co-operation implies a compulsory regulating system: the militant form of structure which the dominant impose ramifies throughout. Ancient Peru furnished an extreme case; and the Ottoman Empire may be instanced. Social constitutions of this kind, in which races having aptitudes for forming unlike structures co-exist, are in states of unstable equilibrium. Any considerable shock dissolves the organization; and in the absence of unity of tendency, re-establishment of it is difficult if not impossible. In cases where the conquering and conquered, though widely unlike, intermarry extensively, a kindred effect is produced in another way. The conflicting tendencies towards different social types, instead of existing in separate individuals, now exist in the same individual. The half-caste, inheriting from one line of ancestry proclivities adapted to one set of institutions, and from the other line of ancestry proclivities adapted to another set of institutions, is not fitted for either. He is a unit whose nature has not been moulded by any social type, and therefore cannot, with others like himself, evolve any social type. Modern Mexico and the South American Republics, with their perpetual revolutions, show us the result. It is observable, too, that where races of strongly-contrasted natures have mixed more or less, or, remaining but little mixed, occupy adjacent areas subject to the same government, the equilibrium maintained so long as that government keeps up the coercive form, shows itself to be unstable when the coercion relaxes. Spain with its diverse peoples, Basque, Celtic, Gothic, Moorish, Jewish, partially mingled and partially localized, shows us this result.

Small differences, however, seem advantageous. Sundry instances point to the conclusion that a society formed from nearly-allied peoples of which the conquering eventually mingles with the conquered, is relatively well fitted for progress. From their fusion results a community which, determined in its leading traits by the character common to the two, is prevented by their differences of character fron being determined in its minor traits—is left capable of taking on new arrangements wrought by new influences: medium plasticity allows those changes of structure constituting advance in heterogeneity. One example is furnished us by the Hebrews who, notwithstanding their boasted purity of blood, resulted from a mixing of many Semitic varieties in the country east of the Nile and who, both in their wanderings and after the conquest of Palestine, went on amalgamating kindred tribes. Another is supplied by the Athenians, whose progress had for antecedent the mingling of numerous immigrants from other Greek states with the Greeks of the locality. The fusion by conquest of the Romans with other Aryan tribes, Sabini, Sabelli, and Samnites, preceded the first ascending stage of the Roman civilization. And our own country, peopled by different divisions of the Aryan race, and mainly by varieties of Scandinavians, again illustrates this effect produced by the mixture of units sufficiently alike to co-operate in the same social system, but sufficiently unlike to prevent that social system from becoming forthwith definite in structure.

Admitting that the evidence where so many causes are in operation cannot be satisfactorily disentangled, and claiming only probability for these inductions respecting social constitutions, it remains to point out their analogy to certain inductions respecting the constitutions of individual living things. Between organisms widely unlike in kind, no progeny can arise: the physiological units contributed by them respectively to form a fertilized germ, cannot work together so as to produce a new organism. Evidently as, while multiplying, each class of units tends to build itself into its peculiar type of structure, their conflict prevents the formation of any structure. If the two organisms are less unlike in kind—belonging, say, to the same genus though to different species—the two structures which their two groups of physiological units tend to build up, being tolerably similar, these can, and do, co-operate in making an organism that is intermediate. But this, though it will work, is imperfect in its latest-evolved parts: there results a mule incapable of propagating. If, instead of different species, remote varieties are united, the intermediate organism is not infertile; but many facts suggest the conclusion that infertility results in subsequent generations: the incongruous working of the united structures, though longer in showing itself, comes out ultimately. And then, finally, if instead of remote varieties, varieties nearly allied are united, a permanently-fertile breed results; and while the slight differences of the two kinds of physiological units are not such as to prevent harmonious co-operation, they are such as conduce to plasticity and unusually vigorous growth.

Here, then, seems a parallel to the conclusion indicated above, that hybrid societies are imperfectly organizable—cannot grow into forms completely stable; while societies which have been evolved from mixtures of nearly-allied varieties of man, can assume stable structures, and have an advantageous modifiability.

We class societies, then, in two ways, both having to be kept in mind when interpreting social phenomena.

First, they have to be arranged in the order of their integration, as simple, compound, doubly-compound, trebly-compound. And along with the increasing degrees of evolution implied by these ascending stages of composition, we have to recognize the increasing degrees of evolution implied by growing heterogeneity, general and local.

Much less definite is the division to be made among societies according as one or other of their great systems of organs is supreme. Omitting those lowest types which show no differentiations at all, we have but few exceptions to the rule that each society has structures for carrying on conflict with other societies and structures for carrying on sustentation; and as the ratios between these admit of all gradations, it results that no specific classification can be based on their relative developments. Nevertheless, as the militant type, characterized by predominance of the one, is framed on the principle of compulsory co-operation, while the industrial type, characterized by predominance of the other, is framed on the principle of voluntary co-operation, the two types, when severally evolved to their extreme forms, are diametrically opposed; and the contrasts between their traits are among the most important with which sociology has to deal.

Were this the fit place, some pages might be added respecting a possible future social type, differing as much from the industrial as this does from the militant—a type which, having a sustaining system more fully developed than any we know at present, will use the products of industry neither for maintaining a militant organization not exclusively for material aggrandizement; but will devote them to the carrying on of higher activities. As the contrast between the militant and the industrial types is indicated by inversion of the belief that individuals exist for the benefit of the State into the belief that the State exists for the benefit of individuals; so the contrast between the industrial type and the type likely to be evolved from it is indicated by inversion of the belief that life is for work into the belief that work is for life. But we are here concerned with inductions derived from societies that have been and are, and cannot enter upon speculations respecting societies that may be. Merely naming as a sign, the multiplication of institutions and appliances for intellectual and æsthetic culture, and for kindred activities not of a directly life-sustaining kind but of a kind having gratification for their immediate purpose, I can here say no more.

Returning from this parenthetical suggestion, there remains the remark that to the complications caused by crossings of the two classifications set forth, have to be added the complications caused by unions of races widely unlike or little unlike; which here mix not at all, there partially, and in other cases wholly. Respecting these kinds of constitutions, we have considerable warrant for concluding that the hybrid kind, essentially unstable, admits of being organized only on the principle of compulsory co-operation, since units much opposed in their natures cannot work together spontaneously. While, conversely, the kind characterized by likeness in its units is relatively stable, and under fit conditions may evolve into the industrial type, especially if the likeness is qualified by slight differences.

(H) Social Metamorphoses[1]

Verification of the general view set forth in the last chapter is gained by observing the alterations of social structures which follow alterations of social activities; and here again we find analogies between social organisms and individual organisms. In both there is metamorphosis consequent on change from a wandering life to a settled life; in both there is metamorphosis consequent on change from a life exercising mainly the inner or sustaining system, to a life exercising the outer or expending system; and in both there is a reverse metamorphosis.

The young of many invertebrate creatures, annulose and molluscous, pass through early stages during which they move about actively. Presently comes a settling down in some fit habitat, a dwindling away of the locomotive organs and the guiding appliances which they had, a growth of those other organs now needed for appropriating such food as the environment supplies, and a rapid enlargement of the sustaining system. A transformation opposite in nature is made familiar to us by the passage from larva to imago in insects. Surrounded by food, the future moth or fly develops almost exclusively its sustaining system, has but rudimentary limbs or none at all, and has proportionately imperfect senses. After growing immensely and accumulating much plastic material, it begins to unfold its external organs with their appropriate regulating apparatus, while its organs of nutrition decrease; and it thus fits itself for active dealings with environing existences.

The one truth, common to these opposite kinds of metamorphoses which here concerns us is that the two great systems of structures for carrying on outer activities and inner activities respectively, severally dwindle or develop according to the life the aggregate leads. Though in the absence of social types fixed by repeated inheritance we cannot have social metamorphoses thus definitely related to changes of life arising in definite order, analogy implies that which we have already seen reason to infer; namely, that the outer and inner structures with their regulating systems, severally increase or diminish according as the activities become more militant or more industrial.

[1] From *The Principles of Sociology*, Vol. I, 1876.

Before observing how metamorphoses are caused, let us observe
how they are hindered. I have implied above that where it has not
derived a specific structure from a line of ancestral societies leading
similar lives, a society cannot undergo metamorphoses in a precise
manner and order: the effects of surrounding influences predominate over the effects of inherited tendencies. Here may fitly be
pointed out the converse truth, that where societies descending one
from another in a series have pursued like careers, there results a
type so far settled in its cycle of development, maturity and decay,
that it resists metamorphosis.

Uncivilized tribes in general may be cited in illustration. They
show little tendency to alter their social activities and structures
under changed circumstances, but die out rather than adapt themselves. Even with superior varieties of men this happens; as, for
example, with the wandering hordes of Arabs. Modern Bedouins
show us a form of society which, so far as the evidence enables us to
judge, has remained substantially the same these three thousand
years or more, in spite of contact with adjacent civilizations; and
there is evidence that in some Semites the nomadic type had, even
in ancient times, become so ingrained as to express itself in the
religion. Thus we have the Rechabite injunction: 'Neither shall ye
build house, nor sow corn, nor plant vineyard, nor have any, but all
your days ye shall dwell in tents'; and Mr. E. W. Robertson points
out that:

one of the laws of the ancient Nabatæan confederacy made it a
capital crime to sow corn, to build a house, or plant a tree. . . . It
was a fixed and settled principle in the nomad to reduce the
country he invaded to the condition of a waste and open pastur-
age. . . . He looked upon such a course as a religious duty.

Change from the migratory to the settled state, hindered by per-
sistence of the primitive social type, is also otherwise hindered.
Describing the Hill Tribes on the Kuladyne River, Arracan,
Lieutenant Latter says:

A piece of ground rarely yields more than one crop; in each
successive year other spots are in like manner chosen, till all
those around the village are exhausted; a move is then made to
another locality, fresh habitations are erected, and the same pro-

cess gone through. These migrations occur about every third year, and they are the means by which long periods of time are calculated; thus a Toungtha will tell you that such and such an event occurred so many migrations since.

Evidently a practice of this kind, prompted partly by the restlessness inherited from ancestral nomads, is partly due to undeveloped agriculture—to the absence of those means by which, in a thickly-peopled country, the soil is made permanently fertile. This intermediate state between the wandering and the stationary is common throughout Africa. It is remarked that 'society in Africa is a plant of herbaceous character, without any solid or enduring stem; rank in growth, rapid in decay, and admitting of being burned down annually without any diminution of its general productiveness.' Reade tells us that 'the natives of Equatorial Africa are perpetually changing the sites of their villages'. Of the Bechuanas, Thompson says: 'Their towns are often so considerable as to contain many thousand people; and yet they are removable at the caprice of the chief, like an Arab camp.' And a like state of things existed in primitive Europe: families and small communities in each tribe, migrated from one part of the tribal territory to another. Thus from the temporary villages of hunters like the North American Indians, and from the temporary encampments of pastoral hordes, the transition to settled agricultural communities is very gradual; the earlier mode of life, frequently resumed, is but slowly outgrown.

When studying the social metamorphoses that follow altered social activities, we have therefore to bear in mind those resistances to change which the inherited social type offers, and also those resistances to change caused by partial continuance of old conditions. Further, we may anticipate reversion if the old conditions begin again to predominate.

Of chief interest to us here are the transformations of the militant into the industrial and the industrial into the militant. And especially we have to note how the industrial type, partially developed in a few cases, retrogrades towards the militant type if international conflicts recur.

When comparing these two types we saw how the compulsory co-operation which military activity necessitates, is contrasted with the voluntary co-operation which a developed industrial activity necessitates; and we saw that where the coercive regulating system proper to the one has not become too rigid, the non-coercive regulating system proper to the other begins to show itself as industry flourishes unchecked by war. The great liberalization of political arrangements which occurred among ourselves during the long peace that commenced in 1815, furnishes an illustration. An example of this metamorphis is supplied by Norway, too, in which country absence of war and growth of free institutions have gone together. But our attention is demanded chiefly by the proofs that revived belligerent habits re-develop the militant type of structure.

Not dwelling on the instances to be found in ancient history, nor on the twice-repeated lapse of the rising Dutch Republic into a monarchy under the reactive influences of war, nor on the reversion from parliamentary government to despotic government which resulted from the wars of the Protectorate among ourselves, nor on the effect which a career of conquest had in changing the first French Republic into a military despotism; it will suffice if we contemplate the evidence yielded in recent years. How, since the establishment of a stronger centralized power in Germany by war, a more coercive regime has shown itself, we see in the dealings of Bismarck with the ecclesiastical powers; in the laying down by Moltke of the doctrine that both for safety from foreign attack and guardianship of order at home, it is needful that the supplies for the army should not be dependent on a parliamentary vote; and again in the measures lately taken for centralizing the state-control of German railways. In France we have as usual the chief soldier becoming the chief ruler; the maintenance, in many parts, of that state of siege which originated with the war; and the continuance by a nominally free form of government of many restrictions upon freedom. But the kindred changes of late undergone by our own society, furnish the clearest illustrations; because the industrial type having developed here further than on the continent, there is more scope for retrogression.

Actual wars and preparations for possible wars, have conspired to produce these changes. In the first place, since the accession of Louis Napoleon, which initiated the change, we have had the Crimean War, the war entailed by the Indian Mutiny, the China war, and the more recent wars in Abyssinia and Ashantee.[1] In the second place, and chiefly, there has been the re-development of

[1] And since this was written the Afghan, Zulu, and Egyptian wars.

military organization and feeling here, caused by re-development of them abroad. That in nations as in individuals a threatening attitude begets an attitude of defence, is a truth that needs no proof. Hence among ourselves the recent growth of expenditure for army and navy, the making of fortifications, the formation of the volunteer force, the establishment of permanent camps, the repetitions of autumn manœuvres, the building of military stations throughout the kingdom.

Of the traits accompanying this reversion towards the militant type, we have first to note the revival of predatory activities. Always a structure assumed for defensive action, available also for offensive action, tends to initiate it. As in Athens the military and naval organization which was developed in coping with a foreign enemy, thereafter began to exercise itself aggressively; as in France the triumphant army of the Republic, formed to resist invasion, forthwith became an invader; so is it habitually—so is it now with ourselves. In China, India, Polynesia, Africa, the East Indian Archipelago, reasons—never wanting the aggressor—are given for widening our empire: without force if it may be, and with force if needful. After annexing the Fiji Islands, voluntarily ceded only because there was no practicable alternative, there comes now the proposal to take possession of Samoa. Accepting in exchange for another, a territory subject to a treaty, we ignore the treaty and make the assertion of it a ground for the war with the Ashantees. In Sherbro our agreements with the native chiefs having brought about universal disorder, we send a body of soldiers to suppress it, and presently will allege the necessity of extending our rule over a larger area. So again in Perak. A resident sent to advise becomes a resident who dictates; appoints as sultan the most plastic candidate in place of one preferred by the chiefs; arouses resistance which becomes a plea for using force; finds usurpation of the government needful; has his proclamation torn down by a native, who is thereupon stabbed by the resident's servant; the resident is himself killed as a consequence; then (nothing being said of the murder of the native), the murder of the resident leads to outcries for vengeance, and a military expedition establishes British rule. Be it in the slaying of Karen tribes who resist surveyors of their territory, or be it in the demand made on the Chinese in pursuance of the doctrine that a British traveller, sacred wherever he may choose to intrude, shall have his death avenged on someone, we everywhere find pretexts for quarrels which lead to acquisitions. In the House of Commons and in the Press, the same spirit is shown. During the debate on the Suez Canal purchase, our Prime Minister, referring to the possible annexation of Egypt, said that the English people, wishing the Empire to be maintained, 'will not be alarmed even if it be increased'; and was cheered for so saying. And recently, urging that it is time to blot out Dahomey, the weekly organ of filibustering Christianity exclaims, 'let us take Whydah, and leave the savage to recover it'.

Inevitably along with this partial reversion to the compulsory social system which accompanies partial reversion to the militant type of structure, there goes an appropriate change of sentiments. In essence Toryism stands for the control of the State *versus* the freedom of the individual; and in essence Liberalism stands for the freedom of the individual *versus* the control of the State. But whereas during the previous peaceful period, individual liberty was extended by abolishing religious disabilities, establishing free trade, removing impediments from the press, etc; since the reversion began, the party which affected these changes has vied with the opposite party in multiplying State administrations which diminish individual liberty. How far the principles of free government have been disregarded, and how directly this change is sequent upon the feeling which militant action fosters, is conclusively shown by the Suez Canal business. A step which, to say nothing of the pecuniary cost, committed the nation to entanglements of a serious kind, was taken by its ministry in such manner that its representative body had a nominal, but no real, power of reversing it; and instead of protest against this disregard of constitutional principles, there came general applause. The excuse accepted by all was the military exigency. The prompt action of the co-ordinating centre by which offensive and defensive operations are directed, was said to necessitate this ignoring of Parliament and this suspension of self-government. And the general sentiment, responding to the alleged need for keeping our hold on a conquered territory, not only forgave but rejoiced over this return towards military rule.

Of course social metamorphoses are in every case complicated and obscured by special causes never twice alike. Where rapid growth is going on, the changes of structure accompanying increase of mass are involved with the changes of structure resulting from modification of type. Further, disentanglement of the facts is made difficult when the two great systems of organs for sustentation and external action are evolving simultaneously. This is our own case. That re-development of structures for external action which we have been tracing, and that partial return to a congruous social system, have not arrested the development of the sustaining structures and that social system they foster. Hence sundry changes opposite to those enumerated above. While the revival of ecclesiasticism having for cardinal principle subordination to authority, has harmonized with this reversion towards the militant type, the increase of divisions in the Church, the assertions of individual judgment, and the relaxations of dogma, have harmonized with the contrary movement. While new educational organizations tending towards regimental uniformity, are by each fresh Act of Parliament made more rigid, the old educational organizations in public schools and universities, are being made more plastic and less uniform. While there have been increasing interferences with the employment of labour, wholly at variance with the principles of voluntary co-operation, they have not yet gone far enough to reverse the free-trade policy which industrial evolution has been extending. The interpretation appears to be that while the old compulsory system of regulation has been abolished where pressure had become intolerable, this re-development of it is going on where its pressure has not yet been felt.

Moreover, the vast transformation suddenly caused by railways and telegraphs, adds to the difficulty of tracing metamorphoses of the kinds we are considering. Within a generation the social organism has passed from a stage like that of a cold-blooded creature with feeble circulation and rudimentary nerves, to a stage like that of a warm-blooded creature with efficient vascular system and a developed nervous apparatus. To this more than to any other cause, are due the great changes in habits, beliefs, and sentiments, characterizing our generation. Manifestly, this rapid evolution of distributing and internuncial structures, has aided the growth of both the industrial organization and the militant organization. While productive activities have been facilitated, there has been a furtherance of that centralization characterizing the social type required for offensive and defensive actions.

But notwithstanding these disguising complexities, if we contrast the period from 1815 to 1850 with the period from 1850 to the present time, we cannot fail to see that along with increased armaments, more frequent conflicts, and revived military sentiment, there has been a spread of compulsory regulations. While nominally extended by the giving of votes, the freedom of the individual has been in many ways actually diminished, both by restrictions which ever-multiplying officials are appointed to insist on, and by the forcible taking of money to secure for him, or others at his expense, benefits previously left to be secured by each for himself. And undeniably this is a return towards that coercive discipline which pervades the whole social life where the militant type is predominant.

In metamorphoses, then, so far as they are traceable, we discern general truths harmonizing with those disclosed by comparisons of types. With social organisms as with individual organisms, the structure becomes adapted to the activity. In the one case as in the other, if circumstances entail a fundamental change in the mode of activity, there by-and-by results a fundamental change in the form of structure. And in both cases there is a reversion towards the old type if there is a resumption of the old activity.

Part Four:
Specific Problems and General Concerns:
Conflict and Power in Society

(A) *The Constitution of the State*[1]

It is a tolerably well-ascertained fact that men are still selfish. And that beings answering to this epithet will employ the power placed in their hands for their own advantage is self-evident. Directly or indirectly, either by hook or by crook, if not openly then in secret, their private ends will be served. Granting the proposition that men are selfish, we cannot avoid the corollary that those who possess authority will, if permitted, use it for selfish purposes.

Should anyone need facts in proof of this, he may find them at every page in the nearest volume of history. Under the head—Monarchy, he will read of insatiable cravings after more territory; of confiscations of the subjects' property; of justice sold to the highest bidder; of continued debasements of coinage; and of a greediness which could even descend to share the gains of prostitutes.

He will find Feudalism exemplifying the same spirit by the cruelties inflicted upon serfs; by the right of private war; by the predatory incursions of borderers; by robberies practised on Jews; and by the extortionate tribute wrung from burghers—all of them illustrations of that motto, so characteristic of the system, 'thou shalt want ere I want'.

Does he seek like evidence in the conduct of later aristocracies? He may discover it in every state in Europe: in Spain, where the lands of nobles and clergy were long exempted from direct taxation; in Hungary where, until lately, men of rank were free of all turnpikes, and only the mercantile and working classes paid; in France, before the first revolution, where the *tiers-etat* had to bear all the state burdens; in Scotland, where less than two centuries ago it was the custom of lairds to kidnap the common people, and export them as slaves; in Ireland, where at the rebellion a band of

---

[1] From *Social Statics*, 2nd edition, 1892.

usurping landowners hunted and shot the Catholics as they would game, for daring to claim their own.[1]

If more proofs are wanted that power will be made to serve the purposes of its possessors, English legislation can furnish many such. Take, for example, the significantly named 'Black Act' (9th of George I), which declares that any one disguised and in possession of an offensive weapon 'appearing in any warren, or place where hares or conies have been, or shall be usually kept, and being thereof duly convicted, shall be adjudged guilty of felony, and shall suffer death, as in cases of felony, without benefit of clergy'. Instance again the Inclosure Laws, by which commons were divided amongst the neighbouring landowners, in the ratios of their holdings, regardless of the claims of the poor cottagers. Notice also the manœuvre by which the land tax has been kept stationary, or has even decreased, whilst other taxes have so enormously increased. Add to these the private monopolies (obtained from the king for 'a consideration'), the perversion of the funds of public schools, the manufacture of places, and pensions.

Nor is the disposition to use power for private ends less manifest in our own day. It shows itself in the assertion that an electoral system should give a preponderance to the landed interest. We see it in the legislation which relieves farmers from sundry assessed taxes, that they may be enabled to pay more rent. It is palpably indicated in the Game Laws. The conduct of the squire, who gets his mansion rated at one-third of its value, bears witness to it. It appears in the law enabling a landlord to anticipate other creditors, and to obtain his rent by immediate seizure of his tenant's property. We are reminded of it by the often-mentioned legacy and probate duties. It is implied by the fact that whilst no one dreams of compensating the discharged workman, gentlemen sinecurists must have their 'vested interests' bought up if their offices are abolished. In the tracts of the Anti-Corn Law League it received abundant illustration. It is seen in the votes of the hundred and fifty military and naval members of Parliament. And lastly, we find this self-seeking of those in authority creeps out, even in the doings of the 'Right Reverend Fathers in God' forming the Ecclesiastical Commission, who have appropriated,

---

[1] This passage shows how wrong it is to imagine that no one knew or wrote about class inequality and exploitation before Marx. S.A.

for the embellishment of their own palaces, funds entrusted to them for the benefit of the Church.

But it is needless to accumulate illustrations. Though every historian the world has seen should be subpœnaed as a witness, the fact could not be rendered one whit more certain than it is already. Why ask whether those in power *have* sought their own advantage in preference to that of others? With human nature as we know it, they must have done so. It is this same tendency in men to pursue gratification at the expense of their neighbours that renders government needful. Were we not selfish, legislative restraint would be unnecessary. Evidently, then, the very existence of a state-authority proves that irresponsible rulers will sacrifice the public good to their personal benefit; all solemn promises, specious professions, and carefully-arranged checks and safeguards, notwithstanding.

If, therefore, class-legislation is the *inevitable* consequence of class-power, there is no escape from the conclusion that the interest of the *whole* society can be secured, only by giving power into the hands of the *whole* people.[1]

THE NEAR FUTURE[2]

No other traits of social structure are equally radical with those which result from the relative powers of the social unit and the social aggregate. Chronic warfare, while requiring subordination throughout the successive grades of an army, also requires subordination of the whole society to the army, for which it serves as a commissariat. It requires, also, subordination throughout the ranks of this commissariat: graduated subjection is the law of the whole organization. Conversely, decrease of warfare brings relaxation.

[1] Apart from Malthus and Gaetano Mosca, none of the classics of sociology have given much thought to the problem of which kinds of social structure permit a realization of the democratic ideals, and most of the more recent literature has moved on the plane of what is desirable rather than what is possible. For a modern and realistic treatment of the conditions necessary for the functioning of a democracy see Seymour R. Lipset's *Political Man* (Heinemann, 1960) which deals with the cases where it does more or less operate. Why democracy has failed in all the underdeveloped countries is explained in S. Andreski, *Parasitism and Subversion: the Case of Latin America* (Weidenfeld & Nicolson, 1965) and Pantheon Books, N.Y., 1966), and *The African Predicament: A Study in Pathology of Modernization* (Michael Joseph, 1968).
[2] From *The Principles of Sociology*, Vol. III, 1868.

The desire of everyone to use his powers for his own advantage, which all along generates resistance to the coercion of militancy, begins to have its effect as militancy declines. Individual self-assertion by degrees breaks through its rigid regulations, and the citizen more and more gains possession of himself.

Inevitably, with these forms of social organization and social action, there go the appropriate ideas and sentiments. To be stable, the arrangements of a community must be congruous with the natures of its members. If a fundamental change of circumstances produces change in the structure of the community or in the natures of its members, then the natures of its members or the structure of the community must presently undergo a corresponding change. And these changes must be expressed in the average feelings and opinions. At the one extreme loyalty is the supreme virtue and disobedience a crime. At the other extreme servile submission is held contemptible and maintenance of freedom the cardinal trait of manhood. Between these extremes are endless incongruous minglings of the opposed sentiments.

Hence, to be rightly drawn, our conclusions about impending social changes must be guided by observing whether the movement is towards ownership of each man by others or towards ownership of each man by himself, and towards the corresponding emotions and thoughts. Practically it matters little what is the character of the ownership by others—whether it is ownership by a monarch, by an oligarchy, by a democratic majority, or by a communistic organization. The question for each is how far he is prevented from using his faculties for his own advantage and compelled to use them for others' advantage, not what is the power which prevents him or compels him. And the evidence now to be contemplated shows that submission to ownership by others increases or decreases according to the conditions, no matter whether the embodiment of such others is political, social, or industrial.[1]

This general drift towards a form of society in which private activi-

[1] As the prophetic passages which follow show, at the end of his life Spencer came to the conclusion that rather than towards his dogmatically liberal ideals, the world was moving towards collectivism—which (as pointed out in the introduction) fitted better his general theory of society though not his preferences. On the problem of the general drift of the industrial society see Bertrand Russell, *The Impact of Science on Society* (Allen & Unwin, 1950, 1967), Raymond Aron, *Industrial Society* (Weidenfeld & Nicolson, 1964) and S. Andreski, *The Uses of Comparative Sociology*, chap. 24: 'Communism and Capitalism: Are They Converging?'

ties of every kind, guided by individual wills, are to be replaced by public activities guided by governmental will, must inevitably be made more rapid by recent organic changes, which further increase the powers of those who gain by public administrations and decrease the powers of those who lose by them. Already national and municipal franchises, so framed as to dissociate the giving of votes from the bearing of burdens, have resulted, as was long ago pointed out they must do,[1] in multiplied meddlings and lavish expenditure. And now the extension of similar franchises to parishes will augment such effects. With a fatuity almost passing belief, legislators have concluded that things will go well when the many say to the few: 'We will decide what shall be done and you shall pay for it.' Table conversations show that even by many people called educated, Government is regarded as having unlimited powers joined with unlimited resources; and political speeches make the rustic think of it as an earthly providence which can do anything for him if interested men will let it. Naturally it happens that, as a socialist lecturer writes: 'To get listeners to socialist arguments is to get converts', for the listener is not shown that the benefits to be conferred on each, will be benefits derived from the labours of all, carried on under compulsion. He does not see that he can have the mess of pottage only by surrendering his birthright. He is not told that if he is to be fed he must also be driven.

There seems no avoiding the conclusion that these conspiring causes must presently bring about that lapse of self-ownership into ownership by the community, which is partially implied by collectivism and completely by communism. The momentum of social change, like every other momentum, must work out effects proportionate to its amount, *minus* the resistance offered to it; and in this case there is very little resistance. Could a great spread of cooperative production be counted upon, some hope of arrest might be entertained. But even if its growth justifies the beliefs of its advocates, it seems likely to offer but a feeble check.

In what way the coming transformation will be effected is of course uncertain. A sudden substitution of the régime proposed for the régime which exists, as intended by bearers of the red flag, seems less likely than a progressive metamorphosis. To bring about the change it needs but gradually to extend state regulation and restrain individual action. If the central administration and the multiplying

[1] *Westminster Review*, April 1860; see also *Essays*, vol. iii, p. 358, *et seq.*

G

local administrations go on adding function to function; if year after year more things are done by public agency, and fewer things left to be done by private agency; if the businesses of companies are one after another taken over by the state or the municipality, while the businesses of individuals are progressively trenched upon by official competitors; then, in no long time, the present voluntary industrial organization will have its place entirely usurped by a compulsory industrial organization. Eventually the brain-worker will find that there are no places left save in one or other public department, while the hand-worker will find that there are none to employ him save public officials. And so will be established a state in which no man can do what he likes but every man must do what he is told.

An entire loss of freedom will thus be the fate of those who do not deserve the freedom they possess. They have been weighed in the balances and found wanting: having neither the required idea nor the required sentiment. Only a nature which will sacrifice everything to defend personal liberty of action, and is eager to defend the like liberties of action of others, can permanently maintain free institutions. While not tolerating aggression upon himself, he must have sympathies such as will not tolerate aggression upon his fellows—be they fellows of the same race or of other races. As shown in multitudinous ways throughout this work, a *society organized for coercive action against other societies, must subject its members to coercion. In proportion as men's claims are trampled upon by it externally, will men's claims be trampled upon by it internally.*[1] History has familiarized the truth that tyrant and slave are men of the same kind differently placed. Be it in the ancient Egyptian king subject to a rigid routine of daily life enforced by priests, be it in the Roman patrician, master of bondmen and himself in bondage to the state, be it in the feudal lord possessing his serfs and himself possessed by his suzerain, be it in the modern artisan yielding up to his union his right to make contracts and maltreating his fellow who will not, we equally see that those who disregard others' individualities must in one way or other sacrifice their own. Men thus constituted cannot maintain free institutions. They must live under some system of coercive government; and when old forms of it lose their strength must generate new forms.

Even apart from special evidence, this general conclusion is

[1] The italics are mine. S.A.

forced on us by contemplating the law of rhythm: a law manifested throughout all things from the inconceivably rapid oscillations of a unit of ether to the secular perturbations of the solar system. For, as shown in *First Principles*, rhythm everywhere results from antagonist forces. As thus caused it is displayed throughout social phenomena, from the hourly rises and falls of stock exchange prices to the actions and reactions of political parties; and in the changes, now towards increase of restraints on men and now towards decrease of them, one of the slowest and widest rhythms is exhibited. After centuries during which coercive rule had been quietly diminishing and had been occasionally made less by violence, there was reached in the middle of our century, especially in England, a degree of individual freedom greater than ever before existed since nations began to be formed. Men could move about as they pleased, work at what they pleased, trade with whom they pleased. But the movement which in so large a measure broke down the despotic regulations of the past, rushed on to a limit from which there has commenced a return movement. *Instead of restraints and dictations of the old kinds, new kinds of restraints and dictations are being gradually imposed. Instead of the rule of powerful political classes, men are elaborating for themselves a rule of official classes, which will become equally powerful or probably more powerful— classes eventually differing from those which socialist theories contemplate, as much as the rich and proud ecclesiastical hierarchy of the middle ages differed from the groups of poor and humble missionaries out of which it grew.*[1]

(B) Party Government[2]

. . . Power given in support of a particular policy was used by a ministry to carry out other policies which would never have been approved by the electors had they been consulted.

'Well, but what are we to do?' will be the question asked. 'All these evils are the results of our system of government, and we must make the best of them. We cannot avoid having parties. An

[1] The italics are mine. S.A.
[2] From *Facts and Comments*, 1902.

obedient majority will necessarily enable its leaders to do things at variance with the wishes of those who put it in power. Only by the abolition of party government, which no one thinks possible, can this mischievous working out of things be changed.'

I demur to this conclusion. Were every member of Parliament true to his convictions—did every one resolve that he would not tell falsehoods by his votes—did each cease to regard 'party loyalty' as a virtue, and decide to give effect to his unit of opinion, regard-less of ministerial interests—these over-ridings of the national will by a few gentlemen in Downing Street would be impossible.

'But such a course would bring government to a deadlock', will be rejoined. 'No ministry could continue in office for a month if it could not count upon a body of supporters who would vote for its measures whether they approved of them or not. Ministry after ministry would be thrown out and public business arrested.'

Here is one of those not infrequent cases in which men discuss-ing some proposed change assume that while the change is made other things remain unchanged; whereas it is always to be assumed that other things will change simultaneously. If representatives, or a large proportion of them, decided that they would no longer by their votes say they believed things were good which they really believed were bad, and if, while receiving adequate support on certain main issues, the ministry was frequently left in a minority on minor issues and, in conformity with the present practice, re-signed; and if the like happened with subsequent ministries, it would presently be recognized as unfit that a government approved in its general conduct of affairs should resign because it was de-feated—even often defeated—on subordinate questions, especially if those who usually supported it, but who were about to vote against it, announced that their dissent must not be taken as in-dicating any general dissatisfaction. Only in cases where the defeats of the ministry were frequent enough to show that its policy at large was condemned, would resignation be the sequence, and the appropriate sequence. In all ordinary cases ministers would simply accept the expression of dissent, and instead of resigning withdraw the offending measure.

And now observe what would be the general results. No longer able to pass measures disapproved by the opposition and by many of its own followers, a ministry would be able to pass only such measures as were approved by a majority of representatives of all

parties—or rather, let us say, fragments of parties; and, by implication, would be able to pass only such measures as would probably be approved by most of the constituencies. A ministry which
came into power to achieve one purpose willed by the country,
would not be able subsequently to use its power to achieve purposes not willed by the country but at variance with its will. That
is to say, a ministry would become that which its name implies, a
servant, instead of being what it is now, a master—a servant not, as
originally, of the monarch, but a servant of the house and the
nation.

At present that which we boast of as political freedom consists in
the ability to choose a despot or a group of oligarchs, and after long
misbehaviour has produced dissatisfaction, to choose another
despot or group of oligarchs: having meanwhile been made subject to laws sundry of which are repugnant. Abolish the existing
conventional usage—let each member feel that he may express by
his vote his adverse belief respecting a government measure, without endangering the government's stability, and the whole of this
vicious system would disappear. Constituencies through their
representatives would really come to be the makers of the laws they
live under.

But what if each constituency has bound its representatives to
follow a party leader? Yes, here comes the crux. Political vices
have their roots in the nature of the people. The ability to find
candidates who will bind themselves to party-programmes, and
the wish to find such candidates, are alike indicative of an average
character not fitted for truly free institutions, but fitted only for
those institutions under which despotism is from time to time
mitigated by freedom. Freedom in its full sense—the power to
carry on the activities of life with no greater restrictions than those
entailed by the claims of others to like power—is understood by
very few. Illustrations of the current inability meet us on all sides.
Men who take shares in a company formed for a specified purpose
and then think themselves bound by the vote of a two-thirds
majority to undertake some other purpose, do not perceive that
they are aggressed upon—do not see that those who have entered
into a contract are not bound to do a thing which they have not
contracted to do, and that therefore they are wronged. Ratepayers
who elect members of a municipal government for the local maintenance of order, and for certain public administrations, and then

submit to be taxed for purposes they never dreamt of (as subscrib-
ing capital for a canal) if a majority of the elected body so decide,
fail to understand the nature of liberty. Similarly those who, joining a trade-union, surrender their freedom to make engagements
on their own terms, and allow themselves to be told by their leaders
when to work and when not to work, have no adequate sense of that
fundamental right which every man possesses to make the best of
himself, and to dispose of his abilities in any way he pleases.
Naturally, then, it results that those who represent electors who
are thus vague in their conceptions of freedom, and deficient in the
accompanying sentiment, must be expected to submit to party
dictates, and to say by their votes that they approve things which
they do not approve. For the present there is no probability of anything better, but a probability of something worse; for the retrograde movement now going on towards the militant social type is
inevitably accompanied not by relaxation of authority but by enforcement of it.

(C) The Great Political Superstition[1]

The great political superstition of the past was the divine right of
kings. The great political superstition of the present is the divine
right of parliaments. The oil of anointing seems unawares to have
dripped from the head of the one on to the heads of the many, and
given sacredness to them also and to their decrees.

Here we will take leave to question it. To revive questions supposed to be long since settled may be thought to need some apology; but there is a sufficient apology in the implication above made
clear, that the theory commonly accepted is ill-based or unbased.

To recognize and enforce *the rights of individuals* is at the same
time to recognize and enforce the conditions to a normal social life.
There is one vital requirement for both.

The prerequisite to individual life is in a double sense the prerequisite to social life. The life of a society, in whichever of two
senses conceived, depends on maintenance of individual rights. If

[1] From *The Man Versus the State*, 1884.

it is nothing more than the sum of the lives of citizens, this implication is obvious. If it consists of those many unlike activities which citizens carry on in mutual dependence, still this aggregate impersonal life rises or falls according as the rights of individuals are enforced or denied.

Study of men's politico-ethical ideas and sentiments, leads to allied conclusions. Primitive peoples of various types show us that before governments exist, immemorial customs recognize private claims and justify maintenance of them. Codes of law independently evolved by different nations, agree in forbidding certain trespasses on the persons, properties and liberties of citizens; and their correspondences imply, not an artificial source for individual rights, but a natural source. Along with social development, the formulating in law of the rights pre-established by custom, becomes more definite and elaborate. At the same time, government undertakes to an increasing extent the business of enforcing them. While it has been becoming a better protector, government has been becoming less aggressive—has more and more diminished its intrusions on men's spheres of private action. And lastly, as in past times laws were avowedly modified to fit better with current ideas of equity, so now, law-reformers are guided by ideas of equity which are not derived from law but to which law has to conform.

Here, then, we have a politico-ethical theory justified alike by analysis and by history. What have we against it?

A fashionable counter-theory which proves to be unjustifiable. On the one hand, while we find that individual life and social life both imply maintenance of the natural relation between efforts and benefits, we also find that this natural relation, recognized before government existed, has been all along asserting and re-asserting itself, and obtaining better recognition in codes of law and systems of ethics. On the other hand those who, denying natural rights, commit themselves to the assertion that rights are artificially created by law, are not only flatly contradicted by facts, but their assertion is self-destructive: the endeavour to substantiate it, when challenged, involves them in manifold absurdities.

Nor is this all. The re-institution of a vague popular conception in a definite form on a scientific basis, leads us to a rational view of the relation between the wills of majorities and minorities. It turns out that those co-operations in which all can voluntarily unite, and in the carrying on of which the will of the majority is rightly supreme, are co-operations for maintaining the conditions requisite to individual and social life. Defence of the society as a whole against external invaders, has for its remote end to preserve each citizen in possession of such means as he has for satisfying his desires, and in possession of such liberty as he has for getting further means. And defence of each citizen against internal invaders, from murderers down to those who inflict nuisances on their neighbours, has obviously the like end—an end desired by everyone save the criminal and disorderly. Hence it follows that for maintenance of this vital principle, alike of individual life and social life, subordination of minority to majority is legitimate; as implying only such a trenching on the freedom and property of each, as is requisite for the better protecting of his freedom and property. At the same time it follows that such subordination is not legitimate beyond this since, implying as it does a greater aggression upon the individual than is requisite for protecting him, it involves a breach of the vital principle which is to be maintained.

Thus we come round again to the proposition that the assumed divine right of parliaments, and the implied divine right of majorities are superstitions. While men have abandoned the old theory respecting the source of state authority, they have retained a belief in that unlimited extent of State-authority which rightly accompanied the old theory, but does not rightly accompany the new one. Unrestricted power over subjects, rationally ascribed to the ruling man when he was held to be deputy god, is now ascribed to the ruling body, the deputy godhood of which nobody asserts.

Reduced to its lowest terms, every proposal to interfere with citizens' activities further than by enforcing their mutual limitations, is a proposal to improve life by breaking through the fundamental conditions to life. When some are prevented from buying beer that others may be prevented from getting drunk, those who make the law assume that more good than evil will result from interference with the normal relation between conduct and consequences, alike in the few ill-regulated and the many well-regulated. A government which takes fractions of the incomes of multitudinous people for the purpose of sending to the colonies some who have not prospered here, or for building better industrial dwellings, or for making public libraries and public museums, etc, takes for granted that, not only proximately but ultimately, increased general happiness will result from transgressing the essential requirement to general happiness—the requirement that each shall enjoy all those means to happiness which his actions, carried on without aggression, have brought him. In other cases we do not thus let the immediate blind us to the remote. When asserting the sacredness of property against private transgressors, we do not ask whether the benefit to a hungry man who takes bread from a baker's shop is or is not greater than the injury inflicted on the baker: we consider, not the special effects, but the general effects which arise if property is insecure. But when the state exacts further amounts from citizens, or further restrains their liberties, we consider only the direct and proximate effects, and ignore the indirect and distant effects which are caused when these invasions of individual rights are continually multiplied. We do not see that by accumulated small infractions of them, the vital conditions to life, individual and social, come to be so imperfectly fulfilled that the life decays.

Yet the decay thus caused becomes manifest where the policy is pushed to an extreme. Anyone who studies, in the writings of MM. Taine and de Tocqueville, the state of things which preceded the French Revolution, will see that that tremendous catastrophe came about from so excessive a regulation of men's actions in all their details and such an enormous drafting away of the products of their actions to maintain the regulating organization, that life was fast becoming impracticable. The empirical utilitarianism of that day, like the empirical utilitarianism of our day, differed from rational utilitarianism in this, that in each successive case it contemplated only the effects of particular interferences on the actions of particular classes of men, and ignored the effects produced by a multiplicity of such interferences on the lives of men at large. And if we ask what then made, and what now makes, this error possible, we find it to be the political superstition that governmental power is subject to no restraints.

When that 'divinity' which 'doth hedge a king', and which has left a glamour around the body inheriting his power, has quite died away—when it begins to be seen clearly that, in a popularly-governed nation, the government is simply a committee of management; it will also be seen that this committee of management has no intrinsic authority. The inevitable conclusion will be that its authority is given by those appointing it, and has just such bounds as they choose to impose. Along with this will go the further conclusion that the laws it passes are not in themselves sacred; but that whatever sacredness they have, it is entirely due to the ethical sanction—an ethical sanction which, as we find, is derivable from the laws of human life as carried on under social conditions. And there will come the corollary that when they have not this ethical sanction they have no sacredness, and may rightly be challenged.

The function of liberalism in the past was that of putting a limit to the powers of kings. The function of true liberalism in the future will be that of putting a limit to the powers of parliaments.

(D) Imperialism and Slavery[1]

'You shall submit. We are masters and we will make you acknowledge it!' These words express the sentiment which sways the British nation in its dealings with the Boer republics; and this sentiment it is which, definitely displayed in this case, pervades indefinitely the political feeling now manifesting itself as imperialism. Supremacy, where not clearly imagined, is vaguely present in the background of consciousness. Not the derivation of the word only, but all its uses and associations, imply the thought of predominance—imply a correlative subordination. Actual or potential coercion of others, individuals or communities, is necessarily involved in the conception.

There are those, and unhappily they form the great majority, who think there is something noble (morally as well as historically) in the exercise of command—in the forcing of others to abandon their own wills and fulfil the will of the commander. I am not about to contest this sentiment. I merely say that there are others, unhappily but few, who think it ignoble to bring their fellow creatures into subjection, and who think the noble thing is not only to respect their freedom but also to defend it. Leaving this matter undiscussed, my present purpose is to show those who lean towards imperialism, that the exercise of mastery inevitably entails on the master himself some form of slavery, more or less pronounced. The uncultured masses, and even the greater part of the cultured,

[1] From *Facts and Comments*, 1902

will regard this statement as absurd; and though many who have read history with an eye to essentials rather than trivialities know that this is a paradox in the right sense—that is, true in fact though not seeming true—even they are not fully conscious of the mass of evidence establishing it, and will be all the better for having illustrations recalled. Let me begin with the earliest and simplest, which well serves to symbolize the whole.

Here is a prisoner with hands tied and a cord round his neck (as suggested by figures in Assyrian bas-reliefs) being led home by his savage conqueror who intends to make him a slave. The one, you say, is captive and the other free? Are you quite sure the other is free? He holds one end of the cord, and unless he means to let his captive escape, he must continue to be fastened by keeping hold of the cord in such way that it cannot easily be detached. He must be himself tied to the captive while the captive is tied to him. In other ways his activities are impeded and certain burdens are imposed on him. A wild animal crosses the track, and he cannot pursue. If he wishes to drink of the adjacent stream he must tie up his captive lest advantage be taken of his defenceless position. Moreover he has to provide food for both. In various ways, then, he is no longer completely at liberty; and these ways adumbrate in a simple manner the universal truth that the instrumentalities by which the subordination of others is effected, themselves subordinate the victor, the master, or the ruler.

The coincidence in time between the South African war and the recent outburst of imperialism, illustrates the general truth that militancy and imperialism are closely allied—are, in fact, different manifestations of the same social condition. It could not indeed be otherwise. Subject races or subject societies do not voluntarily submit themselves to a ruling race or a ruling society: their subjection is nearly always the effect of coercion. An army is the agency which achieved it, and an army must be kept ever ready to maintain it. Unless the supremacy has actual or potential force behind it there is only federation, not imperialism. Here, however, as above implied, the purpose is not so much to show that an imperial society is necessarily a militant society, as to show that in proportion as liberty is diminished in the societies over which it rules, liberty is diminished within its own organization.

The earliest records furnish an illustration. Whether in the times of the pyramid-builders the power of the Egyptian autocrat, which effected such astounding results, was qualified by an elaborate system of restraints, we have no evidence; but there is proof that in later days he was the slave of the governmental organization.

> The laws subjected every action of his private life to as severe a scrutiny as his behaviour in the administration of affairs. The hours of washing, walking, and all the amusements and occupations of the day, were settled with precision, and the quantity as well as the quality of his food were regulated by law.[1]

Moreover the relation between enslavement of foreign peoples and enslavement of the nation which conquered them, is shown by an inscription at Karnak, which describes 'how bitterly the country was paying the price of its foreign conquests, in its oppression by its standing army'.[2]

Turn we now to a society of widely different type but exhibiting the same general truths—that of Sparta. The conquering race, or Spartans proper, who had beneath them the Perioeci and the Helots, descendants of two subject races, were not only supreme over these but twice became the supreme race of the Peloponnesus. What was the price they paid for their 'imperial' position? The individual Spartan, master as he was over slaves and semi-slaves, was himself in bondage to the incorporated society of Spartans. Each led the life not which he himself chose but the life dictated by the aggregate of which he formed one unit. And this life was a life of strenuous discipline, leaving no space for culture, or art, or poetry, or other source of pleasure. He exemplified in an extreme degree the Grecian doctrine that the citizen does not belong to himself nor to his family but to his city.

If instead of the small and simple community of Sparta we take the vast and complex empire of Rome, we find this essential connection between imperialism and slavery even more conspicuous. I do not refer to the fact that three-fourths of those who peopled Italy in imperial days were slaves, chained in the fields when at work, chained at night in their dormitories, and those who were porters chained to the doorways—conditions horrible to contemplate—but I refer to the fact that the nominally free part of the

---

[1] *Manners and Customs of the Ancient Egyptians*, Birch's ed. of Wilkinson, Vol. I, 166.
[2] Flinders Petrie, *History of Egypt*, ii, 252.

community consisted of grades of bondmen. Not only did citizens stand in that bondage implied by military service, complete or partial, under subjection so rigid that an officer was to be dreaded more than an enemy, but those occupied in civil or semi-civil life, were compelled to work for the public. 'Everyone was treated in fact as a servant of the state . . . the nature of each man's labour was permanently fixed for him.' The society was formed of fighting serfs, working serfs, cultivating serfs, official serfs. And then what of the supreme head of this gigantic bureaucracy into which Roman society had grown—the emperor? He became a puppet of the Pretorian guard, which while a means of safety was a cause of danger. Moreover he was in daily bondage to routine. As Gibbon says, 'the emperor was the first slave of the ceremonies he imposed'. Thus in a conspicuous manner Rome shows how, as in other cases, a society which enslaves other societies enslaves itself.

The same lesson is taught by those ages of seething confusion— of violence and bloodshed—which the collapse of the Roman Empire left: an empire which dwells in the minds of the many as something to be admired and emulated—the many who forgive any horrors if only their brute love of mastery is gratified, sympathetically when not actually. Passing over those sanguinary times in which the crimes of Clovis and Fredegonde and Brunehaut were typical, we come in the slow course of things to the emergence of the feudal regime—a regime briefly expressed by the four words, suzerains, vassals, serfs, slaves—a regime which, along with the perpetual struggles for supremacy among local rulers and consequent chronic militancy, was characterized by the unqualified power of each chief or ruler, count or duke, within his own territory —a graduated bondage of all below him. The established form— 'I am your man', uttered by the vassal on his knees with apposed hands, expressed the relation of one grade to another throughout the society; and then, as usual, the master of slaves was himself enslaved by his appliances for maintaining life and power. He had the perpetual burden of arms and coat of mail, and the precautions to be taken now against assassination now against death by poison. And then when we come to the ultimate state in which the subordination of minor rulers by a chief ruler had become complete, and all counts and dukes were vassals of the king, we have not only the bondage entailed on the king by state business with its unceasing anxieties, but the bondage of ceremonial with its dreary round. Speaking of this in France in the time of Louis le Grand, Madame de Maintenon remarks: 'Save those only who fill the highest stations, I know of none more unfortunate than those who envy them. If you could only form an idea of what it is!'

Merely referring to the extreme subjection of the ruler to his appliances for ruling which was reached in Japan, where the god-descended Mikado, imprisoned by the requirements of his sacred state, was debarred from ordinary freedoms, and in whose recluse life there were at one time such penalties as sitting for three hours daily on the throne—passing over, too, the case of China, where, as Professor Douglas tells us of the emperor 'his whole life is one continual round of ceremonial observances', and 'from the day on which he ascends the throne to the time when he is carried to his tomb in the Eastern Hills, his hours and almost minutes have special duties appointed to them by the Board of Rites', we may turn now to the conspicuous example furnished by Russia. Along with that unceasing subjugation of minor nationalities by which its imperialism is displayed, what do we see within its own organization? We have its vast army, to service in which every one is actually or potentially liable; we have an enormous bureaucracy ramifying everywhere and rigidly controlling individual lives; we have an expenditure ever outrunning resources and calling for loans. As a result of the pressure felt personally and pecuniarily, we have secret revolutionary societies, perpetual plots, chronic dread of social explosions; and while everyone is in danger of Siberia, we have the all-powerful head of this enslaved nation in constant fear for his life. Even when he goes to review his troops, rigorous precautions have to be taken by a supplementary army of soldiers, policemen and spies, some forming an accompanying guard, some lying in wait here and there to prevent possible attacks; while similar precautions, which from time to time fail, have ever to be taken against assassination by explosion, during drives and railway journeys. What portion of life is not absorbed in government business and religious observances is taken up in self-preservation.

And now what is the lesson? Is it that in our own case imperialism and slavery, everywhere else and at all times united, are not to be united? Most will say yes. Nay they will join, as our Poet Laureate lately did in the title to some rhymes, the words 'imperialism and liberty'; mistaking names for things as of old. Gibbon writes:

Augustus was sensible that mankind is governed by names; nor was he deceived in his expectation, that the senate and people would submit to slavery, provided they were respectfully assured that they still enjoyed their ancient freedom.[1]

'Free!' thinks the Englishman, 'how can I be other than free if by my vote I share in electing a representative who helps to determine the national transactions, home and foreign?' Delivering a ballot-paper he identifies with the possession of those unrestrained activities which liberty implies; though, to take but one instance, a threatened penalty every day reminds him that his children must be stamped with the state pattern, not as he wills but as others will. But let us note how, along with the nominal extension of constitutional freedom, there has been going on actual diminution of it. There is first the fact that the legislative functions of parliament have been decreasing while the ministry has been usurping them. Important measures are not now brought forward and carried by private members, but appeal is made to the government to take them up: the making of laws is gradually lapsing into the hands of the executive. And then within the executive itself the tendency is towards placing power in fewer hands. Just as in past times the cabinet grew out of the privy council by a process of restriction, so now a smaller group of ministers is coming to exercise some of the functions of the whole group. Add to which we have subordinate executive bodies, like the Home Office, the Board of Trade, the Board of Education, and the Local Government Board, to which there have been deputed the powers both of making certain kinds of laws and enforcing them: government by administrative order. In like manner by taking for government purposes more and more of the time which was once available for private members; by the cutting down of debates by the closure; and now by requiring the vote for an entire department to be passed *en bloc*, without criticism of details, we are shown that while extension of the franchise has been seeming to increase the liberties of citizens, their liberties have been decreased by restricting the spheres of action of their representatives. All these are stages in that concentration of power which is the concomitant of imperialism.[2] And how this tendency

[1] *Decline and Fall of the Roman Empire*, 68.
[2] Even while I have the proof in hand there come the new rules of procedure, further diminishing the freedom of members.

works out where militancy becomes active, we are shown by the measures taken in South Africa—the proclamation of martial law by a governor, who thereby becomes in so far a despot, and the temporary suspension of constitutional government: a suspension which many so-called loyalists would make complete.

Passing by this, however, let us note the extent to which the citizen is the servant of the community in disguised ways. Certain ancient usages will best make this clear. During times when complete slavery was mingled with serfdom, the serf, tied to his plot, rendered to his lord or seigneur many dues and services. These services, or *corvees*, varied, according to the period and the place, from one day's labour to six days' labour in the week—from partial slavery to complete slavery. Labours and exactions of these kinds were most of them in course of time commuted for money, the equivalence between so much tax paid to the lord and so much work done for him, being thus distinctly recognized. Now in so far as the burden is concerned, it comes to the same thing if for the feudal lord we substitute the central government, and for local money payments we substitute general taxes. The essential question for the citizen is what part of his work goes to the power which rules over him, and what part remains available for satisfying his own wants. Labour demanded by the state is just as much *corvee* to the state as labour demanded by the feudal lord was *corvee* to him, though it may not be called so, and though it may be given in money instead of in kind; and to the extent of this *corvee* each citizen is a serf to the community. Some five years ago M. Guyot calculated that in France, the civil and military expenditure absorbs some thirty per cent of the national produce, or, in other words, that ninety days annually of the average citizen's labour is given to the state under compulsion.

Though to a smaller extent, what holds in France holds here. Not forgetting the heavy burden of state-*corvees* which the imperialism of past days bequeathed to us—the 150 millions of debt incurred for the American war and the 50 millions we took over with the East India Company's possessions, the interest on both of which entails on citizens extra labour annually, let us limit ourselves to the burdens imperialism now commits us to. From a statistical authority second to none, I learn that 100 millions of annual expenditure requires from the average citizen the labour of one day in every seventeen, that is to say, nearly eighteen days in the year. As the present permanent expenditure on army and navy plus the interest on the debt recently contracted amounts to about 76 millions, it results that 13½ days' labour per annum is thus imposed on the average citizen as *corvee*. And then there comes the £153,000,000 spent, and to be spent, on the South African and Chinese wars, to which may be added, for all the subsequent costs of pensions, repairs, compensations, and reinstatements, a sum which will raise the total to more than £200,000,000. What is the taxation which direct expenditure and interest on loans will entail, the reader may calculate. He has before him the data for an estimate of the extra number of days annually, during which imperialism will require him to work for the government—extra number, I say, because to meet the ordinary state expenditure, there must always be a large number of days spent by him as a state labourer. Doubtless one who is satisfied by names instead of things, as the Romans were, will think this statement absurd; but he who understands by freedom the ability to use his powers for his own ends, with no greater hindrance than is implied by the like ability of each other citizen, will see that in whatever disguised ways he is obliged to use his abilities for state purposes, he is to that extent a serf of the state; and that as fast as our growing imperialism augments the amount of such compulsory service, he is to that extent more and more a serf of the state.

And then beyond the roundabout services given by the citizen under the form of direct taxes and under the form of indirect taxes, severally equivalent to so many days' work that would else have elevated the lives of himself and his belongings, there will presently come the actual or potential service as a soldier, demanded by the State to carry out an imperialist policy—a service which, as those in South Africa can tell us, often inflicts under the guise of fine names a slavery harder than that which the Negro bears, with the added risk of death.

Even were it possible to bring home to men the extent to which their lives are, and presently will be still more, subordinated to state requirements, so as to leave them less and less owned by themselves, little effect would be produced. So long as the passion for mastery over-rides all others the slavery that goes along with imperialism will be tolerated. Among men who do not pride themselves on the possession of purely human traits, but on the possession of traits which they have in common with brutes, and in whose mouths 'bulldog courage' is equivalent to manhood—among people who take their point of honour from the prize-ring, in which the combatant submits to pain, injury, and risk of death in the determination to prove himself 'the better man', no deterrent considerations like the above will have any weight. So long as they continue to conquer other peoples and to hold them in subjection, they will readily merge their personal liberties in the power of the state, and hereafter as heretofore accept the slavery that goes along with imperialism.

(E) Patriotism[1]

Were anyone to call me dishonest or untruthful he would touch me to the quick. Were he to say that I am unpatriotic, he would leave me unmoved. 'What, then, have you no love of country?' That is a question not to be answered in a breath.

The early abolition of serfdom in England, the early growth of relatively free institutions, and the greater recognition of popular claims after the decay of feudalism had divorced the masses from the soil, were traits of English life which may be looked back upon with pride. When it was decided that any slave who set foot in England became free; when the importation of slaves into the Colonies was stopped; when twenty millions were paid for the emancipation of slaves in the West Indies; and when, however unadvisedly, a fleet was maintained to stop the slave trade, our countrymen did things worthy to be admired. And when England gave a home to political refugees and took up the causes of small states struggling for freedom, it again exhibited noble traits which excite affection. But there are traits, unhappily of late more frequently displayed, which do the reverse. Contemplation of the acts by which England has acquired over eighty possessions—settlements, colonies, protectorates, etc—does not arouse feelings of satisfaction. The transitions from missionaries to resident agents, then to officials having armed forces, then to punishments of those who resist their rule, ending in so-called 'pacification'—these processes

1 From *Facts and Comments*, 1902.

of annexation, now gradual and now sudden, as that of the new Indian province and that of Barotziland, which was declared a British colony with no more regard for the wills of the inhabiting people than for those of the inhabiting beasts—do not excite sympathy with their perpetrators. Love of country is not fostered in me on remembering that when, after our Prime Minister had declared that we were bound in honour to the Khedive to reconquer the Sudan, we, after the re-conquest, forthwith began to administer it in the name of the Queen and the Khedive—practically annexing it; nor when, after promising through the mouths of two colonial ministers not to interfere in the internal affairs of the Transvaal, we proceeded to insist on certain electoral arrangements, and made resistance the excuse for a desolating war.[1] Nor does the national character shown by a popular ovation to a leader of filibusters, or by the according of a university honour to an arch-conspirator, or by the uproarious applause with which undergraduates greeted one who sneered at the 'unctuous rectitude' of those who opposed his plans of aggression, appear to me lovable. If because my love of country does not survive these and many other adverse experiences I am called unpatriotic—well, I am content to be so called.

To me the cry—'Our country, right or wrong!' seems detestable. By association with love of country the sentiment it expresses gains a certain justification. Do but pull off the cloak, however, and the contained sentiment is seen to be of the lowest. Let us observe the alternative cases.

Suppose our country is in the right—suppose it is resisting invasion. Then the idea and feeling embodied in the cry are righteous. It may be effectively contended that self-defence is not only justified but is a duty. Now suppose, contrariwise, that our country is the aggressor—has taken possession of others' territory, or is forcing by arms certain commodities on a nation which does not want them, or is backing up some of its agents in 'punishing' those those who have retaliated. Suppose it is doing something which, by the hypothesis, is admitted to be wrong. What is then the implication of the cry? The right is on the side of those who oppose us; the wrong is on our side. How in that case is to be expressed

---

[1] We continue to hear repeated the transparent excuse that the Boers commenced the war. In the far west of the US, where every man carries his life in his hand and the usages of fighting are well understood, it is held that he is the aggressor who first moves his hand towards his weapon. The application is obvious.

the so-called patriotic wish? Evidently the words must stand—
'Down with the right, up with the wrong!' Now in other relations
this combination of aims implies the acme of wickedness. In the
minds of past men there existed, and there still exists in many
minds, a belief in a personalized principle of evil—a Being going
up and down in the world everywhere fighting against the good
and helping the bad to triumph. Can there be more briefly expressed the aim of that Being than in the words—'Up with the
wrong and down with the right'? Do the so-called patriots like the
endorsement?

Some years ago I gave expression to my own feeling—anti-
patriotic feeling, it will doubtless be called—in a somewhat start-
ling way. It was at the time of the second Afghan war, when, in
pursuance of what were thought to be 'our interests', we were invading Afghanistan. News had come that some of our troops were
in danger. At the Athenaeum Club a well-known military man—
then a captain but now a general—drew my attention to a telegram
containing this news, and read it to me in a manner implying the
belief that I should share his anxiety. I astounded him by reply-
ing: 'When men hire themselves out to shoot other men to order,
asking nothing about the justice of their cause, I don't care if they
are shot themselves.'

I foresee the exclamation which will be called forth. Such a
principle, it will be said, if accepted, would make an army impossible and a government powerless. It would never do to have each
soldier use his judgment about the purpose for which a battle is
waged. Military organization would be paralysed and our country
would be a prey to the first invader.

Not so fast, is the reply. For one war an army would remain just
as available as now—a war of national defence. In such a war every
soldier would be conscious of the justice of his cause. He would not
be engaged in dealing death among men about whose doings, good
or ill, he knew nothing, but among men who were manifest transgressors against himself and his compatriots. Only aggressive war
would be negatived, not defensive war.

Of course it may be said, and said truly, that if there is no aggressive war there can be no defensive war. It is clear, however, that
one nation may limit itself to defensive war when other nations do
not. So that the principle remains operative.

But those whose cry is—'Our country, right or wrong!' and who would add to our eighty-odd possessions others to be similarly obtained, will contemplate with disgust such a restriction upon military action. To them no folly seems greater than that of practising on Monday the principles they profess on Sunday.

(F) The Man Versus the State: Postscript[1]

So long as the religion of enmity predominates over the religion of amity, the current political superstition must hold its ground. While throughout Europe the early culture of the ruling classes is one which every day of the week holds up for admiration those who in ancient times achieved the greatest feats in battle, and only on Sunday repeats the injunction to put up the sword—while these ruling classes are subject to a moral discipline consisting of six-sevenths pagan example and one-seventh Christian precept, there is no likelihood that there will arise such international relations as may make a decline in governmental power practicable, and a corresponding modification of political theory acceptable. While among ourselves the administration of colonial affairs is such that native tribes who retaliate on Englishmen by whom they have been injured, are punished, not on their own savage principle of life for life, but on the improved civilized principle of wholesale massacre in return for single murder, there is little chance that a political doctrine consistent only with unaggressive conduct will gain currency. While the creed men profess is so interpreted that one of them who at home addresses missionary meetings, seeks, when abroad, to foment a quarrel with an adjacent people whom he wishes to subjugate, and then receives public honours after his death, it is not likely that the relations of our society to other societies will become such that there can spread to any extent that doctrine of limited governmental functions accompanying the diminished governmental authority proper to a peaceful state. A nation which, interested in ecclesiastical squabbles about the ceremonies of its humane cult, cares so little about the essence of that

[1] From *The Man Versus the State*, 1884.

cult that filibustering in its colonies receives applause rather than reprobation, and is not denounced even by the priests of its religion of love, is a nation which must continue to suffer from internal aggressions, alike of individuals on one another and of the state on individuals. It is impossible to unite the blessings of equity at home with the commission of inequities abroad.

Of course there will arise the question—why, then, enunciate and emphasize a theory at variance with the theory adapted to our present state?

Beyond the general reply that it is the duty of everyone who regards a doctrine as true and important to do what he can towards diffusing it, leaving the result to be what it may be, there are several more special replies, each of which is sufficient.

In the first place an ideal, far in advance of practicability though it may be, is always needful for right guidance. If, amid all those compromises which the circumstances of the times necessitate, or are thought to necessitate, there exist no true conceptions of better and worse in social organization—if nothing beyond the exigencies of the moment are attended to, and the proximately best is habitually identified with the ultimately best, there cannot be any true progress. However distant may be the goal, and however often intervening obstacles may necessitate deviation in our course towards it, it is obviously requisite to know whereabouts it lies.

Again, while something like the present degree of subjection of the individual to the state, and something like the current political theory adapted to it, may remain needful in presence of existing international relations; it is by no means needful that this subjection should be made greater and the adapted theory strengthened. In our days of active philanthropy, hosts of people eager to achieve benefits for their less fortunate fellows by the shortest methods, are busily occupied in developing administrative arrangements of a kind proper to a lower type of society—are bringing about retrogression while aiming at progression. The normal difficulties in the way of advance are sufficiently great, and it is lamentable that they should be made greater. Hence, something well worth doing may be done, if philanthropists can be shown that they are in many cases insuring the future ill-being of men while eagerly pursuing their present well-being.

Chiefly, however, it is important to impress on all the great truth, at present but little recognized, that a society's internal and external policies are so bound together that there cannot be an essential improvement of the one without an essential improvement of the other. A higher standard of international justice must be habitually acted upon before there can be conformity to a higher standard of justice in our national arrangements. The conviction that a dependence of this kind exists, could it be diffused among civilized peoples, would greatly check aggressive behaviour towards one another; and, by doing this, would diminish the coerciveness of their governmental systems while appropriately changing their political theories.

(G) Re-Barbarization[1]

All societies, be they those savage tribes which have acquired some political structure or those nations which have grown vast by conquering adjacent nations, show that the cardinal trait of fighting peoples is the subjection of man to man and of group to group. Graduated subordination, which is the method of army organization, becomes more and more the method of civil organization where militancy is chronic; since where militancy is chronic, the civil part becomes little else than a commissariat supplying the wants of the militant part, and is more and more subject to the same discipline. Further, familiar facts prove that emergence from those barbaric types of society evolved by chronic militancy, brings with it a decrease of this graduated subordination, and there results, as recent centuries have shown, an increase of freedom. To which let it be added that where, as among ourselves, the militant activities have for ages been less marked and the militant organization less pronounced, the growth of free institutions begins earlier and advances further. An obvious corollary is that a cardinal trait in the process of re-barbarization is the regrowth of graduated subordination. Let us contemplate the facts.

The United States furnishes a fit looking-glass. Since the days when there grew up local 'bosses' to whom clusters of voters were obedient, there has been a development of 'bosses' whose authorities extend over wider areas; until now a few men . . . mainly

[1] From *Facts and Comments*, 1902.

determine the elections, municipal and central. Conventions formed of delegates supposed to represent the wills of their respective localities, have become bodies which merely register the decisions of certain heads who nominally advise but practically dictate. And so completely has this system submerged the traditions of individual freedom, that now the assertion of such freedom has become a discredit, and the independent citizen, here and there found, who will not surrender his right of private judgment, bears the contemptuous name of 'mugwump'.

In England the caucus, not yet supreme over the individual, has still in large measure deprived him of what electoral freedom he had during the generation following the Reform Bill; when, as I know from personal experience, the initiative of each citizen (even a non-elector) was of some effect. Now, governing bodies in each constitutency undertake to judge for all members of their respective parties, who are obliged to accept the candidates chosen for them. Practically these bodies have become electoral oligarchies. Similarly in the House of Commons itself, this retrogressive movement, shown in ways described some pages back, is shown in further ways. There is the change which a few years ago cut off 'the privilege of ventilating grievances before going into Committee of Supply'—cut off that which was the primary privilege of burgesses sent up from their respective constituencies in early days; since, on the rectification or mitigation of grievances, partially depended the granting of supplies. And then, recently, a kindred resolution has negatived the right of moving amendments to the motion for going into Committee of Ways and Means. Retrogression is thus shown by increasingly subordinating the citizen, alike as elector and as representative.

Ecclesiastical movements now going on, show us a kindred change.

For these twenty years there has been at work a widespread cause, which few will at first recognize as a cause, but the effects of which analysis will make clear.

I make these remarks a propos of the Salvation Army. The word is significant—army; as are the names for the ranks, from the so-called 'General', descending through brigadiers, colonels, majors, down to local sub-officers, all wearing uniforms. This system is like in idea and in sentiment to that of an actual army. Then what are the feelings appealed to? The 'Official Gazette of the Salvation

Army' is entitled *The War Cry*; and the motto conspicuous on the title-page is 'Blood and Fire'. Doubtless it will be said that it is towards the principle of evil, personal or impersonal—towards 'the devil and all his works'—that the destructive sentiments are invoked by this title and this motto. So it will be said that in a hymn, conspicuous in the number of the paper I have in hand, the like *animus* is displayed by the expressions which I cull from the first thirty lines:—'Made us warriors for ever, Sent us in the field to fight . . . We shall win with fire and blood . . . Stand to your arms, the foe is nigh, The powers of hell surround . . . The day of battle is at hand! Go forth to glorious war'. These and others like them are stimuli to the fighting propensities, and the excitements of song joined with martial processions and instrumental music, cannot fail to raise high those slumbering passions which are ready enough to burst out even in the intercourse of ordinary life. Such appeals as there may be to the gentler sentiments which the creed inculcates, are practically lost amid these loud-voiced invocations.

Not in the Salvation Army alone but in the church services held on the occasion of the departure of troops for South Africa, certain hymns are used in a manner which substitutes for the spiritual enemy the human enemy. Thus for a generation past, under cover of the forms of a religion which preaches peace, love, and forgiveness, there has been a perpetual shouting of the words 'war' and 'blood', 'fire' and 'battle', and a continual exercise of the antagonistic feelings.

This diffusion of military ideas, military sentiments, military organization, military discipline, has been going on everywhere. There is the competing body, the Church Army, which, not particularly obtrusive, we may presume from its name follows similar lines; and there is, showing more clearly the ecclesiastical bias in the same direction, the Church Lads' Brigade, with its uniform, arms, and drill. In these as in other things the clerical and the military are in full sympathy. The Reverend Dr Warre, headmaster of Eton, reads a paper at the United Service Institution, arguing that in the public secondary schools there should be diffusion of the elements of military science, as well as exercise in military drill, manoeuvres, use of fire-arms, etc. So, too, another headmaster, the Reverend Mr Gull, in a lecture to the College of Preceptors under chairmanship of the Reverend Mr Bevan, tells us that there are seventy-nine cadet-corps in various public schools; that efforts are being made to 'organize drill in elementary schools and for boys in the lower ranks of life'; that a committee of the Headmasters' Conference resolved unanimously that in public secondary schools boys over fifteen should receive military drill and instruction; and that, by the suggestion of these 'reverend' headmasters, a Military Instruction Bill, embodying their views and favoured by the War Office, has been brought before both Houses of Parliament.[1] Similarly during the Guthrie Commemoration at Clifton College, the headmaster, the Reverend Canon Glazebrook, in presence of two bishops, glorified the part which those educated at Clifton had taken in the South African War: enlarging with pride on 'so noble a contribution in such a patriotic cause' as the nineteen old Cliftonians who had fallen; dilating, too, on the increasing zeal of the school in military matters. And now at Cambridge the Senate urges that the University should take steps towards the organization of instruction in military sciences.

More conspicuous growths of like nature have taken place. Fifty years ago we had no such incidents as the 'passages of arms' or tournaments now held periodically, nor had we any military and naval exhibitions. Showing the utter change of social sentiment, it was resolved at a Mansion House meeting that the Great Exhibition of 1851, which was expected to inaugurate universal peace, should be commemorated in 1901 by a Naval and Military Exhibition: an anti-militant display having for its jubilee a militant display!

The temper generated by these causes has resulted in the outbursts of violence occurring all over England in thirty towns large and small, where those who entertain opinions disliked by the majority respecting our treatment of the Boers, have been made the victims of mobs—mobs which not only suppressed even private meetings and ill-treated those who proposed to take part in them, kicking and even tarring them in the public streets, but attacked the premises of those who were known to be against the war, smashing shop-windows, breaking into houses, and even firing into them. And now after these breaches of the law, continued for two years, have been habitually condoned by the authorities, we find leading newspapers applauding the police for having 'judiciously refrained' from interfering with a mob in its ill-treatment of Stop-the-War speakers! Surely a society thus characterized and thus governed is a fit habitat for hooligans.

[1] See *Educational Times*, 1 June, 1901.

Naturally along with this exaltation of brute force in its armed form, as seen in military organizations, secular and sacred, as well as in the devotion of teaching institutions to fostering it, and along with these manifestations of popular passion, showing how widely the trait of coerciveness, which is the essential element in militancy, has pervaded the nation, there has gone a cultivation of skilled physical force under the form of athleticism. The word is quite modern . . . in my early days 'sports', so called, were almost exclusively represented by one weekly paper, *Bell's Life in London*. . . . Since then, the growth has been such that there are professionals and there are courses of training; so that what was originally a game has become a business. Football, in my boyhood, occupying no public attention, has now provision made for it in every locality, and its leading contests between paid players, draw their tens of thousands—nay even a hundred thousand—spectators, whose natures are such that police are often required for the protection of referees. It may, indeed, be remarked that this game, which has now become the most popular, is also the most brutalizing; for the merciless struggles among the players, and the intensity of their antagonisms, prove, even without the frequent inflictions of injuries and occasional deaths, that the game approaches as nearly to a fight as lack of weapons allows.

Meanwhile, to satisfy the demand journalism has been developing, so that besides sundry daily and weekly papers devoted wholly to sports, the ordinary daily and weekly papers give reports of 'events' in all localities, and not unfrequently a daily paper has a whole page occupied with them. Literature, journalism and art, have all been aiding in this process of re-barbarization. For a long time there have flourished novel-writers who have rung the changes on narratives of crime and stories of sanguinary deeds. Others have been supplying boys and youths with tales full of plotting and fighting and bloodshed: millions of such having of late years been circulated;[1] and there have been numerous volumes of travel in which encounters with natives and the killing of big game have been the advertised attractions. Various war-books have followed in the wake of Professor Creasy's *Fifteen Decisive Battles of the World* with its thirty-odd editions; and now . . . as indicating most clearly the state of national feeling, we have the immense popularity of Mr Rudyard Kipling, in whose writings one-tenth of nominal

[1] See *Academy*, 5 June, 1897.

Christianity is joined with nine-tenths of real paganism; who idealizes the soldier and glories in the triumphs of brute force; and who, in depicting school-life, brings to the front the barbarizing activities and feelings and shows little respect for a civilizing culture.

So, too, the literature of the periodicals reeks with violence. Not content with battles and great captains of recent times, editors have, to satisfy the appetites of readers, gone back to the remote past as well as to the near past. The life and conquests of Alexander the Great have been set forth afresh with illustrations; and in serial articles, as also in book form, Napoleon has again served as a subject for biography: Wellington and Nelson, too, have been resuscitated. Nay, even memoirs of celebrated pirates and privateers have been exhumed to meet the demand. At the same time the fiction filling our monthly magazines has been mainly sanguinary. Tales of crimes and deeds of violence, drawings of men fighting, men overpowered, men escaping, of daggers raised, pistols levelled— these, in all varieties of combination, have appealed to our latent savagery. . . . So has it been with our pictorial newspapers. Even before the recent wars there were ever found occasions for representing bloody combats, or else the appliances of destruction naval and military, or else the leading men using them.

Thus on every side we see the ideas and feelings and institutions appropriate to peaceful life, replaced by those appropriate to fighting life. The continual increases of the army, the formation of permanent camps, the institution of public military contests and military exhibitions, have conduced to this result. The drills and displays and competitions of civilian soldiers (not uncalled-for when they began) have gone on exercising the combative feelings. Perpetual excitements of the destructive passions which, in *The War Cry* and in the hymns of General Booth's followers, have made battle and blood and fire familiar, and under the guise of fighting against evil have thrust into the background the gentler emotions, have done the like. Similarly in schools, military organization and discipline have been cultivating the instinct of antagonism in each rising generation. More and more the spirit of conflict has been exercised by athletic games, interest in which has been actively fostered first by the weekly press and now by the daily press; and with increase of the honours given to physical prowess there has been decrease of the honours given to mental prowess.

Meanwhile literature and art have been aiding. Books treating of battles, conquests and the men who conducted them, have been widely diffused and greedily read. Periodicals full of stories made interesting by killing, with accompanying illustrations, have every month ministered to the love of destruction; as have, too, the weekly illustrated journals. In all places and in all ways there has been going on during the past fifty years a recrudescence of barbaric ambitions, ideas and sentiments and an unceasing culture of blood-thirst.

(H) Conclusions[1]

How long this phase of social life to which we are approaching will last, and in what way it will come to an end, are of course questions not to be answered. Probably the issue will be here of one kind and there of another. A sudden bursting of bonds which have become intolerable may in some cases happen: bringing on a military despotism. In other cases practical extinction may follow a gradual decay, arising from abolition of the normal relation between merit and benefit, by which alone the vigour of a race can be maintained. And in yet further cases may come conquest by peoples who have not been emasculated by fostering their feebles—peoples before whom the socialistic organization will go down like a house of cards, as did that of the ancient Peruvians before a handful of Spaniards.

But if the process of evolution which, unceasing throughout past time, has brought life to its present height, continues throughout the future, as we cannot but anticipate, then, amid all the rhythmical changes in each society, amid all the lives and deaths of nations, amid all the supplantings of race by race, there will go on that adaptation of human nature to the social state which began when savages first gathered together into hordes for mutual defence—an adaptation finally complete. Many will think this a wild imagination. Though everywhere around them are creatures with structures and instincts which have been gradually so moulded as to subserve their own welfares and the welfares of their species, yet the immense majority ignore the implication that human beings

[1] From *The Principles of Sociology*, Vol. III, 1896.

too have been undergoing in the past, and will undergo in the future, progressive adjustments to the lives imposed on them by circumstances. But there are a few who think it rational to conclude that what has happened with all lower forms must happen with the highest form—a few who infer that, among types of men, those most fitted for making a well-working society will, hereafter as heretofore, from time to time emerge and spread at the expense of types less fitted, until a fully fitted type has arisen.

The view thus suggested must be accepted with qualifications. If we carry our thoughts as far forward as palaeolithic implements carry them back, we are introduced, not to an absolute optimism but to a relative optimism.

Social evolution throughout the future, like social evolution throughout the past, must, while producing step after step higher societies, leave outstanding many lower ... but ... in time to come, a federation of the highest nations, exercising supreme authority (already foreshadowed by occasional agreements among 'the Powers'), may, by forbidding wars between any of its constituent nations, put an end to the re-barbarization which is continually undoing civilization.

When this peace-maintaining federation has been formed, there may be effectual progress towards that equilibrium between constitution and conditions—between inner faculties and outer requirements—implied by the final stage of human evolution. Adaptation to the social state, now perpetually hindered by anti-social conflicts, may then go on unhindered; and all the great societies, in other respects differing, may become similar in those cardinal traits which result from complete self-ownership of the unit and exercise over him of nothing more than passive influence by the aggregate. On the one hand, by continual repression of aggressive instincts and exercise of feelings which prompt ministration to public welfare, and on the other hand by the lapse of restraints, gradually becoming less necessary, there must be produced a kind of man so constituted that while fulfilling his own desires he fulfils also the social needs. Already, small groups of men, shielded by circumstances from external antagonisms, have been moulded into forms of moral nature so superior to our own, that, as said of the Let-htas, the account of their goodness 'almost savours of romance'; and it is reasonable to infer that what has even now happened on a small scale may, under kindred conditions, eventually happen on a large scale. Long studies, showing among other things the need for certain qualifications above indicated, but also revealing facts like that just named, have not caused me to recede from the belief expressed nearly fifty years ago that: 'the ultimate man will be one whose private requirements coincide with public ones. He will be that manner of man who, in spontaneously fulfilling his own nature, incidentally performs the functions of a social unit; and yet is only enabled so to fulfil his own nature by all others doing the like.'

(I) *General Considerations on Social Philosophy*[1]

The course of civilization could not possibly have been other than it has been. Whether a perfect social state might have been at once established; and why, if it might have been, it was not— why for unnumbered ages the world was filled with inferior creatures only—and why mankind was left to make it fit for human life by clearing it of these—are questions that need not be discussed here. But given an unsubdued earth; given the being—man, appointed to overspread and occupy it; given the laws of life what they are; and no other series of changes than that which has taken place, could have taken place.

For be it remembered, that the ultimate purpose of creation —the production of the greatest amount of happiness—can be fulfilled only under certain fixed conditions. Each member of the race fulfilling it, must not only be endowed with faculties enabling him to receive the highest enjoyment in the act of living but must be so constituted that he may obtain full satisfaction for every desire, without diminishing the power of others to obtain like satisfaction: nay, to fulfil the purpose perfectly, must derive pleasure from seeing pleasure in others. Now, for beings thus constituted to multiply in a world already tenanted by inferior creatures—creatures that must be dispossessed to make room— is a manifest impossibility. By the definition such beings must lack

From *Social Statics*, 1897.

all desire to exterminate the races they are to supplant. They must, indeed, have a repugnance to exterminating them, for the ability to derive pleasure from seeing pleasure involves the liability to pain from seeing pain: the sympathy by which either of these results is effected, simply having for its function to reproduce observed emotions, irrespective of their kind. Evidently, therefore, having no wish to destroy—to destroy giving them, on the contrary, disagreeable sensations—these hypothetical beings, instead of subjugating and overspreading the earth, must themselves become the prey of pre-existing creatures, in whom destructive desires predominate. How then are the circumstances of the case to be met? Evidently the aboriginal man must have a constitution adapted to the work he has to perform, joined with a dormant capability of developing into the ultimate man when the conditions of existence permit. To the end that he may prepare the earth for its future inhabitants—his descendants, he must possess a character fitting him to clear it of races endangering his life, and races occupying the space required by mankind. Hence he must have a desire to kill, for it is the universal law of life that to every needful act must attach a gratification, the desire for which may serve as a stimulus. He must further be devoid of sympathy, or must have but the germ of it, for he would otherwise be incapacitated for his destructive office. In other words, he must be what we call a savage and must be left to acquire fitness for social life as fast as the conquest of the earth renders social life possible.

Whoever thinks that a thoroughly-civilized community could be formed out of men qualified to wage war with the pre-existing occupants of the earth—that is, whoever thinks that men might behave sympathetically to their fellows, whilst behaving unsympathetically to inferior creatures, will discover his error on looking at the facts. He will find that human beings are cruel to one another in proportion as their habits are predatory. The Indian whose life is spent in the chase delights in torturing his brother man as much as in killing game. His sons are schooled into fortitude by long days of torment, and his squaw made prematurely old by hard treatment. The treachery and vindictiveness which Bushmen or Australians show to one another and to Europeans, are accompaniments of that never-ceasing enmity existing between them and the denizens of the wilderness. Amongst partially-civilized nations the two characteristics have ever borne the same relationship.

Thus the spectators in the Roman amphitheatres were as much delighted by the slaying of gladiators as by the death-struggles of wild beasts. The ages during which Europe was thinly peopled, and hunting a chief occupation, were also the ages of feudal violence, universal brigandage, dungeons, tortures. Here in England a whole province depopulated to make game preserves, and a law sentencing to death the serf who killed a stag, show how great activity of the predatory instinct and utter indifference to human happiness coexisted. In later days, when bull-baiting and cock-fighting were common pastimes, the penal code was far more severe than now; prisons were full of horrors; men put in the pillory were maltreated by the populace; and the inmates of lunatic asylums, chained naked to the wall, were exhibited for money, and tormented for the amusement of visitors. Conversely, amongst ourselves a desire to diminish human misery is accompanied by a desire to ameliorate the condition of inferior creatures. Whilst the kindlier feeling of men is seen in all varieties of philanthropic effort, in charitable societies in associations for improving the dwellings of the labouring classes, in anxiety for popular education, in attempts to abolish capital punishment, in zeal for temperance reformation, in ragged schools, in endeavours to protect climbing boys, in inquiries concerning 'labour and the poor', in emigration funds, in the milder treatment of children, and so on, it also shows itself in societies for the prevention of cruelty to animals, in acts of parliament to put down the use of dogs for purpose of draught, in the condemnation of steeplechases and *battues*, in the late inquiry why the pursuers of a stag should not be punished as much as the carter who maltreats his horse, and lastly, in vegetarianism. Moreover, to make the evidence complete, we have the fact that men, partially adapted to the social state, retrograde on being placed in circumstances which call forth the old propensities. The barbarizing of colonists, who live under aboriginal conditions, is universally remarked. The back settlers of America, amongst whom unavenged murders, rifle duels, and lynch law prevail—or, better still, the trappers, who leading a savage life have descended to savage habits, to scalping, and occasionally even to cannibalism—sufficiently exemplify it.

But, indeed, without collecting from so wide a field, illustrations of the truth that the behaviour of men to the lower animals and their behaviour to each other, bear a constant relationship, it becomes clear that such is the fact, on observing that the same

H

impulses govern in either case. The blind desire to inflict suffering, distinguishes not between the creatures who exhibit that suffering, but obtains gratification indifferently from the agonies of beast and human being—delights equally in worrying a brute, and in putting a prisoner to the rack. Conversely, the sympathy which prevents its possessor from inflicting pain, that he may avoid pain himself, and which tempts him to give happiness that he may have happiness reflected back upon him, is similarly undistinguishing. As already said, its function is simply to reproduce in one being the emotions exhibited by other beings; and every one must have noticed that it extracts pleasure from the friskiness of a newly-unchained dog, or excites pity for an ill-used beast of burden, as readily as it generates fellow feeling with the joys and sorrows of men.

So that only by giving us some utterly different mental constitution could the process of civilization have been altered. Assume that the creative scheme is to be wrought out by natural means, and it is necessary that the primitive man should be one whose happiness is obtained at the expense of the happiness of other beings. It is necessary that the ultimate man should be one who can obtain perfect happiness without deducting from the happiness of others. After accomplishing its appointed purpose, the first of these constitutions has to be moulded into the last. And the manifold evils which have filled the world for these thousands of years—the murders, enslavings and robberies—the tyrannies of rulers, the oppressions of class, the persecutions of sect and party, the multiform embodiments of selfishness in unjust laws, barbarous customs, dishonest dealings, exclusive manners and the like—are simply instances of the disastrous working of this original and once needful constitution, now that mankind has grown into conditions for which it is not fitted—are nothing but symptoms of the suffering attendant upon the adaptation of humanity to its new circumstances.

But why, it may be asked, has this adaptation gone on so slowly? Judging from the rapidity with which habits are formed in the individual, and seeing how those habits, or rather the latent tendencies toward them, become hereditary, it would seem that the needful modification should have been completed long ago. How, then, are we to understand the delay?

The answer is that the new conditions to which adaptation has been taking place have themselves grown up but slowly. Only when a revolution in circumstances is at once both marked and permanent, does a decisive alteration of character follow. If the demand for increase of power in some particular faculty is great and unceasing, development will go on with proportionate speed. And, conversely, there will be an appreciable dwindling in a faculty altogether deprived of exercise. But the conditions of human life have undergone no changes sudden enough to produce these immediate results.

Thus, note in the first place that the warfare between man and the creatures at enmity with him has continued up to the present time, and over a large portion of the globe is going on now. Note further that where the destructive propensities have almost fulfilled their purpose, and are on the eve of losing their gratification, they make to themselves an artificial sphere of exercise by game-preserving, and are so kept in activity after they would otherwise have become dormant. But note chiefly that the old predatory disposition is in a certain sense self-mantained. For it generates between men and men a hostile relationship, similar to that which it generates between men and inferior animals; and by doing so provides itself a lasting source of excitement. This happens inevitably. The desires of the savage acting, as we have seen, indiscriminately, necessarily lead him to perpetual trespasses against his fellows and consequently to endless antagonisms—to quarrels of individuals, to fightings of tribes, to feuds of clan with clan, to wars of nations. And thus being by their constitutions made mutual foes, as well as foes to the lower races, men keep alive in each other the old propensities after the original need for them has in great measure ceased.

Hitherto, then, human character has changed but slowly, because it has been subject to two conflicting sets of conditions. On the one hand, the discipline of the social state has been developing it into the sympathetic form, whilst on the other hand, the necessity for self-defence partly of man against brute, partly of man against man, and partly of societies against each other, has been maintaining the old unsympathetic form. And only where the influence of the first set of conditions has exceeded that of the last, and then only in proportion to the excess, has modification taken place. Amongst tribes who have kept each other's anti-social characteristics in full activity by constant conflict, no advance has

H*

been possible. But where warfare against man and beast has ceased to be continuous, or where it has become the employment of but a portion of the people, the effects of living in the associated state have become greater than the effects of barbarizing antagonisms, and progress has resulted.

Regarded thus, civilization no longer appears to be a regular unfolding after a specific plan, but seems rather a development of man's latent capabilities under the action of favourable circumstances; which favourable circumstances, mark, were certain some time or other to occur. Those complex influences underlying the higher orders of natural phenomena, but more especially those underlying the organic world, work in subordination to the law of probabilities. A plant, for instance, produces thousands of seeds. The greater part of these are destroyed by creatures that live upon them, or fall into places where they cannot germinate. Of the young plants produced by those which do germinate, many are smothered by their neighbours; others are blighted by insects, or eaten up by animals; and *in the average of cases*, only one of them produces a perfect specimen of its species which, escaping all dangers, brings to maturity seeds enough to continue the race. Thus is it also with every kind of creature. Thus is it also, as M. Quetelet has shown, with the phenomena of human life. And thus was it even with the germination and growth of society. The seeds of civilization existing in the aboriginal man, and distributed over the earth by his multiplication, were certain in the lapse of time to fall here and there into circumstances fit for their development; and, in spite of all blightings and uprootings, were certain, by sufficient repetition of these occurrences, ultimately to originate a civilization which should outlive all disasters and arrive at perfection.

Whilst the continuance of the old predatory instinct after the fulfilment of its original purpose, has retarded civilization by giving rise to conditions at variance with those of social life, it has subserved civilization by clearing the earth of inferior races of men. The forces which are working out the great scheme of perfect happiness, taking no account of incidental suffering, exterminate such sections of mankind as stand in their way with the same sternness that they exterminate beasts of prey and herds of useless ruminants. Be he human being or be he brute, the hindrance must be got rid of. Just as the savage has taken the place of lower creatures, so must he, if he have remained too long a savage, give place to his superior. And, observe, it is necessarily to his superior that, in the great majority of cases, he does give place. For what are the prerequisites to a conquering race? Numerical strength, or an improved system of warfare; both of which are indications of advancement. Numerical strength implies certain civilizing antecedents. Deficiency of game may have necessitated agricultural pursuits, and so made the existence of a larger population possible; or distance from other tribes may have rendered war less frequent, and so have prevented its perpetual decimations; or accidental superiority over neighbouring tribes, may have led to the final subjugation and enslaving of these: in any of which cases the comparatively peaceful condition resulting, must have allowed progress to commence. Evidently, therefore, from the very beginning, the conquest of one people over another has been, in the main, the conquest of the social man over the anti-social man.

In another mode, too, the continuance of the unsympathetic character has indirectly aided civilization whilst it has directly hindered it; namely, by giving rise to slavery. It has been observed —and, as it seems, truly enough—that only by such stringent coercion as is exercised over men held in bondage, could the needful power of continuous application have been developed. Devoid of this, as from his habits of life the aboriginal man necessarily was (and as, indeed, existing specimens show), probably the severest discipline continued for many generations was required to make him submit contentedly to the necessities of his new state. And if so, the barbarous selfishness which maintained that discipline, must be considered as having worked a collateral benefit, though in itself so radically bad.

Let not the reader be alarmed. Let him not fear that these admissions will excuse new invasions and new oppressions. Nor let anyone who fancies himself called upon to take nature's part in this matter, by providing discipline for idle Negroes or others, suppose that these dealings of the past will serve for precedents. Rightly understood, they will do no such thing. That phase of civilization during which forcible supplantings of the weak by the strong, and systems of savage coercion, are on the whole advantageous, is a phase which spontaneously and necessarily gives birth to these things. It is not in pursuance of any calmly-reasoned conclusions respecting nature's intention that men conquer and enslave their fellows—it is not that they smother their kindly feelings to subserve civilization; but it is that as yet constituted they care little what suffering they inflict in the pursuit of gratification, and even think the achievement and exercise of mastery honourable. As soon, however, as there arises a perception that these subjugations and tyrannies are not right—as soon as the sentiment to which they are repugnant becomes sufficiently powerful to suppress them, it is time for them to cease. The question altogether hinges upon the amount of moral sense possessed by men; or, in other words, upon the degree of adaptation to the social state they have undergone. Unconsciousness that there is anything wrong in exterminating inferior races, or in reducing them to bondage, presupposes an almost rudimentary state of men's sympathies and their sense of human rights. The oppressions they then inflict and submit to, are not, therefore, detrimental to their characters—do not retard in them the growth of the social sentiments, for these have not yet reached a development great enough to be offended by such doings. And hence the aids given to civilization by clearing the earth of its least advanced inhabitants, and by forcibly compelling the rest to acquire industrial habits, are given without moral adaptation receiving any corresponding check. Quite otherwise is it, however, when the flagitiousness of these gross forms of injustice begins to be recognized. Then the times give proof that the old regime is no longer fit. Further progress cannot be made until the newly-felt wrong has been done away or diminished. Were it possible under such circumstances to uphold past institutions and practices (which, happily, it is not), it would be at the expense of a continual searing of men's consciences. The feelings whose predominance gives possibility to an advanced social state would be constantly repressed—kept down on a level with the old arrangements, to the stopping of all further progress; and before those who have grown beyond one of these probationary states could reinstitute it, they must resume that inferior character to which it was natural. Before a forced servitude could be again established for the industrial discipline of eight hundred thousand Jamaica blacks, the thirty millions of English whites who established it would have to retrograde in all things—in truthfulness, fidelity, generosity, honesty and even in material condition; for to diminish men's moral sense is to diminish their fitness for acting

together, and, therefore, to render the best producing and distributing organizations impracticable. Another illustration this of
the perfect economy of nature. Whilst the injustice of conquests
and enslavings is not perceived, they are on the whole beneficial;
but as soon as they are felt to be at variance with the moral law,
the continuance of them retards adaptation in one direction, more
than it advances it in another: a fact which our new preacher of the
old doctrine, that might is right, may profitably consider a little.

Contrasted as are their units, primitive communities and advanced ones must essentially differ in the principles of their
structure. Like other organisms, the social organism has to pass in
the course of its development through temporary forms, in which
sundry of its functions are fulfilled by appliances destined to disappear as fast as the ultimate appliances become efficient. Associated humanity has larval appendages analogous to those of individual creatures. As in the common Triton of our ponds, the
external lungs or bronchiæ dwindle away when the internal lungs
have grown to maturity; and as during the embryo stage of the
higher vertebrata, temporary organs appear, serve their purpose
awhile, and are subsequently reabsorbed, leaving only signs of their
having been; so, in the earlier forms of the body politic do there
exist institutions which after answering their ends for a time are
superseded and become extinct.

But deciduous institutions imply deciduous sentiments. Dependent as they are upon popular character, established political
systems cannot die out until the feeling which upholds them dies
out. Hence during man's apprenticeship to the social state there
must predominate in him some impulse corresponding to the
arrangements requisite; which impulse diminishes as the probationary organization made possible by it, merges into the ultimate
organization. The nature and operation of this impulse now demand our attention.

'I had so great a respect for the memory of Henry IV,' said the
celebrated French robber and assassin, Cartouche, 'that had a
victim I was pursuing taken refuge under his statue on the Pont
Neuf, I would have spared his life.' An apt illustration, this, of the
coexistence of profound hero-worship with the extremest savageness, and of the means hero-worship affords whereby the savage
may be ruled. The necessity for some such sentiment to bind men
together whilst they are as yet unsympathetic, has been elsewhere

shown. For the anti-social man to be transformed into the social man, he must live in the social state. But how can a society be maintained when, by the hypothesis, the aggressive desires of its members are destructive of it? Evidently its members must possess some counterbalancing tendency which shall keep them in the social state despite the incongruity—which shall make them submit to the restraint imposed—and which shall diminish as adaptation to the new circumstances renders restraint less needful. Such counterbalancing tendency we have in this same sentiment of hero-worship; a sentiment which leads men to prostrate themselves before any manifestation of power, be it in chief, feudal lord, king or constitutional government, and makes them act in subordination to that power.

Facts illustrating this alleged connection between strength of hero-worship and strength of the aggressive propensities, together with other facts illustrating the simultaneous decline of both, were given when the matter was first discussed. Now, however, we may appropriately examine the evidence in detail. The proposition is that in proportion as the members of a community are barbarous that is, in proportion as they show a lack of moral sense by seeking gratification at each other's expense, in the same proportion will they show depth of reverence for authority. What, now, are the several indications of deficient moral sense? First on the list stands disregard of human life; next, habitual violation of personal liberty; next to that, theft, and the dishonesty akin to it. Each of these, if the foregoing theory be true, we ought to find most prevalent where the awe of power is most profound.

Well, is it not a fact that grovelling submission to despotic rule flourishes side by side with the practice of human sacrifices, infanticide, and assassination? We find suttees and thuggees amongst a race who have ever been abject slaves. In some of the Pacific isles, where the immolation of children to idols, and the burying of parents alive, are common, 'so high is the reverence for hereditary chieftainship that it is often connected with the idea of divine power'. Complete absolutism uniformly coexists with cannibalism. We read of human hecatombs in connection with the extremest prostration of subjects to rulers. In Madagascar, where men are put to death on the most trifling occasions, and where the coast is decorated with skulls stuck on poles, the people are governed on the severest maxims of feudal law, by absolute chieftains under an absolute monarch. The head-hunting Dyaks of Borneo have petty tyrants over them. There is autocratic government, too, for the bloodthirsty Mongolian races. Both positive and negative proof of this association is given by Mr Grote, where he says: 'In no city of historical Greece did there prevail either human sacrifices or deliberate mutilations, such as cutting off the nose, ears, hands, feet, or castration, selling of children into slavery, or polygamy, *or the feeling of unlimited obedience toward one man*; all of them customs, which might be pointed out as existing amongst the contemporary Carthaginians, Egyptians, Persians, Thracians.' If we consult medieval history, there, along with loyalty strongly manifested, are the judicial combats, right of private war, constant wearing of arms, religious martyrdoms and massacres, to prove that life was held in less respect than now. Glancing over modern Europe, we find the assassinations of Italy, the cruelty of the Croats and Czechs, and the Austrian butcheries, illustrating the relationship. Whilst, amongst ourselves, diminished reverence for authority has occurred simultaneously with diminished sanguinariness in our criminal code.

That infringements of personal liberty are greatest where awe of power is greatest, is in some sort a truism, seeing that forced servitude, through which alone extensive violations of human liberty can be made, is impossible, unless the sentiment of power-worship is strong. Thus, the ancient Persians could never have allowed themselves to be considered the private property of their monarchs had it not been for the overwhelming influence of this sentiment. But that such submission is associated with a defect of moral sense is best seen in the acknowledged truth that readiness to cringe is accompanied by an equal readiness to tyrannize. Satraps lorded it over the people as their king over them. The Helots were not more coerced by their Spartan masters than these in turn by their oligarchy. Of the servile Hindoos we are told that 'they indemnify themselves for their passiveness to their superiors by their tyranny, cruelty, and violence to those in their power'. During the feudal ages, whilst the people were bondsman to the nobles, the nobles were vassals to their kings, their kings to the pope. In Russia, at the present moment, the aristocracy are dictated to by their emperor much as they themselves dictate to their serfs. And when to these facts we add the significant one elsewhere dwelt upon, that the treatment of women by their husbands, and children by their parents, has been tyrannical in proportion as the servility of subjects to rulers has been extreme, we have sufficient proof that hero-worship is strongest where there is least regard for human freedom.

Equally abundant evidence exists that the prevalence of theft is similarly associated with a predominance of the loyalty-producing faculty. Books of travels give proof that amongst uncivilized races pilfering and the irresponsible power of chiefs coexist. The same association of dishonesty and submissiveness is found amongst more advanced peoples. It is so with the Hindoos, with the Cinghalese, and with the inhabitants of Madagascar. The piracy of the Malays, and of the Chinese, and the long-continued predatory habits of the Arab races, both on land and sea, exist in conjunction with obedience to despotic rule. 'One quality', says Kohl, 'which the Lettes show, with all enslaved tribes, is a great disposition to thieving.' The Russians, to whom worship of their emperor is a needful luxury, confess openly that they are cheats, and laugh over the confession. The Poles, whose servile salutation is 'I throw myself under your feet', and amongst whom nobles are cringed to by the Jews and citizens, and these again by the people, are certainly not noted for probity. The times when fealty of serfs to feudal barons was strongest were times of universal rapine. 'In Germany a very large proportion of the rural nobility lived by robbery'; their castles being built with a special view to this occupation, and that even by ecclesiastics. Burghers were fleeced, towns were now and then sacked, and Jews were tortured for their money. Kings were as much thieves as the rest. They laid violent hands upon the goods of their vassals, like John of England and Philip Augustus of France; they cheated their creditors by debasing the coinage; they impressed men's horses without paying for them; and they seized the goods of traders, sold them, and pocketed a large part of the proceeds. Meantime, whilst freebooters overran the land, pirates covered the sea, the Cinque Ports and St Malo being the headquarters of those infesting the English Channel.

Between these days and ours, the gradual decline of loyalty—as shown in the extinction of feudal relationships, in the abandonment of divine right of kings, in the reduction of monarchical power, and in the comparative leniency with which treason is now punished —has accompanied an equally gradual increase of honesty, and of regard for people's lives and liberties. By how much men are still deficient in respect for each other's rights, by so much are they still penetrated with respect for authority; and we may even trace in existing parties the constant ratio preserved between these characteristics. It has been shown, for instance, that the unskilled labourers of the metropolis who, instead of entertaining violently democratic opinions, appear to have no political opinions whatever, or, if they think at all, rather lean toward the maintenance of 'things as they are', and part of whom, (the coalwhippers) are extremely proud of their having turned out a man on April 1848, and become special constables for the 'maintenance of law and order' on the day of the great Chartist Demonstration—it has been shown that these same unskilled labourers constitute the most immoral class. The criminal-returns prove them to be nine times as dishonest, five times as drunken, and nine times as savage (shown by the assaults), as the rest of the community. Of like import is the observation respecting convicts, quoted and confirmed by Captain Maconochie, that 'a good prisoner [i.e. a submissive one] is usually a bad man'. If, again, we turn over the newspapers which circulate amongst court satellites, and chronicle the movements of the *haut-ton*, which ascribe national calamities to the omission of a royal title from a new coin, and which apologize for continental despots; we read in them excuses for war and standing armies, sneerings at 'peace-mongers', defences of capital punishment, condemnations of popular enfranchisement, diatribes against freedom of exchange, rejoicings over territorial robberies, and vindications of church-rate seizures: showing that, where belief in the sacredness of authority most lingers, belief in the sacredness of life, of liberty, and of property, is least displayed.

The fact that, during civilization, hero-worship and moral sense vary inversely, is simply the obverse of the fact already hinted, that society is possible so long only as they continue to do this. Where there is insufficient reverence for the Divine Law, there must be supplementary reverence for human law; otherwise there will be complete lawlessness or barbarism. Evidently, if men are to live together, the absence of internal power to rule themselves rightly toward each other, necessitates the presence of external power to enforce such behaviour as may make association tolerable; and this power can become operative only by being held in awe. So that wild races deficient in the allegiance-producing sentiment cannot enter into a civilized state at all, but have to be supplanted by others that can. And it must further follow, that if in any community loyalty diminishes at a greater rate than equity increases, there will arise a tendency toward social dissolution—a tendency which the populace of Paris threaten to illustrate.

How needful the continuance of a savage selfishness renders the continuance of a proportionate amount of power-worship, may be perceived daily. The veneration which produces submission to a government, unavoidably invests that goverment with proportionately high attributes; for being in essence a worship of power, it can be strongly drawn out toward that only which either has great power, or is believed to have it. Hence, the old delusions that rulers can fix the value of money, the rate of wages, and the price of food. The sense of rights, by whose sympathetic excitement men are led to behave justly toward each other, is the same sense of rights by which they are prompted to assert their own claims— their own liberty of action—their own freedom to exercise their faculties, and to resist every encroachment. This impulse brooks no restraint, save that imposed by fellow feeling; and disputes all assumption of extra privilege by whomsoever made. Consequently, it is in perpetual antagonism with a sentiment which delights in subserviency. 'Reverence this authority', suggests power-worship. 'Why should I? who set it over me?' demands instinct of freedom. 'Obey' whispers the one. 'Rebel', mutters the other. 'I will do what your Highness bids', says the one with bated breath. 'Pray, sir,' shouts the other, 'who are you, that you should dictate to me?' 'This man is Divinely appointed to rule over us, and we ought therefore to submit' argues the one. 'I tell you no,' replies the other, 'we have Divinely-endorsed claims to freedom, and it is our duty to maintain them.' And thus the controversy goes on, conduct during each phase of civilization being determined by the relative strengths of the two feelings. Whilst yet too feeble to be operative as a social restraint, moral sense, by its scarcely-heard protest, does not hinder a predominant hero-worship from giving possibility to the most stringent despotism. Gradually, as it grows strong enough to deter men from the grosser trespasses upon each other, does it also grow strong enough to struggle successfully against that excess of coercion no longer required. And when it shall finally have attained sufficient power to give men, by its reflex function, so perfect a regard for each other's rights as to make government needless; then will it also, by its direct function, give men so wakeful a jealousy of their own rights as to make government impossible. A further example, this, of the admirable simplicity of nature. The same sentiment which fits us for freedom, itself makes us free.

Of course the institutions of any given age exhibit the compromise made by these contending moral forces at the signing of their last truce. Between the state of unlimited government arising from supremacy of the one feeling, and the state of no government arising from supremacy of the other, lie intermediate forms of social organization, beginning with 'despotism tempered by assassination', and ending with that highest development of the representative system, under which the right of constituents to instruct their delegates is fully admitted—a system which, by making the nation at large a deliberative body, and reducing the legislative assembly to an executive, carries self-government to the fullest extent compatible with the existence of a ruling power. Of necessity the mixed constitutions that characterize this transition period are in the abstract absurd. The two feelings answering to the popular and monarchical elements, being antagonistic, give utterance to antagonistic ideas. And to suppose that these can be consistently united, is to suppose that *yes* and *no* can be reconciled. The monarchical theory is, that the people are in duty bound to submit themselves with all humility to a certain individual—ought to be loyal to him—ought to give allegiance to him, that is—ought to subordinate their wills to his will. Contrariwise the democratic theory—either as specifically defined, or as embodied in our own constitution under the form of a power to withhold supplies and in the legal fiction that the citizen assents to the laws he has to obey— is, that the people ought *not* to be subject to the will of one, but should fulfil their own wills. Now these are flat contradictions, which no reasoning can harmonize. If a king may rightfully claim obedience, then should that obedience be entire; else there starts up the unanswerable question—why must we obey in this and not in that? But if men should mainly rule themselves, then should they rule themselves altogether? Otherwise it may be asked—why are they their own masters in such and such cases, and not in the rest?

Nevertheless, though these mixed governments, combining as they do two mutually-destructive hypotheses, are utterly irrational in principle, they must of necessity exist, so long as they are in

I

harmony with the mixed constitution of the partially-adapted man. And it seems that the radical incongruity pervading them cannot be recognized by men, whilst there exists a corresponding incongruity in their own natures: a good illustration of the law that opinion is ultimately determined by the feelings, and not by the intellect.

How completely, indeed, conceptions of right and wrong in these matters depend upon the balance of impulses existing in men, may be worth considering a moment. And first, observe that no tracing out of actions to their final good or bad consequences is, by itself, capable of generating approbation, or reprobation, of those actions. Could it do this, men's moral codes would be high or low, according as they made these analyses well or ill, that is— according to their intellectual acuteness. Whence it would follow, that in all ages and nations, men of equal intelligence should have like ethical theories, whilst contemporaries should have unlike ones, if their reflective powers are unlike. But facts do not answer to these inferences. On the contrary, they point to the law above specified. Both history and daily experience prove to us that men's ideas of rectitude correspond to the sentiments and instincts predominating in them. We constantly read of tyrants defending their claims to unlimited sway as being Divinely authorized. The *rights* of rival princes were of old asserted by their respective partisans, and are still asserted by modern legitimists, with the same warmth that the most ardent democrat asserts the rights of man. To those living in the feudal times, so unquestionable seemed the duty of serfs to obey their lords, that Luther (no doubt acting conscientiously) urged the barons to vengeance on the rebellious peasants, calling on all who could 'to stab them, cut them down, and dash their brains out, as if they were mad dogs'. Moreover, we shall find, that absence of the ethical sentiment completely disables the mind from realizing the abstract title of the human being to freedom. Thus, with all his high reasoning powers, Plato could conceive of nothing better for his ideal republic than a system of class despotism; and indeed, up to his time, and long after it, there seems to have existed no man who saw anything wrong in slavery. It is narrated of Colonel D'Oyley, the first governor of Jamaica, that within a few days after having issued an order 'for the distribution to the army of 1701 Bibles', he signed another order for the 'payment of the summe of twenty pounds sterling, out of the impost money, to pay for fifteen doggs, brought by John Hoy, for the hunting of Negroes'. The holding of slaves by ministers of religion in America is a parallel fact. We read that the Chinese cannot understand why European women are treated with respect; and that they attribute the circumstance to the exercise of demoniacal arts by them over the men. Here and there amongst ourselves, analogous phenomena may be detected. For example, Dr Moberly, of Winchester College, has written a book to defend fagging, which he says, as a system of school-government, gives 'more security of essential deepseated goodness than any other which can be devised'. Again, in a recent pamphlet, signed 'A Country Parson', it is maintained, that 'you must convert the Chartist spirit as you would reform the drunkard's spirit, by showing that it is a rebellion against the laws of God'. But the strangest peculiarity exhibited by those deficient in sense of rights—or rather that which looks the strangest to us—is their inability to recognize their own claims. We are told, for instance, by Lieutenant Bernard,[1] that in the Portuguese settlements on the African coast, the free Negroes are 'taunted by the slaves as having no white man to look after them, and see them righted when oppressed'; and it is said that in America the slaves themselves look down upon the free blacks, and call them rubbish. Which anomalous-looking facts are, however, easily conceivable when we remember that here in England, in this nineteenth century, most women defend that state of servitude in which they are held by men.

To account, by any current hypothesis, for the numberless disagreements in men's ideas of right and wrong here briefly exemplified, seems scarcely possible. But on the theory that opinion is a resultant of moral forces, whose equilibrium varies with every race and epoch—that is, with every phase of adaptation—the rationale is self-evident. Nor, indeed, considering the matter closely, does it appear that society could ever hold together were not opinion thus dependent upon the balance of feelings. For were it otherwise, races yet needing coercive government might reason their way to the conclusion that coercive government was bad, as readily as more advanced races. The Russians might see despotism to be wrong, and free institutions to be right, as clearly as we do. And did they see this, social dissolution would ensue; for it is not con-

[1] *Three Years' Cruise in the Mozambique Channel.*

ceivable that they would any longer remain contented under that stringent rule needed to keep them in the social state.

The process by which a change of political arrangements is effected, when the incongruity between them and the popular character becomes sufficient, must be itself in keeping with that character, and must be violent or peaceful accordingly. There are not a few who exclaim against all revolutions wrought out by force of arms, forgetting that the quality of a revolution, like that of an institution, is determined by the natures of those who make it. Moral suasion is very admirable; good for us; good, indeed, for all who can be induced to use it. But to suppose that, in the earlier stages of social growth, moral suasion can be employed or, if employed, would answer, is to overlook the conditions. Stating the case mechanically, we may say that as, in proportion to their unfitness for associated life, the framework within which men are restrained must be strong, so must the efforts required to break up that framework, when it is no longer fit, be convulsive. The existence of a government which does not bend to the popular will —a despotic government—presupposes several circumstances which make any change but a violent one impossible. First, for coercive rule to have been practicable, implies in the people a predominance of that awe of power ever indicative of still lingering savageness. Moreover, with a large amount of power-worship present, disaffection can take place only when the cumulative evils of misgovernment have generated great exasperation. Add to which, that as abundance of the sentiment upholding external rule, involves lack of the sentiments producing internal rule, no such check to excesses as that afforded by a due regard for the lives and claims of others, can be operative. And where there are comparatively active destructive propensities, extreme anger, and deficient self-restraint, violence is inevitable. Peaceful revolutions occur under quite different circumstances. They become possible only when society, no longer consisting of members so antagonistic, begins to cohere from its own internal organization, and needs not be kept together by unyielding external restraints; and when, by consequence, the force required to effect change is less. They become possible only when men, having acquired greater adaptation to the social state, will neither inflict on each other nor submit to, such extreme oppressions, and when therefore, the causes of popular indignation are diminished. They become possible only when character has grown more sympathetic and when, as a result of this, the tendency toward angry retaliation is partially neutralized. Indeed, the very idea that reforms may and ought to be effected peacefully implies a large endowment of the moral sense. Without this, such an idea cannot even be conceived, much less carried out; with this, it may be both.

Hence, we must look upon social convulsions as upon other natural phenomena, which work themselves out in a certain inevitable, unalterable way. We may lament the bloodshed—may wish it had been avoided; but it is folly to suppose that, the popular character remaining the same, things could have been managed differently. *If* such and such events had not occurred, say you, the result would have been otherwise; *if* this or that man had lived, he would have prevented the catastrophe. Do not be thus deceived. These changes are brought about by a power far above individual wills. Men who seem the prime movers are merely the tools with which it works; and were they absent, it would quickly find others. Incongruity between character and institutions is the disturbing force and a revolution is the act of restoring equilibrium. Accidental circumstances modify the process but do not perceptibly alter the effect. They precipitate; they retard; they intensify or ameliorate; but, let a few years elapse, and the same end is arrived at no matter what the special events passed through.

That these violent overturnings of early institutions fail to do what their originators hope, and that they finally result in the setting up of institutions not much better than those superseded, is very true. But it is not the less true that the modifications they effect can be effected in no other way. Non-adaptation necessitates a bad mode of making changes, as well as a bad political organization. Not only must the habitual rule it calls for be severe, but even small ameliorations of this cannot be obtained without much suffering. Conversely, the same causes which render a better social state possible, render the successive modifications of it easier. These occur under less pressure; with smaller disturbance; and more frequently: until, by a gradual diminution in the amounts and intervals of change, the process merges into one of uninterrupted growth.

There is another form under which civilization can be generalized. We may consider it as a progress toward that constitution of man and society required for the complete manifestation of every one's individuality. To be that which he naturally is—to do just what he would spontaneously do—is essential to the full happiness of each, and therefore to the greatest happiness of all. Hence, in virtue of the law of adaptation, our advance must be toward a state in which this entire satisfaction of every desire, or perfect fulfilment of individual life, becomes possible. In the beginning it is impossible. If uncontrolled, the impulses of the aboriginal man produce anarchy. Either his individuality must be curbed, or society must dissolve. With ourselves, though restraint is still needful, the private will of the citizen, not being so destructive of order, has more play. And further progress must be toward increased sacredness of personal claims, and a subordination of whatever limits them.

There are plenty of facts illustrating the doctrine that under primitive governments the repression of individuality is greatest, and that it becomes less as we advance. Referring to the people of Egypt, Assyria, China, and Hindostan, as contrasted with those of Greece, Mr Grote says: 'The religious and political sanction, sometimes combined and sometimes separate, determined for every one his mode of life, his creed, his duties, and his place in society, without leaving any scope for the will or reason of the individual himself.' The ownership of people by rulers, from its pure form under Darius, through its various modifications down to the time of *L'etat c'est moi*, and as even still typified amongst ourselves in the expression, 'my subjects', must be considered as a greater or less merging of many individualities into one. The parallel relationships of slaves or serfs to their master, and of the family to its head, have implied the same thing. In short, all despotisms, whether political or religious, whether of sex, of caste or of custom, may be generalized as limitations of individuality, which it is in the nature of civilization to remove.

From the point of view now arrived at, we may discern how what is termed in our artificial classifications of truth, *morality*, is essentially one with physical truth—is, in fact, a species of transcendental physiology. That condition of things dictated by the law of equal freedom—that condition in which the individuality of each may be unfolded without limit, save the like individualities of others—that condition toward which, as we have just seen, mankind is progressing, is a condition toward which the whole creation tends. Already it has been incidentally pointed out that only by entire fulfilment of the moral law can life become complete; and now we shall find that all life whatever may be defined as a quality, of which aptitude to fulfil this law is the highest manifestation.

A theory of life developed by Coleridge has prepared the way for this generalization. 'By life,' says he, 'I everywhere mean the true idea of life, that most general form under which life manifests itself to us, which includes all other forms. This I have stated to be the *tendency to individuation*; and the degrees or intensities of life to consist in the progressive realizations of this tendency.' To make this definition intelligible, a few of the facts sought to be expressed by it must be specified—facts exemplifying the contrast between low and high types of structure, and low and high degrees of vitality.

Restricting our illustrations to the animal kingdom, and beginning where the vital attributes are most obscure, we find, for instance, in the genus Porifera, creatures consisting of nothing but amorphous semi-fluid jelly, supported upon horny fibres (sponge). This jelly possesses no sensitiveness, has no organs, absorbs nutriment from the water which permeates its mass and, if cut in pieces, lives on, in each part, as before. So that this 'gelatinous film', as it has been called, shows little more individuality than a formless lump of inanimate matter for, like that, it possesses no distinction of parts and, like that also, has no greater completeness than the pieces it is divided into. In the compound polyps which stand next, and with which Coleridge commences, the progress toward individuality is manifest; for there is now distinction of parts. To the originally uniform gelatinous mass with canals running through it, we have superadded, in the Alcyonidæ, a number of digestive sacs, with accompanying mouths and tentacles. Here is, evidently, a partial segregation into individualities—a progress toward separateness. There is still complete community of nutrition; whilst each polyp has a certain independent sensitiveness and contractility. From this stage onwards, there appear to be several routes; one through the Corallidæ, in which the polyp-bearing mass surrounds a calcarous axis, up to the Tubiporidæ, in which the polyps, no longer united, inhabit separate cells, seated in a common calcareous framework. But Coleridge has overlooked the remarkable mode in which these communist polyps are linked with higher individual organisms by the transitional arrangement seen in the common hydrae, or fresh-water polyps of our ponds. These creatures (which are in structure similar to the separate members of the compound animal above described), multiply by gemmation, that is, by the budding out of young ones from the body of the parent. 'During the first period of the formation of these sprouts, they are evidently continuous with the general substance from which they arise; and even when considerably perfected, and possessed of an internal cavity and tentacula, their stomachs freely communicate with that of their parent. . . . As soon as the newly-formed hydra is capable of catching prey, it begins to contribute to the support of its parent; the food which it captures passing through the aperture at its base into the body of the original polyp. At length, when the young is fully formed, and ripe for independent existence, the point of union between the two becomes more and more slender, until a slight effort on the part of either is sufficient to detach them, and the process is completed. . . . Sometimes six or seven gemmæ have been observed to sprout at once from the same hydra; and although the whole process is concluded in twenty-four hours, not unfrequently a third generation may be observed springing from the newly-formed polyps even before their separation from their parent; eighteen have in this manner been seen united into one group.'[1] Now here is a creature which cannot be strictly called either simple or compound. Nominally, it is an individual; practically, it never is so. In the alcyonide polyp many individuals are *permanently* united together: in this genus they are *temporarily* united, in so far as particular individuals are concerned, but otherwise *permanently* so; for there is always a group, though that group keeps changing its members. Indeed, may we not say that the 'tendency to individuation' is here most visible; seeing that the hydræ are, as it were, perpetually striving to become individuals, without succeeding? And may we not further say that in the gradually-decreasing recurrence of this budding, and the simultaneous appearance of a higher method of reproduction by ova (which in the bryozoa coexists with a comparatively languid gemmation), this 'tendency to individuation' is still further manifested?

After complete separateness of organisms has been arrived at, the law is still seen in successive improvements of structure. By greater individuality of parts—by greater distinctness in the nature and functions of these, are all creatures possessing high vitality

[1] *A General Outline of the Animal Kingdom.* By Professor T. R. Jones, F.G.S.

distinguished from inferior ones. Those hydræ just referred to, which are mere bags, with tentacles round the orifice, may be turned inside out with impunity: the stomach becomes skin, and the skin stomach. Here, then, is evidently no speciality of character; the duties of stomach and skin are performed by one tissue, which is not yet *individualized* into two separate parts, adapted to separate ends. The contrast between this state and that in which such a distinction exists, will sufficiently explain what is meant by individuation of organs. How clearly this individuation of organs is traceable throughout the whole range of animal life, may be seen in the successive forms which the nervous system assumes. Thus in the Acrita, a class comprehending all the genera above mentioned, 'no nervous filaments or masses have been discovered, and the neurine or nervous matter is supposed to be diffused in a molecular condition through the body'.[1] In the class next above this, the Nematoneura, we find the first step toward individuation of 'the nervous system: the nervous matter is distinctly aggregated into filaments'.[2] In the Homogangliata, it is still further concentrated into a number of small equal-sized masses—ganglia. In the Heterogangliata, some of these small masses are collected together into larger ones. Finally, in the vertebrata, the greater part of the nervous centres are united to form a brain. And with the rest of the body there has simultaneously taken place just the same process of condensation into distinct systems—muscular, respiratory, nutritive, excretive, absorbent, circulatory, etc.—and of these again into separate parts, with special functions.

The changes of vital manifestation associated with and consequent upon these changes of structure, have the same significance. To possess a greater variety of senses, of instincts, of powers, of qualities—to be more complex in character and attributes, is to be more completely distinguishable from all other created things; or to exhibit a more marked individuality. For, manifestly, as there are some properties which all entities, organic and inorganic, have in common, namely, weight, mobility, inertia, etc.; and as there are additional properties which all organic entities have in common, namely, powers of growth and multiplication; and as there are yet further properties which the higher-organic entities have in common, namely, sight, hearing, etc., then those still higher organic entities possessing characteristics not shared in by the rest, thereby

[1] Jones, op. cit.   [2] Jones, op. cit.

differ from a larger number of entities than the rest, and differ in more points—that is, are more separate, more individual. Observe, again, that the greater power of self-preservation shown by beings of superior type may also be generalized under this same term—a 'tendency to individuation'. The lower the organism, the more is it at the mercy of external circumstances. It is continually liable to be destroyed by the elements, by want of food, by enemies; and eventually is so destroyed in nearly all cases. That is, it lacks power to preserve its individuality; and loses this, either by returning to the form of inorganic matter, or by absorption into some other individuality. Conversely, where there is strength, sagacity, swiftness (all of them indicative of superior structure), there is corresponding ability to maintain life—to prevent the individuality from being so easily dissolved; and therefore the individuation is more complete.

In man we see the highest manifestation of this tendency. By virtue of his complexity of structure, he is furthest removed from the inorganic world in which there is least individuality. Again, his intelligence and adaptability commonly enable him to maintain life to old age—to complete the cycle of his existence; that is, to fill out the limits of this individuality to the full. Again, he is self-conscious; that is, he recognizes his own individuality. And, as lately shown, even the change observable in human affairs, is still toward a greater development of individuality—may still be described as 'a tendency to individuation'.

But note lastly, and note chiefly, as being the fact to which the foregoing sketch is introductory, that what we call the moral law—the law of equal freedom, is the law under which individuation becomes perfect, and that ability to recognize and act up to this law, is the final endowment of humanity—an endowment now in process of evolution. The increasing assertion of personal rights is an increasing demand that the external conditions needful to a complete unfolding of the individuality shall be respected. Not only is there now a consciousness of individuality, and an intelligence whereby individuality may be preserved, but there is a perception that the sphere of action requisite for due development of the individuality may be claimed; and a correlative desire to claim it. And when the change at present going on is complete—when each possesses an active instinct of freedom, together with an active sympathy—then will all the still existing limitations to individuality, be they governmental restraints, or be they the aggressions of men on one another, cease. Then, none will be hindered from duly unfolding their natures; for whilst everyone maintains his own claims, he will respect the like claims of others. Then, there will no longer be legislative restrictions and legislative burdens; for by the same process these will have become both needless and impossible. Then, for the first time in the history of the world, will there exist beings whose individualities can be expanded to the full in all directions. And thus, as before said, in the ultimate man perfect morality, perfect individuation, and perfect life will be simultaneously realized.

Yet must this highest individuation be joined with the greatest mutual dependence. Paradoxical though the assertion looks, the progress is at once toward complete separateness and complete union. But the separateness is of a kind consistent with the most complex combinations for fulfilling social wants; and the union is of a kind that does not hinder entire development of each personality. Civilization is evolving a state of things and a kind of character, in which two apparently conflicting requirements are reconciled. To achieve the creative purpose—the greatest sum of happiness, there must on the one hand exist an amount of population maintainable only by the best possible system of production; that is, by the most elaborate subdivision of labour; that is, by the extremest mutual dependence: whilst on the other hand, each individual must have the opportunity to do whatever his desires prompt. Clearly these two conditions can be harmonized only by that adaptation humanity is undergoing—that process during which all desires inconsistent with the most perfect social organization are dying out, and other desires corresponding to such an organization are being developed. How this will eventuate in producing at once perfect individuation and perfect mutual dependence may not be at once obvious. But probably an illustration will sufficiently elucidate the matter. Here are certain domestic affections, which can be gratified only by the establishment of relationships with other beings. In the absence of those beings, and the consequent dormancy of the feelings with which they are regarded, life is incomplete—the individuality is shorn of its fair proportions. Now as the normal unfolding of the conjugal and parental elements of the individuality depends on having a family, so when civilization becomes complete, will the normal unfolding of all other elements of the individuality depend upon the existence of the civilized state. Just that kind of individuality will be acquired which finds in the most highly-organized community the fittest sphere for its manifestation—which finds in each social arrangement a condition answering to some faculty in itself—which could not, in fact, expand at all, if otherwise circumstanced. The ultimate man will be one whose private requirements coincide with public ones. He will be that manner of man who, in spontaneously fulfilling his own nature, incidentally performs the functions of a social unit; and yet is only enabled so to fulfil his own nature by all others doing the like.

How truly, indeed, human progress is toward greater mutual dependence, as well as toward greater individuation—how truly the welfare of each is daily more involved in the welfare of all—and how truly, therefore, it is the interest of each to respect the interests of all, may, with advantage, be illustrated at length; for it is a fact of which many seem woefully ignorant. Men cannot break that vital law of the social organism—the law of equal freedom, without penalties in some way or other coming round to them. Being themselves members of the community, they are affected by whatever affects it. Upon the goodness or badness of its state depends the greater or less efficiency with which it administers to their wants; and the less or greater amount of evil it inflicts upon them. Through those vicious arrangements that hourly gall them, they feel the cumulative result of all sins against the social law; their own sins included. And they suffer for these sins, not only in extra restraints and alarms, but in the extra labour and expense required to compass their ends.

That every trespass produces a reaction, partly general and partly special—a reaction which is extreme in proportion as the trespass is great, has been more or less noticed in all ages. Thus the remark is as old as the time of Thales, that tyrants rarely die natural deaths. From his day to ours, the thrones of the East have been continually stained with the blood of their successive occupants. The early histories of all European states, and the recent history of Russia, illustrate the same fact; and if we are to judge by his habits, the present Czar lives in constant fear of assassination. Nor is it true that those who bear universal sway, and seem able to do as they please, can really do so. They limit their own freedom in limiting that of others: their despotism recoils, and puts them also in bondage. We read, for instance, that the Roman emperors were the puppets of their soldiers. 'In the Byzantine palace,' says Gibbon, 'the emperor was the first slave of the ceremonies he imposed.' Speaking of the tedious etiquette of the time of Louis le Grand, Madame de Maintenon remarks; 'Save those only who fill the highest stations, I know of none more unfortunate than those who envy them. If you could only form an idea of what it is!' The same reaction is felt by slave-owners. Some of the West India planters have acknowledged that before Negro emancipation they were the greatest slaves on their estates. The Americans, too, are shackled in various ways by their own injustice. In the south, the whites are self-coerced, that they may coerce the blacks. Marriage with one of the mixed race is forbidden; there is a slave-owning qualification for senators; a man may not liberate his own slaves without leave; and only at the risk of lynching dare anyone say a word in favour of abolition.

It is, indeed, becoming clear to most that these gross transgressions return upon the perpetrators—that 'this even-handed justice commends the ingredients of our poisoned chalice to our own lips'; but it is not yet clear to them that the like is true of those lesser transgressions they are themselves guilty of. Probably the modern maintainers of class power can see well enough that their feudal ancestors paid somewhat dearly for keeping the masses in thraldom. They can see that, what with armours and hidden mail, what with sliding panels, secret passages, dimly lighted rooms, precautions against poison, and constant fears of surprise and treachery, these barons had but uncomfortable lives of it at the best. They can see how delusive was the notion that the greatest wealth was to be obtained by making serfs of the people. They can see that in Jacqueries and Gallician massacres, when bondsmen glut their vengeance by burning castles and slaughtering the inmates, there arrive fatal settlements of long-standing balances. But they cannot see that their own inequitable deeds, in one way or other, come home to *them*. Just as these feudal nobles mistook the evils they suffered under for unalterable ordinations of nature, never dreaming that they were the reflex results of tyranny, so do their descendants fail to perceive that many of their own unhappinesses are similarly generated.

And yet, whilst in some cases it is scarcely possible to trace the secret channels through which our misbehaviour to others returns upon us, there are other cases in which the reaction is palpable. An audience rushing out of a theatre on fire, and in their eagerness to get before each other jamming up the doorway so that no one can get through, offers a good example of unjust selfishness defeating itself. An analogous result may be witnessed at the American ordinaries, where the attempts of greedy guests to get more than a fair share have generated a competition in fast eating which not only frustrates these attempts, but entails on all, immediate loss of enjoyment and permanent ill-health. In such cases it is clear enough, that by trespassing upon the claims of others, men hurt themselves also. The reaction is here direct and immediate. In all other cases, however, reaction is equally sure, though it may come round by some circuitous route, or after a considerable lapse of time, or in an unrecognized form. The country squire who thinks it a piece of profound policy to clear his estate of cottages, that he may saddle some other place with the paupers, forgets that land-owners in neighbouring parishes will eventually defeat him by do-ing the same; or that if he is so situated as to settle his labourers upon towns, the walking of extra miles to and fro must gradually lower the standard of a day's work, raise the cost of cultivation, and, in the end, decrease rent. Nor does he see that by the overcrowded bedrooms and neglected drainage and repairs to which this policy leads, he is generating debility or disease, and raising his poors'-rates in one way, whilst he lowers them in another. The Dorsetshire farmer who pays wages in tailings of wheat charged above market price, imagines he is economizing. It never occurs to him that he loses more than the difference by petty thefts, by the destruction of his hedges for fuel, by the consequent pounding of his cattle, and by the increase of country rates, for the prosecution of robbers and poachers. It seems very clear to the tradesman that all extra profit made by adulterating goods, is so much pure gain; and for a while, perhaps, it may be. By-and-by, however, his competitors do as he does—are in a measure compelled to do so—and the rate of profit is then brought down to what it was before. Meanwhile the general practice of adulteration has been encouraged—has got into other departments—has deteriorated the articles our shop-keeper buys; and thus, in his capacity of consumer, he suffers from the vicious system he has helped to strengthen. When, during Negro apprenticeship, the West India planters had to value slaves who wished to buy themselves off, before 'the Queen's free', they no doubt thought it cunning to make oath to a higher worth per day than the true one. But when, awhile after, having to pay wages, they had their own estimates quoted to them, and found that the Negroes would take nothing less, they probably repented of their dishonesty. It is often long before these recoils come; but they do come nevertheless. See how the Irish landlords are at length being punished for their rack-renting, their evictions, their encouragement of middlemen, and their utter recklessness of popular welfare. Note, too, how for having abetted those who wronged the native Irish, England has to pay a penalty, in the shape of loans which are not refunded, and in the misery produced by the swarms of indigent immigrants who tend to bring down her own people to their level. Thus, be they committed by many or by few—be they seen in efforts to despoil foreigners by restrictive duties, or in a tradesman's trickeries—breaches of equity are uniformly self-defeating. Whilst men continue social units, they cannot transgress the life principle of society without disastrous consequences somehow or other coming back upon them.

Not only does the ultimate welfare of the citizen demand that he should himself conform to the moral law; it equally concerns him that everyone should conform to it. This interdependence which the social state necessitates makes all men's business his business, in a more or less indirect way. To people whose eyes do not wander beyond their ledgers, it seems of no consequence how the affairs of mankind go. They think they know better than to trouble themselves with public matters, making enemies and damaging their trade. Yet if they are indeed so selfish as to care nothing about their fellow-creatures, whilst their own flesh-pots are well-filled, let them learn that they have pounds, shillings and pence interest at stake. Mere pocket prudence should induce them to further human welfare, if no higher motive will. To help in putting things on a juster footing will eventually pay. The diffusion of sound principles and the improvement of public morality, end in diminishing household expenses. Can they not see that when buying meat and bread and groceries, they have to give something toward maintaining prisons and police? Can they not see that in price of a coat they are charged a large percentage to cover the tailor's bad debts? Every transaction of their lives is in some way hampered by the general immorality. They feel it in the rate of interest demanded for capital, which (neglecting temporary variations) is high in proportion as men are bad.[1] They feel it in the amount of attorneys' bills; or in having to suffer robbery, lest the law should commit on them greater robbery. They feel it in their share of the two and a half millions a year, which our metallic currency costs. They feel it in those collapses of trade, which follow extensive gambling speculations. It seems to them an absurd waste of time to help in spreading independence amongst men; and yet, did they call to mind how those railway shares, which they bought at a premium, went down to a ruinous discount because the directors cringed to a rich bully, they would learn that the prevalence of a manly spirit may become of money-value to them. They suppose themselves unconcerned in the quarrels of neighbouring nations; and yet, on examination, they will find that a Hungarian war by the loans it calls for, or a Danish blockade by its influence upon our commerce, more or less remotely affects their profits, in whatever secluded nook of England they may live. Their belief is that they are not at all interested in the good government of India, and yet a little reflection would show them that they continually suffer from those fluctuations of trade consequent upon the irregular and insufficient supply of cotton from America—fluctuations which would probably have ceased had not India been exhausted by its extravagance. Not interested? Why even the better education of the Chinese is of moment to them, for Chinese prejudice shuts out English merchants. Not interested? Why they have a stake in the making of American railways and canals, for these ultimately affect the price of bread in England. Not interested? Why the accumulation of wealth by every people on the face of the earth concerns them; for whilst it is the law of capital to overflow from those places where it is abundant, to those where it is scarce, rich nations can never fully enjoy the fruits of their own labour until other nations are equally rich. The well-ordering of human affairs in the remotest and most insignificant communities is beneficial to all men: the ill-ordering of them calamitous to all men. And though the citizen may be but slightly acted upon by each particular good or evil influence at work within his own society, and still more slightly by each of those at work within other societies—although the effect on him may be infinitesimal, yet it is on the cumulative

---

[1] When dishonesty and improvidence are extreme, capital cannot be had under 30 to 40 per cent, as in the Burmese Empire, or in England, in the time of King John.—See *Mill's Political Economy*.

results of myriads of these infinitesimal influences that his happiness or misery depends.

Still more clearly seen is this ultimate identity of personal interests, when we discover how essentially *vital* is the connection between each person and the society of which he is a unit. We commonly enough compare a nation to a living organism. We speak of 'the body politic', of the functions of its several parts, of its growth, and of its diseases, as though it were a creature. But we usually employ these expressions as metaphors, little suspecting how close is the analogy, and how far it will bear carrying out. So completely, however, is a society organized upon the same system as an individual being, that we may almost say there is something more than analogy between them. Let us look at a few of the facts. Observe first, that the parallel gains immensely in reasonableness, when we learn that the human body is itself compounded of innumerable microscopic organisms, which possess a kind of independent vitality, which grow by imbibing nutriment from the circulating fluids, and which multiply, as the infusorial monads do, by spontaneous fission. The whole process of development, beginning with the first change in the ovum and ending with the production of an adult man, is fundamentally a perpetual increase in the number of these cells by the mode of fissiparous generation. On the other hand, that gradual decay witnessed in old age, is in essence a cessation of this increase. During health, the vitality of these cells is subordinated to that of the system at large, and the presence of insubordinate cells implies disease. Thus, smallpox arises from the intrusion of a species of cell, foreign to that community of cells of which the body consists, and which, absorbing nourishment from the blood, rapidly multiplies by spontaneous division, until its progeny have diffused themselves throughout the tissues; and if the excreting energies of the constitution fail to get rid of these aliens, death ensues. In certain states of body, indigenous cells will take on new forms of life, and by continuing to reproduce their like, give origin to parasitic growths, such as cancer. Under the microscope, cancer can be identified by a specific element, known as the cancer-cell. Besides those modifications of cell-vitality, which constitute malignant diseases, there occasionally happens another in which cells, without any change in their essential nature, rebel against the general governing force of the system; and, instead of ceasing to grow, whilst yet invisible to the naked eye, expand to a considerable size, sometimes even reaching several inches in diameter. These are called Hydatids or Acephalocysts, and have, until lately, been taken for internal parasites or entozoa. Still closer appears the relationship between tissue cells and the lowest independent organisms, on finding that there exists a creature called the Gregarina, very similar in structure to the Hydatid, but which is admitted to be an entozoon. Consisting as it does of a cell-membrane, enclosing fluid and a solid nucleus, and multiplying as it does by the spontaneous fission of this nucleus and subsequent division of the cell-walls, the Gregarina differs from a tissue-cell merely in size, and not in forming part of the organ containing it. Thus there may coexist in the same organism cells of which that organism is constituted, others which should have helped to build it up, but which are insubordinate or partially separate, and others which are naturally separate, and simply reside in its cavities. Hence we are warranted in considering the body as a commonwealth of monads, each of which has independent powers of life, growth, and reproduction; each of which unites with a number of others to perform some function needful for supporting itself and all the rest; and each of which absorbs its share of nutriment from the blood. And when thus regarded, the analogy between an individual being and a human society in which each man, whilst helping to subserve some public want absorbs a portion of the circulating stock of commodities brought to his door, is palpable enough.

A still more remarkable fufilment of this analogy is to be found in the fact that the different kinds of organization which society takes on, in progressing from its lowest to its highest phase of development, are essentially similar to the different kinds of animal organization. Creatures of inferior type are little more than aggregations of numerous like parts—are moulded on what Professor Owen terms the principle of vegetative repetition; and in tracing the forms assumed by successive grades above these, we find a gradual diminution in the number of like parts, and a multiplication of unlike ones. In the one extreme there are but a few functions, and many similar agents to each function: in the other, there are many functions, and few similar agents to each function. Thus the visual apparatus in a fly consists of two groups of fixed lenses, numbering in some species 20,000. Every one of these lenses produces an image; but as its field of view is extremely narrow, and as there exists no power of adaptation to different distances, the vision obtained is probably very imperfect. Whilst the mammal, on the other hand, possesses but two eyes, each of these includes numerous appendages. It is compounded of several lenses, having different forms and duties. These lenses are capable of various focal adjustments. There are muscles for directing them to the right and to the left, to the ground and to the sky. There is a curtain (the iris) to regulate the quantity of light admitted. There is a gland to secrete, a tube to pour out, and a drain to carry off the lubricating fluid. There is a lid to wipe the surface, and there are lashes to give warning on the approach of foreign bodies. Now the contrast between these two kinds of visual organ is the contrast between all lower and higher types of structure. If we examine the framework employed to support the tissues, we find it consisting in the Annelida (the common worm, for instance) of an extended series of rings. In the Myriapoda, which stand next above the Annelida, these rings are less numerous and more dense. In the higher Myriapoda they are united into a comparatively few large and strong segments, whilst in the Insecta this condensation is carried still further. Speaking of analogous changes in the crustaceans, the lowest of which is constructed much as the centipede, and the highest of which (the crab) has nearly all its segments united, Professor Jones says: 'And even the steps whereby we pass from the Annelidan to the Myriapod and from thence to the insect, the scorpion, and the spider, seem to be repeated as we thus review the progressive development of the class before us.' Mark again, that these modifications of the exo-skeleton are completely paralleled by those of the endo-skeleton. The vertebra are numerous in fish and in the ophidian reptiles. They are less numerous in the higher reptiles; less numerous still in the quadrupeds; fewest of all in man: and whilst their number is diminished, their forms and the functions of their appendages are varied, instead of being, as in the eel, nearly all alike. Thus, also, is it with locomotive organs. The spines of the echinus and the suckers of the star-fish are multitudinous. So likewise are the legs of the centipede. In the crustaceans we come down to fourteen, twelve and ten; in the arachnidans and insects to eight and six; in the lower mammalia to four; and in man to two. The successive modifications of the digestive cavity are of analogous nature. Its lowest form is that of a sack with but one opening. Next it is a tube with two openings, having different offices. And in higher creatures, this tube, instead of being made up of absorbents from end to end—that is, instead of being an aggregation of like parts—is modified into many unlike ones, having different structures adapted to the different stages into which the assimilative function is now divided. Even the classification under which man, as forming the genus Bimana, is distinguished from the most nearly related genus Quadrumana, is based on a diminution in the number of organs that have similar forms and duties.

Now just this same coalescence of like parts, and separation of unlike ones—just this same increasing subdivisions of function—takes place in the development of society. The earliest social organisms consist almost wholly of repetitions of one element. Every man is a warrior, hunter, fisherman, builder, agriculturist, toolmaker. Each portion of the community performs the same duties with every other portion; much as each portion of the polyp's body is alike stomach, skin and lungs. Even the chiefs, in whom a tendency toward separateness of function first appears, still retain their similarity to the rest in economic respects. The next stage is distinguished by a segregation of these social units into a few distinct classes—soldiers, priests and labourers. A further advance is seen in the sundering of these labourers into different castes, having special occupations, as amongst the Hindoos. And, without further illustration, the reader will at once perceive that from these inferior types of society up to our own complicated and more perfect one, the progress has ever been of the same nature. Whilst he will also perceive that this coalescence of like parts, as seen in the concentration of particular districts, and this separation of agents having separate functions, as seen in the more and more minute division of labour, are still going on.

Significant of the alleged analogy is the further fact consequent upon the above, that the sensitiveness exhibited by societies of low and high structure differs in degree, as does the sensitiveness of similarly-contrasted creatures. That peculiar faculty possessed by inferior organisms of living on in each part after being cut in pieces, is a manifest corollary to the other peculiarity just described; namely, that they consist of many repetitions of the same elements. The ability of the several portions into which a polyp has been divided, to grow into complete polyps, obviously implies that each portion contains all the organs needful to life; and each portion can be thus constituted only when those organs recur in every part of the original body. Conversely, the reason why any member of a more highly-organized being cannot live when separated from the rest is, that it does not include all the vital elements, but is dependent for its supplies of nutriment, nervous energy, oxygen, etc, upon the members from which it has been cut off. Of course, then, the earliest and latest forms of society, being similarly distinguished in structure, will be similarly distinguished in susceptibility of injury. Hence it happens that a tribe of savages may be divided and subdivided with little or no inconvenience to the several sections. Each of these contains every element which the whole did—is just as self-sufficing, and quickly assumes the simple organization constituting an independent tribe. Hence, on the contrary, it happens, that in a community like our own no part can be cut off or injured without all parts suffering. Annihilate the agency employed in distributing commodities, and much of the rest would die before another distributing agency could be developed. Suddenly sever the manufacturing portion from the agricultural portion, and the one would expire outright whilst the other would long linger in grievous distress. This interdependence is daily shown in commercial changes. Let the factory hands be put on short time, and immediately the colonial produce markets of London and Liverpool are depressed. The shopkeeper is busy or otherwise, according to the amount of the wheat crop. And a potato blight may ruin dealers in consols.

Thus do we find, not only that the analogy between a society and a living creature is borne out to a degree quite unsuspected by those who commonly draw it, but also that the same definition of life applies to both. This union of many men into one community —this increasing mutual dependence of units which were originally independent—this gradual segregation of citizens into separate bodies, with reciprocally subservient functions—this formation of a whole, consisting of numerous essential parts—this growth of an organism, of which one portion cannot be injured without the rest feeling it—may all be generalized under the law of individuation. The development of society, as well as the development of man and the development of life generally, may be described as a tendency to individuate—*to become a thing*. And rightly interpreted, the manifold forms of progress going on around us, are uniformly significant of this tendency.

Returning now to the point whence we set out, the fact that public interests and private ones are essentially in unison, cannot fail to be more vividly realized when so vital a connection is found to subsist between society and its members. Though it would be dangerous to place implicit trust in conclusions founded upon the analogy just traced, yet harmonizing as they do with conclusions deducible from everyday experience, they unquestionably enforce these. When, after observing the reactions entailed by breaches of equity, the citizen contemplates the relation in which he stands to the body politic—when he learns that it has a species of life, and conforms to the same laws of growth, organization, and sensibility that a being does—when he finds that one vitality circulates through it and him, and that whilst social health, in a measure, depends upon the fulfilment of some function in which he takes part, his happiness depends upon the normal action of every organ in the social body—when he duly understands this, he must see that his own welfare and all men's welfare are inseparable. He must see that whatever produces a diseased state in one part of the community must inevitably inflict injury upon all other parts. He must see that his own life can become what it should be only as fast as society becomes what it should be. In short, he must become impressed with the salutary truth, that no one can be perfectly free till all are free; no one can be perfectly moral till all are moral; no one can be perfectly happy till all are happy.

'The ultimate man will be one whose private requirements coincide with public ones. He will be that manner of man who, in spontaneously fulfilling his own nature, incidentally performs the functions of a social unit; and yet is only enabled so to fulfil his own nature by all others doing the like.'

Bibliography

Herbert Spencer's Writings

The Synthetic Philosophy

First Principles. First edition, 1862; second edition, 1867; third edition, 1875; fourth edition, 1880; fifth edition, 1884; sixth edition, and finally revised, 1900. Reprinted with an additional appendix and a new index, 1904.

Principles of Biology. Vol. 1, 1864; Vol. 2, 1867; revised and enlarged edition, Vol. 1, 1898; Vol. 2, 1899.

Principles of Psychology. First edition, 1855; second edition, Vol. 1, 1870; Vol. 2, 1872; third edition, 1880; fourth edition, 1899.

The Principles of Sociology. Vol. 1, first edition, 1876; second edition, 1877; third and enlarged edition, 1885; Vol. 2, Part IV, 1879; Part V, 1882; Vol. 3, Part VI, 1885; Parts VII and VIII, 1896.

Principles of Ethics. Vol. 1, Part 1, 1879; Parts II and III, 1892; Vol. 2, Part IV, 1891; Parts V and VI, 1893.

Other Works

Social Statics. First edition, 1855; abridged and revised edition, 1892.

Education. First edition, 1861; cheap edition, 1878; sixpenny edition, published by the Rationalist Press Association, 1903. Reprinted 1905.

The Study of Sociology. International Scientific Series, first edition, 1873; second to seventh editions, 1873–78; library edition, 1880.

The Man Versus the State. First edition, 1884; reprinted with abridged and revised edition of *Social Statics*, 1892.

Essays. First series, 1857; second series, 1863; third series, 1874; revised edition in three volumes, 1890.

Various Fragments. First edition, 1897; enlarged edition, 1900.

Facts and Comments. 1902.

Autobiography. In two volumes, 1904.

Descriptive Sociology. (Classified and arranged by Herbert Spencer). Division I—Uncivilized Societies: Lowest Races, Negrito Races and Malayo–Polynesian Races, by Dr David Duncan (1874); African Races (other than Arab), by Dr David Duncan (1876); American Races, by Dr David Duncan (1878). Division II—Civilized Societies, extinct or decayed: Mexicans, Central Americans, Chibchas and

Peruvians, by Dr Richard Scheppig (1874); Hebrews and Phoenicians, by Dr Richard Scheppig (1880). Division III—Civilized Societies, recent or still flourishing: English, by James Collier (1873); French, by James Collier (1881). *Issued by the Herbert Spencer Trustees:* Division I—Uncivilized Societies: Lowest Races, a new edition brought up to date by the original compiler, Dr Duncan (1925); African Races, a new edition, practically re-written and greatly enlarged, by Emil Torday (1930); The Heritage of Solomon. Division II—Civilized Societies, extinct or decayed: Greeks, Hellenic Period, by Sir J. P. Mahaffy and Prof. W. A. Goligher, LL.D. (1910); Ancient Egyptians, by Sir W. Flinders Petrie (1925); Greeks, Hellenistic Period, by Prof. W. A. Goligher, LL.D. (1928); Mesopotamia, by Reuben Levy, Litt.D. (1929); Ancient Rome (issued in incomplete form). Division III—Civilized Societies, recent or still flourishing: Chinese, by E. T. C. Warner (1910); Islam, by Reuben Levy, 2 vols. (1933). Division I—Uncivilized Societies: The Heritage of Solomon (Ancient Palestine), by Prof. John Garstang, LL.D. Division II—Civilized Societies, extinct or decayed: Ancient Romans, by Dr E. H. Alton and Prof. W. A. Goligher.

A comprehensive list of Herbert Spencer's articles on all kinds of subjects, including engineering, and of copious older literature about him is in J. Rumney, *Herbert Spencer's Sociology* (Williams and Norgate, 1934), which is the only book devoted exclusively to Spencer's sociology.

The most recent editions of Spencer's works are:
S. L. Andreski, *Principles of Sociology* (abridged edition) (Macmillan. 1969).
D. G. Macrae, *Spencer, the Man Versus the State* (Penguin, 1969).
R. L. Carneiro. *The Evolution of Society* (selection from Spencer) (Chicago, 1967).

Index

Hume, David, 17, 25, 32
Huxley, T. H., 28

imperialism, 3, 194–202; allied with militancy, 195; citizen servant of the community, 200–1; diminution of freedom, 194–202; master entailed in slavery, 194–202
Inclosure Laws, 182
indefinite to the definite, 92–104; in the arts, 102–4; in language, 99; in organisms, 95–7; in the sciences, 100–2; in societies, 97–9
individuation, tendency to, 235, 236, 238, 249; joined with mutual dependence, 239, 240
industrial social type, 160–5; political rights, 163; principle of voluntary co-operation, 164, 169, 172, 176; religious rights, 162; representational government, 163; supremity of citizens' will, 163; transformation into the militant, 172, 174
integration, 60, 62, 68, 69, 70–4; & disintegration, 56, 57, 58; in groups of like entities, 70; longitudinal, 65, 66; of matter & dissipation of motion, 69, 73, 75, 92; in music, 72; in painting, 72; primary & secondary, 63–4; social, 108, 126, 131; transverse, 66; in uncivilized societies, 67–8

Jones, Professor, 247

Kepler, Johannes, 101
Kipling, Rudyard, 211
Kropotkin, Prince, Mutual Aid, 26
Kant, Immanuel, 7

law: enforcement, 191; formulation, 191; law-making in the hands of executives, 199; proclamation of martial law, 200. See also Divine Law & moral law

liberalism, 175; function, 194
Luther, Martin, 230

Machajski, Waclaw, 29
Maine, Henry Summer, 15
Maintenon, Mme. de, 198, 241
Malinowski, B. K., 21, 23, 24
Malthus, Thomas, 20, 183n.
man: aboriginal, 216, 221, 234; conquest of social over anti-social, 220–2; development of latent capabilities, 220; warfare with creatures at enmity, 219. See also ultimate man
Man Versus the State, The, extracts from, 205–7
Marx, Karl, 3, 8, 15, 17, 19, 20, 28, 29, 30; & Engels, 25, 31; comparison with Spencer, 18, 28–9
Medawar, Sir Peter, The Art of the Soluble, 7
migration, 171, 172
militancy, 3, 209–13; & athleticism, 211; for boys, 209, 212; coercion, 184, 211; in literature, 211–13; martial law, 200
militant social type, 154–60, 190; chief as political head, 155; discipline, 158, 159; principle of compulsory co-operation, 168–9, 172; sacrifices, 157; social gradations, 156, 158; trait characterizing, 160; transformation into industrial social type, 172–4, 175
military despotism, 213
Military Instruction Bill, 210
military organization, 14
Military Organization in Society (Andreski), 2, 19
Mill, John Stuart, 30
Millar, John, 15, 25
monarchical theory, 229
Montesquieu, Baron Charles de, 15, 25; De l'Esprit des Lois, 16
moral law, 234, 235, 238, 240
Morgan, Lewis Henry, 31
Mosca, Gaetano, 183n.
Mutual Aid (Kropotkin), 26